REVELATION
DRAMA OF THE AGES

REVELATION

DRAMA OF THE AGES

HERBERT
LOCKYER

WHITAKER
HOUSE

REVELATION: DRAMA OF THE AGES

ISBN: 978-1-60374-556-7
Printed in the United States of America
© 1980, 2012 by Ardis A. Lockyer

Whitaker House
1030 Hunt Valley Circle
New Kensington, PA 15068
www.whitakerhouse.com

Library of Congress Cataloging-in-Publication Data (pending)

1 2 3 4 5 6 7 8 9 10 11 ⨆ 19 18 17 16 15 14 13 12

DEDICATION

To my dear son, Herbert Lockyer Jr.,
a faithful minister of the Word.

CONTENTS

PART ONE:

THE FACTS AND FEATURES OF REVELATION

1

CANONICITY, AUTHOR, AND TITLE

The book of Revelation is a great and worthy consummation of Scripture. It can be looked upon as a second Genesis—the beginning of the new world of perfected spiritual life in the city of God. As Genesis is the book of first things, Revelation is the book of last things.

The book of Revelation was admitted to the Canon of Scripture on its own merits and, apart from the question of authorship, was admitted with comparatively few dissenting voices. As an integral part of the Holy Scriptures, Revelation should not be neglected because of its highly symbolic nature.

Although liberal theologians may dispute the Johannine authorship of Revelation, their objections do not move us from the position that John, the beloved disciple who wrote the gospel of John and the three epistles of John, was also the writer of Revelation. The testimony of the early church as to John's authorship cannot be ignored. Revelation is quoted with the author's name earlier than any other New Testament book, except for 1 Corinthians. In both his gospel and his epistles, John wrote in the third person, but in Revelation, he named himself five times (see Revelation 1:1, 4, 9; 21:2; 22:8) and wrote in the first person.

In most cases, the writers of the Holy Scriptures did not title their respective books. The title of Revelation is not *The Revelation of Saint John the Divine*, as if to suggest that the apostle possessed some special sanctity. The book contains *The Revelation of Jesus Christ*, which was *given to* John. (See Revelation 1:1–3.) John was the recipient, not the author, of Revelation. Often, the book is mistakenly referred to as "Revelations," but, while it contains various visions that John received in the spirit, these were essentially one, being received in one day—namely, *"the Lord's Day"* (Revelation 1:10). The unity of the entire book is expressed in the two opening words: *"The Revelation..."* (verse 1).

2

AUDIENCE, DATE, AND PURPOSE

The original audience of readers of Revelation were the members of the churches in Asia Minor, which was remarkable for the number and wealth of its cities. The seven churches named in Revelation were important centers from which the gospel spread eastward and westward. Revelation is for the universal church, as well as for all the churches of succeeding generations. Here, Christ reveals Himself to *"all the churches"* (Revelation 2:23). What a mighty spiritual renewal would be experienced today if all churches would live in the light of this final book of the Bible!

With the City of Ephesus as a center point, John directed the churches of Asia Minor in spiritual matters. He even directed them while he was a prisoner of Rome on the Island of Patmos near the end of the reign of Emperor Domitian, around 90 A.D. However, Tertullian, one of the early church fathers, felt that Revelation was written during the Neronic persecution, around 64 A.D. Many modern scholars favor this earlier date.

The purpose of Revelation is indicated in its prologue. The book was written to reveal things *"which must shortly come to pass"* (Revelation 1:1). Among the activities of the Holy Spirit, these two are to be distinguished: to *"guide you into all truth"* (John 16:13) and to *"show you things to come"* (verse 13). The former is found particularly in the Gospels and the Epistles, and the latter is found particularly in Revelation. In this book of practical prophecy, the Lord's people are encouraged to practice endurance and faithfulness by the vision of the final overthrow of evil and God's eternal triumph of righteousness.

3

FORM, CONNECTIONS, AND SCHEME

There is a sense in which Revelation is the Christian philosophy of world history. It glows with poetic and prophetic enthusiasm. It is a book of wars, but it is also a book of final, triumphant peace. The word *revelation* signifies an unveiling, a drawing back, the removal of a veil that had covered a manifestation of truth. Thus, the book contains divine secrets revealed by God to Christ, and by Christ to the apostle John and to the church.

In imagery, scope, and expression, Revelation resembles the book of Daniel and, for this reason, has been called "the Daniel of the New Testament." Both in his gospel and in his epistles, John indicated some of the same ideas found in Revelation—namely, the conflict between faith and unbelief, and the ultimate victory of faith. The basic teachings of Revelation also can be found in the prophecies of Christ in Matthew 24. The language used in the opening of the sixth seal (see Revelation 6:12–17) is similar to that used by Old Testament prophets in their unfolding of the day of the Lord.

Revelation is a unified whole, and it provides a prophetic outline of the course of church history from the apostolic period to its translation at Christ's return, and also of the subsequent judgments to overtake a godless, guilty world. In style, Revelation is apocalyptic, and the movement of its great drama unfolds on a scale of peerless grandeur. The earth staggers under the shock of battle and strokes of judgment. Exposed to view are both the unending horrors of the abyss and the eternal joys of heaven.

The order of events is as follows:

1. The present dispensation will culminate in apostasy and in a period of unprecedented trial.

2. The "Man of Sin" will be fully manifested, will assume political supremacy, and will claim religious homage.

3. The true church of Christ will be "raptured" to heaven, and the Man of Sin will establish a covenant with the Jews. After violating his agreement with them, he will gather forces against them from other nations and seek to destroy God's people.

4. Jesus Christ will appear in great glory and destroy the Man of Sin and the false prophet. He will cast the devil, who inspired them, into the bottomless pit for a thousand years.

5. The millennial period will then be inaugurated. Sin will be suppressed but not exterminated. Christ will rule with a rod of iron, and universal peace and blessing will be enjoyed.

6. The loosing of Satan will result in the deception of the nations who follow him in earth's last revolt. This will be met by disastrous punishment for the rebels and their leader.

7. The last judgment will be set up, and Christ, as the supreme Judge, will preside at the condemnation of the ungodly.

8. The eternal age, with its permanent destinies, will begin after Jesus delivers up the kingdom to the Father. Then, God will be all in all.

4

KEY WORDS
AND KEYNOTE VERSE

JUDGMENT

Revelation is a book burdened with judgment, beginning at the house of God and continuing until the wicked are finally punished. The word *"judge,"* or *"judgment,"* is used nine times in the book.

PROPHECY

This word is used seven times in Revelation, showing that the contents of the book are future rather than past history.

WITNESS

This word is used six times—four times as *"witness"* and twice as *"martyr."* (These are translated from the same Greek word.) The testimony, or witness, of Jesus is given either by Him or by others about Him. *"Testimony"* and *"testify"* occur twelve times in Revelation.

The keynote verse is Revelation 1:7: *"Behold, he cometh."* The repetition of the phrase "I come quickly" six times (Revelation 2:5, 16; 3:11; 22:7; 22:12, 20) reminds us that the risen and ever-living

Christ is coming as the Vindicator to take to Himself His power and His kingdom. This hope assures us of the ultimate, unfailing justice of God. The key to the future is found in the pierced hands of Christ, in whom we have a treasure, the full value of which is scarcely realized even now.

5

CHARACTERISTICS
AND CHRISTOLOGY

The book of Revelation is marked with the sign of the cross, with the conflict centering in the person of Christ as *"the Lamb slain from the foundation of the world"* (Revelation 13:8). All through the book is the theme of patient, suffering faith, of brotherly love, and of enduring hope. The grim struggle between light and darkness is depicted in vivid colors. There is little mention of love in Revelation, but much of wrath.

Whatever changing events mark the progress of the conflict, the ultimate outcome is never in doubt. The rivalry of the powers of darkness is illustrated in a series of contrasts:

+ The servants of God are sealed; the antichrist seals his followers.

+ The church is seen as a woman clothed with the sun; the antichrist's apostate church is seen as a woman decked with jewels.

+ The Lamb once slain is alive again; the beast with a deadly head wound lives again.

+ Jehovah is worshipped; the antichrist claims worship.

+ Christ has His true prophets; the antichrist has his false prophet.

Because the book is a revelation of Christ, we expect it to be full of Him—and it is! Christ's person and work dominate its pages. Dr.

G. Campbell Morgan rightly observed that "any study of Revelation that does not concentrate upon Christ, and does not view all else in relation to Him, must bring the reader into an inextricable labyrinth."

Consider the following analysis:

NAMES GIVEN HIM

Jesus Christ (Revelation 1:1, etc.)

Jesus (Revelation 14:12, etc.)

Lord Jesus (Revelation 22:20, etc.)

Lord Jesus Christ (Revelation 22:21, etc.)

Christ (Revelation 20:4, 6)

The Christ of God ("His Christ") (Revelation 11:15; 12:10)

The Lamb (This occurs more than twenty times.)

King of Kings (Revelation 19:16, etc.)

Lord of Lords (Revelation 19:16)

Faithful and True (Revelation 19:11)

The Word of God (Revelation 19:13)

The unknown name (Revelation 19:12)

The root and the offspring of David (Revelation 22:16)

The bright and morning star (Revelation 22:16)

HIS GLORIOUS PERSON

Divine acts, attributes, and names are ascribed to Jesus, in whom dwells the fullness of God.

He is both divine and human, the possessor of two natures. (Revelation 22:16)

He is the first and the last, and everything in between. (Revelation 1:17; 2:8)

He is the living Word of God. (Revelation 19:13)

He is the searcher of hearts. (Revelation 2:23)

He is the Ancient of days. (Revelation 1:14 [based on Daniel 7:9])

He is the Lord of angels. (Revelation 1:1; 22:16)

He is the object of worship and praise. (Revelation 5:8–14; 7:12)

HIS MANIFOLD WORKS

He is faithful in His witness to God and His Word. (Revelation 1:5; 3:14)

He is the conqueror of Satan. (Revelation 3:21; 5:5; 20:10)

He is the crucified One. (Revelation 5:6, 12; 7:14; 13:8)

He is the atoning One. (Revelation 1:5; 7:14)

He is the risen One. (Revelation 1:18; 2:8; 3:21)

He is the exalted King. (Revelation 1:5; 17:14)

He is the coming One. (Revelation 1:7; 19:11, 19; 22:20)

6

INTERPRETATIONS
AND LESSONS

The book of Revelation has long been a battleground between differing schools of theological interpretation. ~~Many of these debates will be solved only through their actual fulfillment.~~

The following are the major systems of interpretation of Revelation.

THE PRETERISTS

Preterists relegate everything in Revelation to the past; they believe that almost all of the prophecies of the book—namely, the destruction of Jerusalem and fall of Rome—were fulfilled during the early centuries of the Christian era. However, when prophecy becomes history, it ceases to be prophecy. Revelation is distinctly referred to as *prophecy*.

THE HISTORICISTS

Historicists interpret Revelation as a progressive study of the fortunes of the church, from her commencement to her consummation. Those who hold this continuously historic view of the book assert that its prophecies are partly fulfilled and partly unfulfilled, with some being fulfilled before our eyes in the present day.

THE FUTURISTS

There are two major groups in this school of interpretation. First are the *simple futurists*, who believe that the first three chapters of Revelation have been fulfilled, and that the remaining chapters refer to the coming appearance of Christ. Second are the *extreme futurists*, who regard all of Revelation as referring to the Lord's coming, with the first three chapters being a prediction for the Jews in the years after Jesus' first resurrection.

A smaller group would be the *tribulationists*, who believe that the church is not raptured at the end of chapter 3 but remains on the earth through the first three-and-a-half years of the tribulation and is not caught up until the last trumpet, in Revelation 11:15. Advocates of this interpretation tell us that we must follow the church through the seals and the trumpets. The visible church is to go through the whole of the tribulation, but the "invisible church" is to be raptured before the last half of this terrible period of judgment breaks upon the guilty earth.

Other *tribulationists* take the church through the entire seven-year period of tribulation. They believe that Christ will not return for His own until He comes in glory and power. However, because the seals, trumpets, and vials are related to judgment and apply to Jews and Gentiles, in reality, the church cannot be on earth after Revelation 3, because the church is not the subject of judicial judgment.

Our understanding of this issue is that the Lord will save His own from the horrors of the tribulation. *"Because thou hast kept the word of my patience, I also will keep thee from the hour of temptation* [tribulation], *which shall come upon all the world, to try them that dwell upon the earth"* (Revelation 3:10; see also 1 Thessalonians 1:10).

THE IDEALISTS

Idealists deny any historical or prophetic meaning of Revelation and instead regard it simply as a collection of symbolic presentations of the conflict between good and evil, and of the ultimate victory of the good. They consider the contents to be mere moral lessons that are applicable to all times and eras.

THE MODERATES

Moderates, as their name implies, lie somewhere in between the historical and futurist interpretations, which can be combined. Those who, in John's day, suffered much at the hands of Rome saw some fulfillment in the prophecies that John wrote, but the persecutions of the first century did not exhaust all of those predictions. Many of them point into the future for complete fulfillment, even as John himself gave us a guide to the interpretation of Revelation in the words of Christ:

> *Write the things which thou hast seen, and the things which are, and the things which shall be hereafter.*
>
> (Revelation 1:19)

"*The things which thou hast seen*" refers to the glorious vision that John speaks of in Revelation 1.

"*The things which are* [now]" refers to church history, as outlined in chapters 2 and 3.

"*The things which shall be hereafter*" refers to all that is to follow the rapture of the church, as shown in chapters 4 through 22.

The complete fulfillment of this final section is, therefore, in the future. Only then will the predictions and promises of the prophets be realized and the kingdom of the Messiah be set up.

J. B. Phillips outlined five important lessons that we can learn from the book of Revelation:

1. The absolute sovereignty of God results in His ultimate purpose to destroy all forms of evil.

2. The inevitable judgments of God will come upon evil, especially the worship of false gods, which include riches, power, and success.

3. The necessity for patient endurance is based on the knowledge that God is in control of all history.

4. The existence of reality—represented with symbols such as the New Jerusalem, apart and secure from the battles and tribulations of earthly life—promises complete spiritual security to those who are faithful to God and His Christ.

5. The glimpse of worship and adoration constantly offered to God and the Lamb demonstrates man's ultimate acknowledgement of godly character when he sees God as He is.

PART TWO:

THE ACTORS AND SCENES
OF REVELATION

The number seven occurs in Revelation more often than any other number, the whole book being constructed around a series of sevens. This number is rich with meaning, representing completeness. The number seven occupies a large part in the Bible as a whole, and it often suggests spiritual perfection.

The Hebrew word for seven is from a root word signifying "to be full," "to be satisfied," or "to have enough of." An early occurrence of the number seven in Scripture is found in an oath between Abraham and Abimelech:

> ...both of them made a covenant. And Abraham set seven ewe lambs of the flock by themselves. And Abimelech said unto Abraham, What mean these seven ewe lambs which thou hast set by themselves? And he said, For these seven ewe lambs shalt thou take of my hand, that they may be a witness unto me, that I have digged this well. Wherefore he called that place Beersheba; because there they sware both of them.
> (Genesis 21:27–31)

In this section, we will explore in detail the significance of the number seven as it pertains to the book of Revelation.

7

THE SEVEN SPIRITS

THE SEVENFOLD MANIFESTATION OF THE HOLY
SPIRIT—REVELATION 1:4

Without a doubt, the book of Revelation is one of the most fascinating and profitable of all the books of the Bible, since, in it, John was able to look down the corridor of time and unfold the divine program of the ages. While there is much in Revelation that we can understand, we will not fully understand the book until the future events outlined within it are actually fulfilled.

IT IS A BOOK OUT OF A PRISON

How greatly prison literature—including Paul's "prison epistles" and John Bunyan's *Pilgrim's Progress*—has enriched the life of the church! Banished to the Island of Patmos by Emperor Domitian around 96 A.D., John, in his lonely cell, received the most remarkable revelation ever granted to mankind.

Rome, the city of seven hills, was to the west of John's island prison, and Palestine, the Euphrates River, and Babylon all were to the east. It was amid these geographical surroundings that the apostle John received his vision, perhaps helping to explain why all of these places figure prominently in the text.

IT IS A BOOK OF PROPHECY

The two great prophetic books of the Bible—Daniel and Revelation—must be studied together because each is a counterpart and complement of the other. As previously stated, this is why Revelation has been called "the Daniel of the New Testament." Revelation is predominantly prophetic. The word "prophecy" occurs seven times in Revelation, and, therefore, the book bears the seal of prophecy.

Prophecy represents a declared truth not yet fulfilled. Once a particular prophecy is fulfilled, it ceases to be prophecy and becomes history. Of course, there is a sense in which prophecy is history, told in advance. Solemn warnings are given to those who dare to tamper in any way with the prophecies of Revelation. (See Revelation 22:18–19.)

IT IS A BOOK WITH A BLESSING

Revelation opens with a blessing and closes with a benediction. The blessing is ours if we prayerfully read the book and obey all we read. (See Revelation 1:3.) The benediction is ours if we live in the light of the truth revealed. (See Revelation 22:21.) The word "blessed" occurs seven times in Revelation—"blessing" occurs three more times—and benedictions are scattered throughout the book.

IT IS A BOOK TO BE UNDERSTOOD

Some think we should treat Revelation as an enigma of the church. As one critic put it, "The more it is studied, the less it is understood." What they misunderstand is that this book is a *revelation*—not a mystery or something that is covered up.

The name, as stated before, means "an unveiling," "an uncovering," "drawing aside a curtain," revealing something that can no longer be concealed. While Revelation is highly symbolic, there is hardly a symbol in the book that cannot be explained by some other part of Scripture. Therefore, we must seek to compare Scripture with Scripture. (See 1 Corinthians 2:13.) Revelation contains some three hundred allusions to other parts of Scripture.

What was sealed in the book of Daniel would be made clear at the end-time period of the Gentile age. *"The words are closed up and sealed till the time of the end....But the wise shall understand"* (Daniel 12:9–10). Events mentioned by Daniel are now fully revealed by God to His servants. To the undiscerning mind, much of Revelation may appear to be dark, inexplicable, and impossible to comprehend, but to those who wait upon the Spirit who inspired John to write the book, its plan and purpose are clear. Yet, in all our efforts to understand Revelation, we must bear in mind the wise comment of Bishop Newton: "To explain this book perfectly is not the work of one man and of one age, and probably, it will not be clearly understood till all is fulfilled."

IT IS A BOOK OF HOPE

Hopelessness hangs like a thick cloud over man's aspirations, for ours are the darkest pages in human history. Through the unleashing of revolutionary forces, we are witnessing the suicide of civilization.

Civilized values are perishing. Barbarism and crime are the order of the day. Ours is a broken, bleeding world because of human hatreds. But the clear, unmistakable message of Revelation is the ultimate triumph of good over evil.

There are no guesses here: earth's sorrows are to cease, for a King is coming who will establish a universal reign of peace and righteousness. It is here in this marvelous book of Revelation that we breathe the exhilarating air of final victory over all forces of evil.

IT IS A BOOK WITH A PLAN

John makes it clear that he was divinely instructed to set forth facts concerning One...

+ who *is*—present,
+ who *was*—past, and
+ who *is to come*—future. (See Revelation 1:4.)
+ John writes about...
+ things which he *had seen*—past,
+ things which *are*—present, and
+ things which *shall be hereafter*—future. (See Revelation 1:19.)

The book is stamped with the number seven, which is found forty-five times, suggesting that its structure is composed of a series of sevens. Revelation is not a book made up of unintelligible, fantastic symbols, but it is a book with the only reliable plan we have of the ages to come. (See Revelation 1:3.)

We now take up a most necessary, yet often neglected, aspect of Revelation: its emphasis on the reality and activities of the Holy Spirit, who figures prominently throughout the book, especially in connection with the church that He brought into being at Pentecost. It would seem that a sevenfold relationship is presented in the twenty-two chapters of this book.

1. HIS RELATION TO INSPIRATION

Although Jesus never left behind any direct written message, and the Spirit Himself never directly composed an epistle, both Christ and the Holy Spirit inspired prophets and apostles to set forth truth that they wanted the church and the world to know. Thus, human hands recorded, and human minds received, the divine will and word. As we know, the Holy Spirit is preeminent as the Inspirer of truth: *"The spirit of the LORD spake by me"* (2 Samuel 23:2); *"The Spirit of Christ which was in them did signify, when it testified beforehand the sufferings of Christ, and the glory that should follow"* (1 Peter 1:11); *"Holy men of God spake as they were moved by the Holy Ghost [Holy Spirit]"* (2 Peter 1:21).

The apostle Paul, more than any other New Testament writer, understood, experienced, and declared the manifold ministry of the Holy Spirit. Paul referred to Him as *"the spirit of wisdom and revelation in the knowledge of him"* (Ephesians 1:17). It is the Spirit who draws aside the curtain in connection with the knowledge of Christ. It was in this capacity that He functioned in the heart and mind of the apostle John, enabling him to give us the book of the Revelation of Jesus Christ. While John was the writer of this book, the Holy Spirit was its true Author.

To John came the request, *"What thou seest, write in a book, and send it unto the seven churches..."* (Revelation 1:11), and, as a holy man, he wrote as he was borne along by the Spirit. It is imperative to notice the verbs of experience used here and elsewhere throughout the book:

What thou *seest...*

What thou seest, *write...*

What thou seest, write..., and *send...*

WHAT THOU SEEST

Phrases like "I saw," "I heard," "I looked," and "I beheld" crowd the pages of Revelation, and they indicate the actual experiences of John. The visions he recorded were not figments of his own imagination but were the Holy Spirit's revelation of persons and events. The secret of the symbolic unveiling that John received is found in the repeated phrase "in the Spirit." (See Revelation 1:10; 4:2; 17:3; 21:10.) As a believer of long experience, John was already "in the Spirit," in contrast to his previous, unregenerate condition—when he was "in the flesh."

But, as used by John on four distinct occasions, the phrases "in the Spirit" and "I became in the Spirit" imply an unusual control of all John's faculties by the Spirit, when he found himself taken out of the consciousness of space, sense, and time and transported into another state of being that was not visible to others. During the occasions mentioned by John, he found his whole inner being absorbed by heavenly visions. He was abstracted from the immediate consciousness of outward, earthly forms of life.

Socrates is said to have had the power of detaching himself from the influence of his outward life and standing deep in thought for hours or even days, unconscious of the midday heat or the mocking wonder of his friends. Other "high-souled" men with a burden for the spiritual welfare of their race also were able to practice such detachment. But, with John, it was the *Holy Spirit* who gave him the power of spiritual abstraction.

True, John was a saint and knew much about long periods of communion and meditation, and it was during one of these seasons of spiritual reflection that he found himself transported by the Spirit into the heavenlies. Thus, his own meditative nature, and the sweet and precious memories of Christ, prepared him for extraordinary visions. This transference of the inner being to another realm was also experienced by other Bible saints, who likewise received visions and revelations by a supernatural power, apart from their own natural mind. Their natural powers were held in abeyance while dominated or controlled by the Spirit. (See 1 Kings 18:12; Isaiah 6; Ezekiel 3:12, 14; 37:1; Acts 8:39; 2 Corinthians 12:1–4.)

The combination of the two phrases "*in the isle that is called Patmos*" (Revelation 1:9) and "*in the Spirit*" (verse 10) proves that geographical limitations are no hindrance to spiritual vision. Patmos was the sphere, but *the Spirit* was the atmosphere. That extremely dreary and inhospitable island on the Aegean Sea was no barrier to John's reception of the unveiling of Christ.

All that John saw while in his ecstatic condition was divinely authoritative; hence, his refrains *"These are the true sayings of God"* (Revelation 19:9) and *"These sayings are faithful and true"* (Revelation 22:6).

WHAT THOU SEEST, WRITE

What John witnessed, he had to write down. Guided by the Spirit, he recorded his sublime revelation. Twelve times over, John was told to *write*. We may not be able to write volumes, but what we do write can say volumes if we record what we receive by the Spirit. What Ezekiel saw in vision, he had to tell and transcribe. (See Ezekiel 12:21–25.) With Paul's heavenly revelations, it was different. When caught up into paradise, he heard unspeakable words, but his lips were sealed as to what he saw and heard. (See 2 Corinthians 12:1–7.) His *"thorn in the flesh"* (verse 7) prevented him from celebrating above measure in the abundance of his revelations. But, in John's case, again and again, he warns us about *keeping* those things he received written and recorded. (See, for example, Revelation 1:3.)

WHAT THOU SEEST, WRITE…, AND SEND

How impoverished the church would have been if John had failed to record the revelation granted him by the Holy Spirit! But John obeyed the divine voice and gave the churches of his time this precious unfolding, with the exhortation that it must be read, and with the promise that a divine blessing would rest upon all who read the record and obeyed all its instructions.

2. HIS RELATION TO PROPHECY

From the biblical unfolding of the ministry of the Holy Spirit, we know that He is particularly identified with prophecy. Our Lord declared that the twofold ministry of the Holy Spirit was to guide the apostles into the fullness of truth and to show them things to come. The result of the former is the Gospels and the Epistles, and the result of the latter is Revelation, in which we are shown the consummation to which the other sections of the Bible point. It was this same Holy Spirit who inspired the Old Testament prophets to "testify beforehand" of the grief and glory of Christ. The book of Revelation is stamped with the seal of *prophecy*, for the word occurs seven times in the book. Thus, the *root* of prophecy in all the other books of the Bible reaches its *fruit* in this last book.

In the command to write, John was instructed to outline the main divisions of the Revelation that he had received. *"Write…*

+ *the things which thou **hast seen**, and*
+ *the things which **are**, and*
+ *the things which **shall be** hereafter"* (Revelation 1:19).

Things past refers to the Patmos vision of Christ, in His prerogatives, His Person, and His position. Things *present* refers to church history from Pentecost to the rapture, as seen in chapters 1 through 3. Things *hereafter* refers to all that will follow the removal of the church at Christ's return to the air, as seen in chapters 4 through 22.

Thus, the bulk of Revelation is prophetic; it contains the consummation of all past traditions, and it is the only New Testament book containing so much of a prophetic nature. As a member of the Godhead, the Holy Spirit knows the end from the beginning and was therefore able to give John a panorama of coming events. Here, we have practical prophecy, in which the Lord's people are encouraged to practice endurance and faithfulness by the symbolic vision of the final overthrow of all evil. The ultimate victory of Christ is prophesied, and our hearts are set at rest by the knowledge that the pierced hand of the Lamb holds the key to all the future.

3. HIS RELATION TO PLENITUDE

A phrase that is perplexing to many, *"the seven Spirits,"* occurs four times in Revelation. (See Revelation 1:4; 3:1; 4:5; 5:6.) It indicates the plenitude of the Spirit's power and also His diversified activities. There are not seven Holy Spirits but only one—*"one Spirit"* (Ephesians 4:4). Seven is the number symbolic of perfection, and the Holy Spirit unifies in Himself all the attributes of deity. As the anointing Spirit, He imparts His sevenfold gifts, possesses a sevenfold might, and freely bestows His sevenfold grace. The Holy Spirit was in the prophet Isaiah when He prompted him in Isaiah 11:2–5 to "testify beforehand" that at Christ's return as King, the Spirit would rest upon Him, enabling Him to exercise His governmental offices in a sevenfold way, as...

1. the Spirit of the LORD,

2. the Spirit of wisdom,

3. the Spirit of understanding,

4. the Spirit of counsel,

5. the Spirit of might,

6. the Spirit of knowledge, and

7. the Spirit of the fear of the LORD.

In Zechariah, we read of the governmental operation of the Spirit, who, by His sevenfold ministry, will cause the earth to rejoice. (See Zechariah 4:6, 10.) The apocalyptic phrase *"the seven Spirits"* is, therefore, another way of expressing the fullness, completeness, and diversified attributes and actions of the one Holy Spirit, who is to exercise His diversified governmental action under the authority of the throne of God. (See Luke 4:18–19.)

4. HIS RELATION TO THE GODHEAD

The third Person of the blessed Trinity is coequal, coexistent, and coeternal with the Father and the Son—"three in one, blessed Trinity." As God the Spirit, He shares all the attributes of the Godhead, some of which are emphasized in Revelation.

DEITY

The apostle John repeatedly speaks of the Spirit as being "*of God*," such as "*the seven Spirits of God*" (Revelation 3:1; 4:5; 5:6.) The apostle also associated the Spirit with the slain Lamb. (See Revelation 5:6). He was the promised gift of both the Father and the Son and was equal in substance to both of them. Not only did the Spirit come from God, but He also is an integral part of the Godhead. Luke referred to Him as God. (See Acts 5:3–4.) Thus, we love, worship, and obey Him as *God the Spirit.*

AUTHORITY

Because the word *throne* occurs more than thirty times in Revelation, it is, without doubt, "the book of the throne," and it comes to us with all the authority of God's awesome seat of control. The Holy Spirit is depicted as being *before* this throne and coming to John "*out of* [it]" (Revelation 4:5). Along with the angels and living creatures around and in the midst of the throne, the Spirit shares their association with the judicial authority of God. In the book of Acts, we see the energy and grace of the Spirit in individuals, and, in the Epistles, we see His presence in the church. But the primary thought in Revelation is the pronouncement of the Spirit that God's government on earth is absolutely consistent with the righteous character of the throne. Coming from the throne, the Spirit acts governmentally, from heaven to earth.

We do not view Him in Revelation as the indwelling Comforter of every believer—although He was such to John in the solitude

of his prison cell, and to all the persecuted saints of his time—
but, rather, as God the Spirit, exercising the divine prerogative of
authority. Christ said that when the Spirit came to earth in His
fullness, He would not speak on His own initiative or authority
but would declare only what He had heard. (See John 16:13–15.)
And here, John writes that the Spirit functions in this way, coming
to John from the throne with its authoritative message of God.

HOLINESS

Another attribute of deity that the Spirit exhibits is that of
spotless holiness. *"Our God is a consuming fire"* (Hebrews 12:29);
therefore, He cannot tolerate anything alien to His thrice-holy
nature. How could He countenance anything contrary to His own
being?

It is the same with the Spirit, who is one with the Father and
the Son in their hatred of sin. This is the significance of the symbolic description of the Spirit as *"seven lamps of fire burning before
the throne"* (Revelation 4:5). As *"seven lamps of fire,"* His is the
perfection of the holiness that the throne represents—a holiness
searching out and destroying all that is contrary to the holy nature
of the Trinity.

> Eternal Light! eternal Light!
> How pure the soul must be
> When, placed within Thy searching sight,
> It shrinks not, but with calm delight,
> Can live, and look on Thee.[1]

Walter Scott observed that the symbol used in Revelation 4:5
denotes "the fullness of the Spirit in governmental action. The
Spirit here is not viewed as saving men through the preaching of
the gospel, nor in any of His varied services in the church, but is

---

1. Thomas Binney, "Eternal Light," 1826.

here witnessed in moral keeping with the throne itself." The *lamps* suggest illumination, while *fire* suggests a cleansing, purifying, and energizing element. As the inextinguishable flame, the Spirit illuminates, purges, and destroys. His is complete, active discernment of all matters and affairs in judgment.

> Come as the Fire, and purge our hearts
> Like sacrificial flame,
> Till our whole souls an offering be
> In love's redeeming name.[2]

OMNISCIENCE

Omni means "all," and *science* means "knowledge." Omniscience, or all-knowledge, is an attribute unique to deity. Perfect knowledge, discernment, hindsight, foresight, and insight are exclusive to the Godhead. In a remarkable passage, the number seven is mentioned three times in connection with the Spirit as the One *"having seven horns and seven eyes, which are the seven Spirits of God"* (Revelation 5:6). If the fullness of administration in government is implied in the phrase *"the seven Spirits of God,"* then perfect intelligence is suggested by *"seven eyes."* (See Zechariah 3:9.) The sevenfold Spirit represents *"the eyes of the LORD, which scan to and fro throughout the whole earth"* (Zechariah 4:10 NKJV), searching out everything that deserves divine judgment.

An eye is the symbol of inner knowledge and wisdom, as when Paul prayed that the eyes of the understanding of the Ephesians might be enlightened. (See Ephesians 1:18.) Paul, likewise, had no doubt as to the omniscience of the Spirit, who *"searcheth all things, yea, the deep things of God"* (1 Corinthians 2:10). Nothing can be hidden from Him who discerns all things. What a sobering thought it is that those seven eyes of the Spirit can scan all the thoughts in your heart and mine!

2. Andrew Reed, "Spirit Divine, Attend Our Prayer," 1829.

OMNIPOTENCE

Horns represent kings or royal powers, as well as power, strength, and glory. In the seven horns associated with the Holy Spirit, we have the truth of perfect power and strength. (See Revelation 5:6.) Job declared that he knew God could do everything (see Job 42:2), and Jesus proclaimed, *"All authority has been given to Me in heaven and on earth"* (Matthew 28:18 NKJV). The book of Acts is eloquent with the truth of the Spirit's omnipotence; in Revelation, where judicial authority is prominent, the Spirit is mantled with the perfection of power to enforce every divine edict pronounced against the seemingly great powers of earth.

In these days of impotency of earthly rulers, we should encourage ourselves in the glorious truth of divine omnipotence and sovereignty. In the narrower realm of our own lives, when difficulties appear to be insurmountable and needs arise that we feel can never be met, may we remember the Holy Spirit with His *"seven horns"* and trust Him as "the Spirit of power" to manifest His omnipotence on our behalf. The mighty Spirit is never weak at any point.

O Holy Ghost, of sevenfold might,
All graces come from Thee.[3]

OMNIPRESENCE

Omnipresence is the ability to be everywhere at the same time. Our finite minds cannot understand the mystery of this attribute of the Godhead. Yet it is a fact that we can never get away from the Spirit, who is everywhere. This is what David meant when he asked,

Whither shall I go from thy spirit? or whither shall I flee from thy presence? (Psalm 139:7)

---

3. Henry W. Baker, "O Holy Ghost, Thy People Bless," 1874.

Even if David had the wings of the morning to take him to the uttermost parts of the earth, what would happen when he got there? The Spirit would be there to lead and protect him! (See verses 9–10.) Those "seven eyes" of His, *"which scan to and fro throughout the whole earth"* (Zechariah 4:10 NKJV), bring us to another phrase of John's:

> *And I beheld, and, lo, **in the midst of the throne** and of the four beasts, and in the midst of the elders, stood a Lamb as it had been slain, having seven horns and seven eyes, which are the seven Spirits of God **sent forth into all the earth.***
>
> (Revelation 5:6)

There are two phrases to combine in this verse: *"in the midst of the throne"* and *"sent forth into all the earth,"* both of which concern the activities of the Holy Spirit. In this age, the Spirit is related to the church, but in the judgments indicated in Revelation, He is associated with the government of earth from heaven. His eyes search out all those deserving of divine punishment, no matter who they are in all the earth, and, by His power, He will see to it that the dictates of the throne are obeyed. Woe to the inhabitants of a godless earth when the Spirit leaves the throne to destroy the evil forces!

PERSONALITY

The majority of the references to the Spirit in Revelation refer to what the Spirit *says*:

> *…the Spirit saith unto the churches….*   (Revelation 2:29)

> *Yea, saith the Spirit….*   (Revelation 14:13)

> *The Spirit and the bride say, Come.*   (Revelation 22:17)

That the Spirit is not a mere influence or emanation from God is proven by the fact that He can speak specifically, or *"expressly,"* as Paul wrote 1 Timothy 4:1. Articulate speech is possible only where there is personality. Because the Holy Spirit possessed all the true elements of personality, He controlled John's thoughts and emotions and used them as the medium of expression. If only people in this age of grace would respond to the pleading voice of the Spirit as He beseeches sinners to be reconciled in God!

5. HIS RELATION TO THE CHURCH

While the bulk of Revelation is taken up with Christ's governmental control of earth and the Spirit's association with this control, in the letters to the seven churches, we have the sevenfold repetition of the phrase *"what the Spirit saith unto the churches"* (Revelation 2:7, 11, 17, 29; 3:6, 13, 22). The majority of references to the Spirit are found in these seven letters.

Since bringing the church, which is the Lord's body, to birth at Pentecost, the Spirit has been the Administrator of her affairs. In the book of Acts, where we have the establishment and expansion of the church, the Spirit's presence and authority dominate the scene. If the church is spiritually impotent today, it is because she has lost the truth concerning the lordship of the Spirit, who distributes His gifts among her members as He wills.

After Revelation 3, the Spirit rules from the throne in a judicial capacity throughout the earth. But when our Lord returns to the church with final exhortations, the Spirit is again identified with the church, Christ's "bride." He voices with her the desire for Christ to redeem His promise to take His bride to Himself: *"The Spirit and the bride say, Come"* (Revelation 22:17). This is the last glimpse of the Holy Spirit we have in the Bible, and what a blessed glimpse it is!

6. HIS RELATION TO INDIVIDUALS

As the way is prepared during the great tribulation for Christ's universal reign, the masses are dealt with in a corporate way. Churches, peoples, tongues, and nations are dealt with en masse. But in the church section of Revelation, a remarkable feature of each of the seven letters is the way in which the Spirit is linked to individual believers. The letters are addressed by Christ to the churches, but it is the responsibility of each member in those churches to heed what He has said. And because it is the ministry of the Spirit to take the truth and reveal it to us—to uncover its inner meaning to our minds—in each letter, we read, *"He that hath an ear, let him hear what the Spirit saith unto the churches."*

At Pentecost, the Spirit dealt with people en masse, and, as a result of His effusion, He saved them, thousands at a time. But with the necessity of the seven churches' spiritual rectification, the responsibility is on the members, as individuals, to listen to the voice of rebuke, and to repent. After all, any church is made up of individual people, and if each person seeks to walk in the Spirit and experience His power, then the church as a whole will be blessed. Are your ears tuned to the voice of the Spirit as He speaks to the churches today? The same personal responsibility is emphasized at the beginning and the end of the book:

> *Blessed is he that readeth, and they that hear the words of this prophecy, and keep those things which are written therein.*
>
> (Revelation 1:3)

> *And the Spirit and the bride say, "Come!" And let him who hears say, "Come!" And let him who thirsts come. Whoever desires, let him take the water of life freely. For I testify to everyone who hears the words of the prophecy of this book: if anyone adds to these things, God will add to him the plagues*

that are written in this book; and if anyone takes away from
the words of the book of this prophecy, God shall take away his
part from the Book of Life, from the holy city, and from the
things which are written in this book.

(Revelation 22:17–19 NKJV)

May grace be ours to respond immediately to the vital, private
call to every opened ear!

7. HIS RELATION TO ETERNITY

How inspiring it is to know that the Holy Spirit is the Herald
of resurrection and of our eternal bliss and rewards. This last
glimpse of Him is most precious in its significance.

THE AGENT IN RESURRECTION

Having had a share in the resurrection of Christ from the
dead, the Holy Spirit is the Agent in the resurrection of saints.
"The Spirit of him that raised up Jesus from the dead" (Romans 8:11)
will also raise up those who are the Lord's from the dead. This
brings us to the resurrection of the two witnesses after they had
been slain in the very place where Jesus was crucified.

The death of God's final two prophets because of their
pronouncements of divine judgment cause tremendous glee
among the godless. As William Newell expresses it, "A regular
Christmastime-of-hell ensues," for *"they that dwell upon the earth*
shall rejoice over them, and make merry, and shall send gifts one to
another" (Revelation 11:10). The identity of these two witnesses—
over which there is much conjecture—does not presently concern
us. What impresses us is that their fearless testimony before the
earth is given over to Satan and to the antichrist. The multitudes
who hear them preach of human wickedness kill the valiant heralds and leave their mutilated bodies in the streets of the city for

three-and-a-half days. (See Revelation 11:9.) Excursions are made into Jerusalem to see and to gloat over the unburied corpses of these prophets of God.

But when man does his worst to his fellow man, God steps in and does His best for those who suffer in His cause. Thus we read, *"The Spirit of life from God entered into them, and they stood upon their feet"* (Revelation 11:11). Then, they are raptured to heaven with their enemies watching their ascension. (See verse 12.) Such a resurrection and ascension wipe the hellish grin from the faces of the murderers of the witnesses, and they become terrified. Dead in Christ, the two men rise again and are caught up—a foretaste of what will happen when Jesus returns for His true church. (See 1 Thessalonians 4:13–18.)

Paul proclaimed that Jesus was declared to be *"the Son of God with power, according to the spirit of holiness, by the resurrection from the dead"* (Romans 1:4). It is this same Spirit of holiness who quickens with divine life and energy those two dead bodies discarded on the Jerusalem streets. What impresses us about this particular activity of the Spirit is the fact that He raises the two dead witnesses after exactly three-and-a-half days. Another half day, and corruption would have begun to claim their corpses. God, however, does not allow His holy ones to undergo corruption. It was on the third day that Jesus arose. You will recall that Martha felt that the resurrection of her brother Lazarus was impossible, for she said, *"Lord, by this time he stinketh: for he hath been dead four days"* (John 11:39). God is able to raise the dead, no matter how long they have been in the grave.

THE HERALD OF ETERNAL BLISS

What a precious glimpse John gives us of the ministry of the Spirit in connection with the blessedness of all the holy dead! The loving voice from heaven said to John, *"Write, Blessed are the dead which die in the Lord from henceforth: Yea, saith the Spirit, that they may rest from their labors; and their works do follow them"* (Revelation 14:13).

The Spirit came as the bequeathed Comforter, and the early church knew what it was to walk *"in the comfort of the Holy Ghost"* (Acts 9:31). It is in this role of Consoler that He addresses His message to all saints—a message with a threefold assurance.

THE REJOICING OF THE DEAD

"Blessed [happy] *are the dead which die in the Lord from henceforth"* (Revelation 14:13). Is there any significance in the words *"from henceforth"*? I think there is. The word *"henceforth"*—a definite time mark—indicates the nearness of the end, and that the blessing is just about to be entered into by those who face the most terrible juncture in human history. But the message is always true for all who die in the Lord in any age. Only those who die in the Lord have the right to rejoice, because they know that although their dust will repose in the grave until the resurrection, they themselves will pass at death into the presence of the Lord to share His life forever. As soon as they are absent from the body, they are at home with the Savior. How different it is with all who die in their sins! For them, there is no rejoicing, only eternal sorrow.

THE REST OF THE DEAD

"...that they may rest from their labors" (Revelation 14:13). Among *"so great a cloud of witnesses"* (Hebrews 12:1) in heaven, none will shine more brightly than the saints of the great tribulation, who will serve and suffer under the most appalling circumstances. How the Spirit's word of rich consolation will be appreciated by those tribulation saints, who, after walking in the vigor of their faith, will enter into their everlasting rest! Toil and tears, sorrow and suffering, will be forever past. They will rest from a service laden with hardship, pain, and death as they find themselves

translated to heaven to enjoy a most blessed service and to serve their Lord day and night forever.

THE REWARD OF THE DEAD

"...*their works do follow them*" (Revelation 14:13). The works of those saints raised and taken up accompany them, and immediate reward is theirs. The righteous Judge will appraise the true value of their works and will reward each saint according to his or her work. As will be seen from the letters to the seven churches, the Holy Spirit is definitely related to rewards for overcomers. (See Revelation 2, 3.)

Of course, *all* who are in Christ will enjoy the eternal rest that comes through dying. Our hope is that we will still be alive when He comes, and will, therefore, have the joy of going to heaven without dying.

O joy! O delight!
Should we go without dying![4]

But whether we are among the dead or the living at Christ's return, our works go with us, and at the judgment seat, our service will be the basis of reward. "*Every man's work shall be made manifest: for the day shall declare it, because it shall be revealed by fire; and the fire shall try every man's work of what sort it is*" (1 Corinthians 3:13). Some of us will be "*saved; yet so as by fire*" (verse 15). Because we are in Christ, we shall be in heaven, but it will be with a saved soul and a lost life. No credit will be ours when the Judge rewards the consecrated service of the saints.

God grant that for each of us, there will be a full reward! May ours be the benediction, "*Well done, good and faithful servant... enter into the joy of your lord*" (Matthew 25:21, 23 NKJV).

---

4. H. L. Turner, "Christ Returneth," 1878.

8

THE SEVENFOLD VISION

THE HEAVEN-DRAWN PICTURE OF
CHRIST—REVELATION 1:12–18

Prominent among the many aspects of Revelation is the fact that it is a book about a Person, Christ Himself being the central subject. As noted previously, Dr. G. Campbell Morgan once observed, "Any study of Revelation which does not concentrate upon Christ, and does not view all else in relation to Him, must bring the reader into an inextricable labyrinth." Thus, the first five words of Revelation declare its nature and purpose: "*The Revelation of Jesus Christ.*" It is not "The Revelation of St. John the Divine," but the unveiling of the One whom John dearly loved.

Nor is it "The Revelations of Jesus Christ." It is singular, not the plural. It is "*The **Revelation** of Jesus Christ,*" of which there are many facets. Within this book, Christ is revealed and exalted more fully than in any other book of the Bible. Allusions to Him abound, as in the twenty or more references to Christ as "the Lamb." Three broad divisions of the book are:

1. Chapters 1–3: Christ and His saints

2. Chapters 4–19: Christ and the old world

3. Chapters 20–22: Christ and the new world

In the Gospels, we see Christ serving and suffering. In Acts, He is alive forever, working through His church. In Revelation, He is the supreme Hero, conquering all of His foes.

As we watch the interplay of good and evil, and the thickening plots of the drama, we welcome the portrayal of Jesus as the coming Executive of divine government, and as the Dispenser of both retribution and reward. Here is the presentation of the King and His kingdom, and the King taking His kingdom by force.

Christ is the key to the book, the Holy Spirit is our Guide, and our own spirituality is the measure of our appreciation of a full-length portrait of our Savior.

In many ways, the opening chapter is one of the most remarkable of the book, since it affords a summary of all that is to follow. Names, titles, and symbols of Christ used in this initial chapter are scattered and enlarged upon throughout the book.

No other book in the Bible unveils the presence, Person, and power of the Lord Jesus Christ as Revelation, which claims to be a marvelous panorama of our Lord Himself, and not merely of events in connection with His triumph. The book opens with Christ as the Revealer of Himself. (See Revelation 1:1–3.) Because this is a revelation of Jesus Christ, the book takes on added significance and becomes tremendously important. Here, He is depicted as the central Figure holding the keys of destiny. In spite of demons and men, Christ moves undefeated through the fascinating and fast-moving drama of the book. Note the five authoritative "I am's" of the opening chapter, and compare them with the other "I am's" that John gives us in his gospel.

One of the special features of this first chapter is the authentic picture of Christ it provides. Here is a portrait that no artist has been able to paint. The chapter abounds in titles and superlatives, and it takes all of them to describe Him who has no equal.

THE PROLOGUE (REVELATION 1:1-3)

With modern treatments of Revelation, we have no sympathy whatsoever. Their blatant assertions that John borrowed the vision of his book from ancient apocalyptic literature, giving us merely a patchwork of heathen folklore, are flatly contradicted by the simple statement that John provides of the origin and order of what he saw and wrote. The apostle has not given us a collection of heathen visions that have been "Christianized." Rather, Christ has shown us a preview of His final conquest over all the antagonistic forces. And because this revelation was God-given, it is our solemn obligation to bow in reverence as we study it.

In Revelation we have what we might call a ladder with five rungs:

1. God

2. Christ

3. Angel

4. John

5. Servants

God gave the revelation to Christ, since it concerns Him. Christ, in turn, gave it to His angel, and, thereafter, angels remain prominent features throughout the book. The angelic messenger then communicated the revelation to John, who recorded what he received for the enlightenment and edification of the saints of all ages. Such an order corresponds to the conclusion: *"And he said unto me, These sayings are faithful and true: and the Lord God of the holy prophets sent his angel to show unto his servants the things which must shortly be done"* (Revelation 22:6).

No one was better fitted than John to act as the appointed channel of this sublime revelation. This is evident from what the Gospels record of his intimate fellowship with Christ. John was Christ's close friend, whom He loved very much. He is also described as leaning upon the bosom of Jesus. (See John 13:23.) And it was John who wrote the words of Jesus regarding the Spirit's ability to show the servants of Christ *"things to come"* (John 16:13).

Before we proceed further with our study, it is essential to pause and ask ourselves, *Am I spiritually fit to read and receive blessing from the Lord through my reading of this great book?* Our humble attitude should be simple: *"That which I see not teach thou me: if I have done iniquity, I will do no more"* (Job 34:32).

In sending this revelation to John through His angel, Jesus *"signified it"* (Revelation 1:1), or "sign-ified" it, meaning He used signs, or symbols, in its impartation. In dealing with these symbols, we must seek to interpret them in light of their usage elsewhere in Scripture. We must compare symbol with symbol and thereby guard ourselves from the extravagances of interpretation, of which so many expositors have been guilty.

We should also consider *when* it was that John saw all the things he wrote down at a later date. He wrote that he was *"in the isle that is called Patmos"* (Revelation 1:9), and that the vision came to him while *"in the Spirit on the Lord's day"* (verse 10). Two phrases here make an interesting combination: *"in the isle"* and *"in the Spirit."* Evidently, John's geographical limitations were no hindrance to his spiritual vision. A dark dungeon was not able to imprison his free spirit. Is it this way with us? When cramped and confined in circumstances that cut us off from a free world, are we more spiritually able to commune with heaven? In our restricting island, are we also "in the Spirit"?

There are two interpretations of *"the Lord's day."* The usual interpretation is that this particular day was the Sabbath, which John was observing when the vision reached him. It was the day

God had set aside for the worship of His name. And on this best of all days, when the opportunity is ours of turning aside from the world, we can hear God's voice and enter into a spiritual understanding of His Word.

Other scholars believe that the phrase *"the Lord's day"* should be translated as "the day of the Lord." Being *"in the Spirit"* can mean some a unique endowment by which the Holy Spirit projected the mind of John forward into the future, as declared by the Old Testament prophets when they prophesied about the day of the Lord. Isaiah 2:10–22, for example, is treated as a complete summary of Revelation chapters 4 through 19. John may have been carried forward in time by the Spirit to that awesome day, with its judgments, and was made to describe in detail what Daniel and other prophets had foreseen in general.

It may be that the solution can be found in harmonizing both views. While John was meditating on the Sabbath, the Spirit enabled him to look down the corridor of time and unfold the coming "day of the Lord."

Before leaving the prologue, we must consider two phrases. John received a revelation of *"things which must shortly come to pass"* (Revelation 1:1). This word *"shortly"* carries with it the thought of "speed" or "immanency." Once action begins, there will be rapidity of execution. There is no thought here that John expected all his visions to be fulfilled immediately.

The same idea is associated with the declaration *"the time is at hand"* (Revelation 1:3). As Walter Scott expressed it, "Prophecy annihilates time and all intervening and even opposing circumstances, and sets one down on the threshold of accomplishment." To our way of thinking, it seems as if God is delaying the fulfillment of His ultimate purposes as outlined in Revelation, but such seeming delay means more grace for a guilty world.

THE PREROGATIVES (REVELATION 1:4–11)

In authoritative fashion, the apostle John begins this section with his own name: *"John to the seven churches which are in Asia"* (verse 4). Similarly emphatic is the phrase in verse 9: *"I John,...."* The Greek word *apostello* means "to send forth" and describes a messenger commissioned to undertake an important mission. But Scripture also uses this term as applied to Christ: *"the **Apostle** and High Priest of our profession, Christ Jesus"* (Hebrews 3:1). As John began the communication of the revelation sent to him, he affirmed his authority as an apostle, or a "sent one." What he was about to announce was not of his own creation. As a God-sent messenger, John was going to describe *"all things that he saw"* (Revelation 1:2). *"I John"* (verse 9) proclaims the opening of the book containing the second coming of Christ. In the *"I Jesus"* of Revelation 22:16, Christ announced His own coming.

The Lord Jesus Christ is presented in Revelation 1:4 as the One *"which is, and which was, and which is to come."* *"Which is"* refers to the present and reminds us of God's immutability. As "the changeless One," Christ is able to undertake for His own in an ever-changing present. *"Which was"* stretches out over the past and takes us back thousands of years. *"Which is to come"* carries us forward and causes us to remember that what the Lord has been, He will continue to be forever. He is *"the same yesterday, and to day, and for ever"* (Hebrews 13:8).

There is another important truth in verses 4 and 5 of John's salutation, where we find three "froms." *"From him"* (Revelation 1:4) is from God, the independent, self-existent One. *"From the seven Spirits which are before his throne"* (verse 4) designates the Holy Spirit's plenitude of power and diversified activity. Finally, there is *"from Jesus Christ"* (verse 5). Thus, Father, Son, and Holy Spirit are linked together in the communication of this revelation. Here, as elsewhere in the Bible, the triune God is found operating as one.

"Jesus Christ, who is the faithful witness" (Revelation 1:5) lends force to the Lord's command to the church in Smyrna: *"Be thou faithful unto death"* (Revelation 2:10). Christ's life exhibited His teachings and commands. The phrase *"the faithful witness"* describes Christ's relationship to God while here on earth. As a true Prophet, He never failed to declare the entire counsel of God. The word *"witness"* means someone who sees, knows, and then speaks, and is a characteristic word of John—and one he used more than seventy times in his writings.

"Jesus Christ...the first begotten of the dead" (Revelation 1:5) is a wonderfully descriptive title. "Christ is both 'firstfruit' and 'firstborn' of the dead," said Walter Scott. "The former title intimates that He is the first in *time* of the coming harvest of those who sleep. (See 1 Corinthians 15:20, 23.) The latter title signifies that He is first in rank of all who will rise from the dead. 'Firstborn' is the expression of supremacy, of preeminent dignity, and not one of time or of chronological sequence. (See Psalm 89:27.) No matter where, when, or how Christ entered the world, He would necessarily take the first place in virtue of what He is." Such a title also indicates Christ's priestly work.

"Jesus Christ...the prince of the kings of the earth" (Revelation 1:5) portrays the kingly aspect of Christ's work. The kings of the earth have been proud, powerful monarchs, and until the time of Christ's appearing, they will have exercised tremendous influence. But when Christ comes to exercise these sovereign rights of His, He will reign supreme. All imperial scepters will be destroyed and all opposing authorities forever vanquished. As the Lord of Lords, Christ will be Lord over all who exercise authority. Truly the King of Kings, He will be King over all who reign. What a princely rule awaits this misruled earth!

"I am Alpha and Omega, the beginning and the ending" (Revelation 1:8) is repeated as *"I am Alpha and Omega, the first and the last"* (verse 11). Most scholars believe the first part of verse 11 is not in the original text as written by John. This may have been borrowed from Revelation 1:17: *"Fear not; I am the first and the last."* Here, we have one of those divine "I am's" calling attention to Christ's dignity and authority. Alpha and Omega, the first and last letters of the Greek alphabet, suggest that Christ is the beginning and ending of all that applies to God's purposes regarding mankind. He is the first and the last, and everything in between.

Christ appears as the three-tense Being again in Revelation 1:8: *"I am Alpha and Omega, the beginning and the ending, saith the Lord, which is, and which was, and which is to come, the Almighty."* This time, with the addition of *"the Almighty"*—with the unfolding of judgment on the antagonistic forces of hell and earth, and all the hatred to be heaped upon the righteous—it is consoling to have the revelation of the Lord's omnipotent power and sustaining resources confirmed at the outset of the book.

As we shall see, the circumstances of the needy will force them to make constant demands upon such a strong name. Mighty powers will seek to engulf God's people, but the almighty One will be on hand to deliver them. Omnipotence matches itself against proud, arrogant forces—and wins! The great question of Revelation is, "Who shall rule?" There is only one answer to this crucial question: the Lord God Almighty.

And from Jesus Christ, who is the faithful witness, and the first begotten of the dead, and the prince of the kings of the earth. Unto him that loved us, and washed us from our sins in his own blood, and hath made us kings and priests unto God and his Father; to him be glory and dominion for ever and ever. Amen.   (Revelation 1:5–6)

The revelation and recital of Christ's dignities issues in the exultant doxology of the redeemed. Our affections are deeply stirred, and our adoration ascends, as we meditate on all that our blessed Lord is in Himself and how His attributes are exercised on behalf of His own.

"Unto him that loveth us, and loosed us from our sins" (Revelation 1:5 rv). The loosing is over and done with, but the loving goes on forever! *"Having loved his own…he loved them unto the end"* (John 13:1). What comfort the present and unchanging love of the Redeemer brings to the redeemed of any age! During the tribulation period, when the fires of persecution gather around God's people on earth, what triumphant songs of victory will be theirs as they rest in their Deliverer's love!

"[He] *hath made us kings and priests unto God and his Father*" (Revelation 1:6). John does not forget to celebrate the high dignity of the redeemed. Christ, whose love and blood are our confidence and rest, has made His people a kingdom of priests unto God. The Greek word for *"kings"* is singular. *"Kingdom,"* a term that is entirely consistent with the book as a whole, implies that the redeemed are not merely to be governed as subjects but are also to exercise sovereignty. The role in which the saints are to rule is as priests. Here and now, all believers exercise the priestly function (see, for example, Ephesians 2:18; Hebrews 13:15), but Revelation anticipates the exercise of a royal priesthood.

Walter Scott asked, "What is meant by this union of kingly dignity and priestly grace? Zechariah 6:13 states the position exactly: 'He shall be a priest upon his throne.' As we are to reign with Christ, the character of His reign determines the nature of ours. Let us never forget, nor, in practice, sink below our exalted rank. The constant remembrance of it will impart dignity of character and preserve us from the money-loving spirit of the age." Yes, and let the order be noted: "kings and priests"! If we are to intercede effectually, we must constantly reign in life. When, as kings, we triumph over evil within and without, then, as priests, we have liberty and power as we plead the cause of lost and sinful souls.

"To him be glory and dominion for ever and ever" (Revelation 1:6). With this ascription of eternal glory and dominion given to Christ, we see the fulfillment of His visible glory and far-flung dominion, as foretold by holy men of old. As Revelation unfolds, this doxology increases in fullness. Here, it is twofold; by Revelation 4:11, it is threefold; by Revelation 5:13, it is fourfold; and by Revelation 7:12, it is sevenfold.

> *Behold, he cometh with clouds; and every eye shall see him, and they also which pierced him: and all kindreds of the earth shall wail because of him. Even so, Amen.*   (Revelation 1:7)

In this verse, we find the testimony of the second coming of Christ. William Newell rightly called this verse the first great text of Revelation. In Revelation 21:5, we have the second great text: *"Behold, I make all things new."* The announcement of our Lord's glorious advent is introduced with the exclamation *"Behold,"* which stands as a sentinel at the threshold of the book. Here, John is emphasizing the return of our Lord to the earth—that is, His public revelation to the whole world, resulting in the establishment of His kingdom. And every eye, at one time or another, shall witness His public manifestation. By *"they also which pierced him,"* we can understand it to mean both the Jews and the Gentiles. It was John who reminded us that it was a Gentile spear that pierced the Savior's side. (See John 19:33–37.)

As Walter Scott expressed it, "The weak and vacillating representative of Rome, in her imperial greatness, sullied her vaunted reputation for inflexible justice by basely ordering her august Prisoner, whom he thrice declared innocent, to be scourged and crucified." But is there a special reference here to the Jews, since they goaded Pilate into piercing the Savior? (See Zechariah 12:10.) When she sees Christ as He appears, Israel will believe, and, as true morning overtakes Jewish earth-dwellers, she will experience rebirth as a nation.

Let us not lose sight of the general wail of anguish at the coming of the Son of Man. We must not confine the terror to the two tribes of Judah and Benjamin, nor to the ten other tribes. The language used is not "the tribes in the land of Israel" but "*all kindreds* [tribes] *of the earth.*" The prophetic word describing men hiding in the caves of the earth from the terror of the Lord is now to be realized. (See Isaiah 2:19.) Then comes the double affirmation to the prophetic testimony: "*Even so*" and "*Amen.*" For both Jew and Gentile, Christ is coming, and to both groups, God's Word is unchangeable.

HIS PERSON (REVELATION 1:12-18)

In this section, John provides an awesome description of the One whose voice he had heard. Symbols of function and of character are identified here with the Son of Man, who shares full and complete deity. The seven parts of the full-length portrait of Christ are easily discernible, and all the features (as we shall indicate more fully in our next section) are scattered among the churches. As we proceed, we must observe that there is a vast difference between our Lord's past sorrow and His future sovereignty. At last, we see the once-scorned Jesus crowned forever as the King of Kings and Lord of Lords!

The book of Revelation is about the Person and power of Christ, with manifold symbols of His activities, functions, and character. Here, we see Jesus related to time and eternity, as well as to the Jew, the Gentile, and the church of God. The part of the first chapter we want to emphasize is the one that shows Christ as the heavenly One with a human appearance. Deity and humanity are combined, and the heavenly and earthly are marvelously mingled together. (See Revelation 1:9–18.) What a vast difference there is between our Lord's past sorrow and His future sovereignty! At last, we see Jesus—once, the object of shame, scorn, and contempt—now crowned with honor and glory.

1. HIS GARMENT AND GIRDLE

In the midst of the seven candlesticks one like unto the Son of man, clothed with a garment down to the foot, and girt about the paps with a golden girdle. (Revelation 1:13)

Christ's position in the midst of the church, symbolized by the seven candlesticks, declares Him to be the Head of the church, and its central power.

Christ's title—the Son of Man—identifies Him with humanity and judgment.

Christ's clothing and girding declare His kingly authority, and also the majesty of His priesthood. The allusion is to the beautiful garments of the high priest under the Levitical order, indicating the personal qualities and official position of the Priest.

Christ's garment was "*down to the foot,*" but it did not cover His feet. Otherwise, John would not have seen their nail prints and worshipped his Lord, whose glorified form was properly clothed. In these days of immodest clothing, garments are as far up from the feet as they dare go. At Calvary, Jesus lost all His garments to the gamblers, but now He is clothed in His beautiful robe as the great High Priest. "*His raiment was white as the light*" (Matthew 17:2).

Christ was also "*girt about the paps with a golden girdle.*" When the girdle is around the loins, service is prominent (see John 13:4–5), but when a girdle is around the breasts, dignified priestly judgment is implied. Being of gold, the girdle portrays Christ's deity and His righteous kingship. As for the breasts, these can imply both calm and repose, or else preparation for judgment.

Robed as the King-Priest, Christ was not seen by John as the Priest at the golden altar with the censer and the burning incense, but rather among the candlesticks with the golden snuffers, as though He was inquiring for the last time whether the lamps of the sanctuary would burn worthy of the place, or whether He would be compelled to remove them soon. All the figures of speech that follow are an expression of judgment—a revelation of the Priest not at the altar with incense, nor even at the lamp stand with oil to feed it, but with snuffers to judge and trim the smoky lamp stand.

This initial vision that John received was not about the pastoral grace of Christ but of His judicial authority. This is why Revelation must be viewed as a book of judgment. *"Judge"* and *"judgment"* appear fifteen times in the book. The seven churches are depicted as being in the place of this judgment, which must always begin at the house of God. (See 1 Peter 4:17.) For an enumeration of the various judgments of Revelation, with Christ as the Judge, the following summary can be noted:

1. Judgment of the church's earthly history (Revelation 2–3)

2. Judgment of the rebellious nations, especially of beast worshippers (Revelation 4–16)

3. Judgment of the system of earth-idolatry (Revelation 17–18)

4. Judgment of the beast, false prophet, kings, and armies at Armageddon (Revelation 19:19–21)

5. Judgment of the devil's permitted career on earth (Revelation 20:1–3)

6. Judgment of the spared nations, in enforced righteousness, justice, and peace, during the millennium (Revelation 20:4–6)

7. Judgment of the rebellious earth upon Satan's release (Revelation 20:7–9)

8. Judgment of Satan in the lake of fire forever (Revelation 20:10)

9. Judgment of the unsaved at the great white throne (Revelation 20:11–15)

Each of the foregoing judgments presents Christ in a special character at each stage of judgment.

2. HIS HEAD AND HAIR

His head and his hairs were white like wool, as white as snow. (Revelation 1:14)

Christ's white, uncovered head easily distinguishes the glorified Person being revealed. Isaiah used the whiteness of wool and snow to describe the cleansing of the heart from the foulness of sin. (See Isaiah 1:18.) In Revelation, it symbolizes the absolute purity and agelessness of the Savior, whose shed blood alone can cleanse us from the vileness of sin, enabling us to walk with Him dressed in white garments.

The uncovered, majestic head of the Son of Man conveys the idea of mature experience and of perfected wisdom coupled with immaculate holiness. Daniel had a similar vision of the One who was *"the Ancient of days"* (Daniel 7:9), whose garment was white as snow and whose hair was like pure wool.

Christ's transfiguration was a preview of the Patmos vision. Peter, James, and John were eyewitnesses of Christ's majesty and were overawed as they saw His face shining with brilliant white light. (See Matthew 17:2.) For a moment, they saw His glory as the Only-begotten of the Father.

For us, white hair is a sign of old age, decay, and nearness to the grave. But this is not the implication in Revelation, for the white-haired One whom John saw is ageless, deathless, and eternal. From eternity to eternity, Jesus is the same, and His years have no end.

Christ always retains the dew of His youth, and yet, He has always been venerable in the eternal wisdom and glory, which He has had with the Father from before the foundation of the world. John, who once saw the head and hairs of his Lord crowned with thorns, now beholds them crowned with the diadem of heaven's glory.

3. HIS EYES OF FIRE

...his eyes were as a flame of fire....   (Revelation 1:14)

The Bible has much to say about the eyes of the Lord, which *"run to and fro throughout the whole earth"* (2 Chronicles 16:9) and *"are in every place, beholding the evil and the good"* (Proverbs 15:3). Eyes, as well as tongues, have a way of speaking, and the eyes of the Lord, beholding the evil and the good, indicate divine discernment, deep penetration, and intimate knowledge. As for the *"flame of fire,"* this represents the attribute of perfect understanding, and the ability to search out the thoughts, intents, and motives of the heart. Everything is exposed by those piercing eyes; no one can escape their scrutiny.

Revelation is a book of fire, where the word occurs seventeen times. Those flame-like eyes of Christ, always fixed on the moving scenes of human life and untiring in reading the hearts of men and the true meaning of all human events and actions, will burn up all that is alien to their holy gaze when their Possessor comes back to earth in His blood-dipped garments. *"All things are naked and open to the eyes of Him to whom we must give account"* (Hebrews 4:13 NKJV).

When Christ was on earth, His loving eyes were often wet with tears over the sins and sorrows of those around Him. Surely there is no passage in Holy Scripture so moving and revealing as the one describing Christ's grief over the death of one He loved: *"Jesus wept"* (John 11:35).

Yet the eyes that John saw in Revelation were not red with tears but with judgment. How grateful we should be that, through grace, we will not have to endure the scathing look of those eyes as they search out and destroy all that is antagonistic to the divine will!

4. HIS FEET AND FURNACE

His feet were like fine brass, as if refined in a furnace.
(Revelation 1:15 NKJV)

Although the glorified Son of Man was *"clothed with a garment down to the foot"* (Revelation 1:13), His feet were not hidden but visible, shining like polished brass. Those feet were bare, even as the feet of the ministering priests of Israel had been bare. As Phillips translates Revelation 1:15, *"His feet shone as the finest bronze glows in the furnace."* The picture is that of "white brass," which is attained in a furnace of white heat. White-heated brass is almost intolerable to the human gaze.

Brass is symbolic not only of strength and endurance but also of the firmness of divine judgment, as seen at the brazen altar and the brazen serpent. (See Exodus 27:1–7; Numbers 21:8–9.) As a composite metal produced by fire, brass is the symbol of the wrath of a thrice-holy God upon sin and sinners. As for the feet, they suggest an unfettered, holy walk, as well as the powerful triumph of judgment. Those blessed feet, which once walked the streets of Jerusalem on errands of mercy, which Mary washed with her tears, and which cruel men pierced with nails at Calvary, are now the feet of the Avenger, as He comes to tread down His foes. (See Ezekiel 22:17–22.)

5. HIS VOICE AND MOUTH

...his voice as the sound of many waters...and out of his mouth went a sharp two-edged sword.

(Revelation 1:15–16)

We group voice and mouth together because they go together, one being necessary to the use of the other. *"Voice"* and *"sound,"* in verse 15, are both translated from the same word that Greeks now use for "phone." The book of Revelation is also a book of the *voice*, which John uses thirty-seven times. The thunderous voice that John heard corresponds to the voice of *"the Ancient of days"* (Daniel 7:9, 13, 22), described by Daniel as *"like the voice of a multitude"* (Daniel 10:6). *"Waters"* are a symbol of raging, turbulent nations. When Christ appears in judgment, His clear, distinct, authoritative voice will calm the clamor of earth. No one will be able to resist the overwhelming power and tranquility of His utterance. When He utters His voice, the earth will melt.

While He was on earth, it was said of Jesus, *"Never man spake like this man"* (John 7:46). Often, that divine voice was heard in strong crying and tears, and at the cross, His foes silenced His mouth through death. But now, all is changed, as Christ's irresistible, articulate, commanding voice silences the loud, insistent voices of godless powers and authorities on earth. As that vibrant voice, once subdued the raging waves of the sea, now sounds forth as the waves of the sea, strong and majestic, it silences the Babel-like sounds of earth. (See Psalm 65:7.)

The imagery of the Bible is explicit in identifying the two-edged sword coming out of Christ's mouth as *"the sword of the Spirit"* (Ephesians 6:17), which is the whole of the infallible Word of God. (See also Hebrews 4:12.) The Word that the voice proclaims will be the basis of judgment and of divine sentence when Christ appears to judge the earth. Being sharper than any two-edged sword, it will lay bare the thoughts and intents of those who dare to make war with the Lamb or with His saints. No carnal weapons will be employed to subdue His adversaries. Instead, He will slay them *"by the words of* [His] *mouth"* (Hosea 6:5). As an old hymn stated,

The sword wherewith Thou dost command
Is in Thy mouth and not Thy hand.

As a *two-edged* sword, the Word either saves or slays, and it is powerful in either discipline or destruction. The two edges of this sword—the Old Testament and the New Testament—have power to cut off sin from man, or else to cut off man in his sin. (See Isaiah 11:4.) The Greek word for *"sword"* is used six times in Revelation. In this church age, those who take any other sword to advance Christ's cause will perish with the weapon to which they have appealed. (See Matthew 26:52.) But those who arm themselves with this powerful sword will find it mighty through God. (See 2 Corinthians 10:4.)

6. HIS RIGHT HAND

He had in his right hand seven stars…. And he laid his right hand upon me, saying unto me, Fear not…the mystery of the seven stars which thou sawest in my right hand.

(Revelation 1:16–17, 20)

The *"right hand"* is used often in Scripture and denotes a position of divine or supreme authority, as well as power and protection. (See Ephesians 1:20; Hebrews 1:3.) We often hear of a qualified person being referred to as "my right-hand man," implying someone who has had authority delegated to him. Being at God's right hand, Christ always acts as His Father would. Holding us in His right hand suggests that we are empowered to serve as He would if He were still here on earth.

What assurance of comfort John must have had when, over-awed by the dazzling vision of his glorified Lord, he felt Christ's right hand upon him and heard His tender voice say, *"Fear not."* This was the same voice that the apostle John heard that day when, while he was toiling with the other disciples against the contrary waves, Jesus bade him not to be afraid. John knew a great deal about that compelling right hand of the Master. Had he not seen it heal the leper, raise a sinking Peter, touch the wounded ear of Malchus, and break the loaves lifted up in benediction? Now the same hand is stretched out to reassure John that the Master he dearly loved was alive forever and had in His right hand the keys of hell and of death.

The seven stars in Christ's right hand are the angels of the seven churches. Who, or what, are these seven angels or stars? Some interpreters have understood the stars to refer to guardian angels, but it is difficult to reconcile this view with angelic warning and reproof and with angelic promise and encouragement. Others take the view that the stars or angels represent the ideal embodiment of the church, just as the forces of nature are symbolized as God's messengers.

The most usual and widely adopted interpretation of the stars, or angels of the churches is that they represent the chief ministers or presiding elders of a congregation—the equivalent of bishops and elders who provided spiritual oversight of the early church. Some scholars suggest that the term is derived from Jewish syn-agogues, where the messenger's recognized office was known by the title "Angel of the Synagogue." Lightfoot's comment should be borne in mind:

> It is conceivable, indeed, that a bishop or chief pastor should be called an angel, or messenger of God, or of Christ, but he would hardly be styled an angel of the church over which he presides.

The imagery John used here is applied elsewhere to teachers, whether true or false. (See Daniel 12:3; Jude 13; Revelation 8:10; 12:4). It is reassuring to know that all who serve the Lord in responsible positions are in His right hand, the place of possession and security. (See John 10:28–30.)

Walter Scott had this to say of the seven stars in Christ's right hand:

> The stars are declared to be the angels or representatives of the churches. The angel of the church is the symbolical representative of the assembly seen in those responsible in it, which indeed all really are. (See Revelation 1:20.) The "stars," as a symbol, are the expression of…
>
> 1. countless multitudes. (See Genesis 15:5.)
>
> 2. eminent persons in authority, civil and ecclesiastical. (See Daniel 8:10; Revelation 6:13; 12:4.)
>
> 3. lesser or subordinate powers in general. (See Genesis 37:9; Revelation 12:1.)

All church authority, all ministry, and all spiritual rule in every assembly is vested in Christ. His competency to give or withhold, to preserve and sustain, every true minister of God is the fundamental idea in the stars being in His right hand. When the eternal security of believers is in question, they are said to be "in His hand" and "in the Father's hand," from whence no power can pluck them. But they are not said to be in His "*right* hand," as here.

Spiritual leaders—we do not say official ones, for all such have not been set in the church of God—are held and maintained in the right hand of the Son of Man. The right hand signifies supreme authority and honor. What a responsible, yet withal honorable, position every ruler in the church occupies.

When Jesus was in the world, going about doing good, His hands were always active in relieving the physical and material needs of men. But the only reward He received for the benefactions of His holy hands was to have them pierced by nails. Now, those who are redeemed by the blood He shed are safe in those hands, which are well able to preserve, protect, and provide for all they hold. Are we among the stars in His right hand? If so, then it is the responsibility of stars to shine. This is the night of our Lord's absence from the earth, and we, as saints, collectively and individually, are the light of the world. As light-bearers amid gathering darkness, we must reflect something of His glory.

7. HIS COUNTENANCE AS THE SUN

His countenance was as the sun shineth in his strength.
                                                    (Revelation 1:16)

John was overwhelmed as he beheld *"the brightness of his glory"* (Hebrews 1:3). The things of earth must have become strangely dim as the apostle gazed upon the undimmed glory of Jesus Christ, of which His transfiguration had been a foregleam.

His face did shine as the sun, and his raiment was white as the light.   (Matthew 17:2)

While Christ was on earth, there had been the veiling of His eternal majesty, but in John's vision, he witnessed His imperial glory and magnificence. The countenance of the face is the window of the soul, and now, all that Christ is within Himself shines forth in beauteous glory.

There is, of course, a vast difference between the glory of the sun and that of the planets. (See 1 Corinthians 15:41.) The sun does not borrow light from any source but is a self-contained source of light and power. The planets, on the other hand, are mere reflectors of the light they receive from the sun. Jesus has a transcendent glory all His own, and it is emphasized in a threefold way:

1. To the world, He is its Light. (See John 8:12.)
2. To Israel, He is the Sun of righteousness. (See Malachi 4:2.)
3. To the church, He is the bright and morning star. (See Revelation 22:16.)

In Christ's humiliation, His face was marred beyond human appearance. At one time, it was covered with vile spittle (see Matthew 26:67), but now, an uncreated glory more brilliant than the midday tropical sun beamed from His face. May the light of that blessed countenance always be upon us!

What was John's response to this blinding vision of Christ? *"When I saw him, I fell at his feet as dead"* (Revelation 1:17). The Scriptures record the overpowering effects of the glorious vision of the Lord in the experience of other saints. Moses, Joshua, Job, Isaiah, Daniel, and Peter all knew what it was to behold God's glory; and in beholding it, they also saw their own sin and weakness. Isaiah said, *"Woe is me! for I am undone; because I am a man of unclean lips...for mine eyes have seen the King, the LORD of hosts"* (Isaiah 6:5). Here in Revelation, John, the apostle who had reclined on his Master's bosom, now falls at His feet as if dead. Although John was the most loving and loved of the disciples, nothing avails now—not even the strength of human affection—in the light of the magnificent, resplendent glory of his Master. Many things have to die in our lives when we are bathed in such glory. The hymnist Frederick Faber must have had this in mind when he wrote,

O everlasting Lord,
By prostrate spirits day and night
Incessantly adored!
How wonderful, how beautiful,

The sight of Thee must be;
Thy endless wisdom, boundless power,
And glorious purity!...
What rapture it will be
Prostrate before Thy throne to lie,
And gaze, and gaze on Thee![5]

After John had fallen as dead at Christ's feet, Jesus reassured him with these words: *"Fear not; I am the first and the last: I am he that liveth, and was dead; and, behold, I am alive for evermore, Amen; and have the keys of hell and of death"* (Revelation 1:17–18).

That gracious right hand of Jesus raised John from his prostrate position, and the voice as the sound of many waters was heard in its consoling tones. There are three *"amens,"* each full of spiritual significance, in this first chapter:

+ To the dying One on the cross (Revelation 1:5–6)

+ To the living One in resurrection (Revelation 1:18)

+ To the coming One in glory (Revelation 1:17)

Three cardinal doctrines of God's holy Word are embraced in these three amens:

+ He died.

+ He lives.

+ He comes.

The Master's reassuring *"Fear not,"* so often repeated by Him, again falls on the ears of the apostle John, comforting him with the fact that his Lord is unchanged—that the heart that beat tenderly in Galilee still throbs with love toward His own, even though He is in glory. As *"the first and the last,"* Jesus reaffirmed His deity, eternity, and absolute supremacy. He is the beginning and the end, and everything in between. (See Revelation 1:8.) As the living One, He proclaimed

5. Frederick W. Faber, "My God, How Wonderful Thou Art," 1849.

Himself to be the Source of life. Life did not commence for Christ in Bethlehem; His birth only revealed what had been His from eternity.

As the One who *"was dead,"* Jesus indicates the voluntary aspect of His death, for His life was not *taken* but *given*. Having power to lay down His life, He alone dismissed His spirit. (See Matthew 27:50.)

As the One who is *"alive forevermore,"* Jesus proclaims that He will never again feel the sting of death: *"Behold, I am alive for evermore."* By His own death, Christ abolished death for all who believe and brought life and immortality to light. Our glorious hope is that we are to share His deathlessness: *"Because I live, ye shall live also"* (John 14:19).

Christ's possession of *"the keys of hell and of death"* denotes His complete mastery over the bodies and souls of all men, with the right, or authority, to open and close as He wills. (See Revelation 3:7–8.) In *Revelation: Introduction and Glorious Vision of Christ*, Walter Scott wrote,

> The right to "open" and "shut" intimates His absolute authority over death and hades, the respective jailers of the dead, and is exercised at His sovereign pleasure. Satan has not now the power of death (Heb. 2:14). For the force of "key" as a symbol of undisputed authority, see Isaiah 22:22; Matthew 16:9.

Having conquered death, the foe which man has ever dreaded, and having proven Himself the Master of the clouded region into which men are ushered by death, Jesus offers Himself to us as the Lord of life and liberty. As His true believers, we live on, and always will, because, as the great Life-giver, He can never again be bound by death. Whether we enter heaven by the way of the grave or the air makes little difference, for we know that through Christ's grace we are to share His changeless years forever.

9

THE SEVEN
GOLDEN CANDLESTICKS

REVELATION 1:20–3:22

On the most important aspects of Revelation for Christians to study are the letters to the seven churches, found in chapters 2 and 3. About one-eighth of the entire book of Revelation is taken up with these remarkable letters. May God give us grace to give prayerful attention to what these letters say. Eager as we may be to grapple with the distinctly prophetic and more spectacular sections of Revelation, may we not be guilty of trying to master other dispensations while at the same time neglecting the dispensation of grace that is presently ours in this church age.

The letters of Christ, dictated from heaven to the seven churches, have been written about more than any other part of Revelation. Special mention should be made of *The Seven Churches*, a monumental classic by Sir William Ramsay. Thomas Cosmades' background book *Nothing Beside Remains* should also be mentioned. Other excellent expositors who have dealt specifically with Revelation include Abraham Kuyper, Walter Scott, William Newell, A. Rice, and Christina Rossetti. Charles Ellicott and Matthew Henry cover Revelation well in their overall Bible communications, as well.

There are several characteristic features of the letters to the seven churches. First of all, the various aspects of Christ's portrait, drawn for us in the first chapter, are parceled out among the churches, with a specific designation being adapted to each church. Christ spoke of *"my church"* in Matthew 16:18. His seven letters to her prove that He is her Head, and, as such, He is concerned about her spiritual welfare.

Another noticeable trait is the use of the number seven. Not only are there seven churches, but declarations and exhortations addressed to them are repeated seven times. We find a sevenfold *"I know"* and a sevenfold *"the Spirit saith."* There is also a sevenfold message for overcomers that is sufficient to sanctify any believer willing to apply the truth to his or her own heart. The general and personal applications of each letter are indicated by the two phrases *"unto the church"* and *"he that hath an ear."*

These letters were sent to actual churches in John's day. While they represent the church universal, the separate assemblies were also viewed as resting on their own bases, and sufficiently distinct for the Lord to walk in their midst. These churches were not seven-in-one, like the manifold attributes of the Holy Spirit, which are represented as the seven Spirits. Instead, each church was independently responsible to the Lord, who governs and controls the church as a whole. Each church was obligated to walk in the light as He is in the light and is the Light. (See 1 John 1:7.) All of the Revelation was sent not only to the seven churches mentioned by name but also to *all* the churches existing at that time and until the rapture. (See Revelation 2:23.)

THE COVERAGE OF THE LETTERS

The immediate readers of Revelation were the members of the seven churches in Asia Minor, from which the gospel had spread both east and west. It is not likely that the members of the churches knew anything about the successive stages of church history, as we do. These letters were addressed to them, and they must have had a humiliating effect.

Why were these particular seven churches chosen? Only two of them are mentioned in the epistles of Paul (Ephesus and Laodicea). Excluded are the prominent churches that the apostle Paul founded in Rome, Galatia, Colosse, Philippi, Corinth, and Thessalonica. Because seven is the number of completion, perhaps we are to understand that these particular seven churches represent the complete church of God during the church age.

The cities in which these churches were located were all on the great Roman post road. The Roman emperors often addressed letters to the cities in the empire, and, in John's time, Ephesus, Smyrna, and Sardis were mighty cities of the world. Therefore, it's probable that these seven churches were chosen not so much because they were the greatest or most important churches of that period but because each one was a *representative* church.

Geographically, these seven churches formed a rough circle, which was in keeping with the vision of their Lord walking in their midst. But the revelation as a whole is for the church as a whole. (See Revelation 22:16.) While Paul addressed his epistles to particular churches, nevertheless, all that he wrote also was meant for all churches in all ages. All that the Bible contains was written for our learning, that we, through patience and comfort of the Scriptures, might have hope. (See Romans 15:4.)

As candlesticks (or, more correctly, "lamp stands"), they emitted a sevenfold light that was dim and uncertain, so the Lord, who is justified in His utterances and vindicated when He judges, dealt with these churches in judgment. Seven churches were enough to exhibit such judgment, for this number indicates the sevenfold— or perfect—expression of the church. Some of the seven were found by Christ's evaluation to be in better condition than the others, but one was not judged by the other; each was responsible for itself. While some churches maintained their purity of life and doctrine longer than others, the whole tone of this church section of Revelation carries a notice of what the end was to be.

Why were these seven churches selected and mentioned in the order in which a traveler would visit them? One answer, suggested by Walter Scott, is worthy of consideration: "The seven selected assemblies form a symbol of the church in its universality in successive periods of its history, as also at any given moment till its final rejection as an unfaithful witness to Christ." The seven letters can be taken, then, as a kind of survey of church history.

The letters may also have a prophetic significance. Some interpreters see the final fulfillment of the letters in the synagogues or assemblies to be found in Asia Minor after the true church has been raptured to heaven. This idea may help to explain some Jewish references in the letters. The commendations and condemnations cited in them have proven prophetic down through this church age. Indeed, there have always been...

+ churches leaving their first love, as Ephesus was.

+ churches enduring persecution and trial, as Smyrna was.

+ churches worldly in practice, as Pergamum was.

+ churches guilty of false teaching, as Thyatira was.

+ churches allowing gross sin, as Sardis did.

+ churches with only a little power, as Philadelphia was.

+ churches denying the deity of Christ, as Laodicea did.

Satanic opposition, as mentioned in John's record of the seven churches, has never ceased. Satan is named a total of eight times in Revelation, and five of these times are in connection with the churches—six times, if we include the name "*devil*" in

Revelation 2:10. All throughout its history, the professing church has been tempted by Satan in various and clever ways.

Exploring the idea of the seven churches being a summary of seven epochs of church history, here are the approximate periods and dates:

1. EPHESUS (REVELATION 2:1–7)
FIRST-LOVE CHURCH (FIRST CENTURY A.D.)

The word *Ephesus* means "desirable" or "first love," which fittingly describes the first century of church history, one that was generally characterized by deep love and ardent zeal for Christ, and also by an unflinching opposition to all false teaching and doctrine. Ephesus was the center of a dense Christian population, and it was through the efforts of John that the main body of pastors in the area was able to stand firm against heresies and false teachings. However, the church that John knew and dearly loved had left her early zeal. The bloom was off the rose. The first light had faded into gloom. (See Acts 20:17–31.)

Ephesus, the renowned capital of the Ionian State, was known as "the light of Asia" and was famous for its wealth, wisdom, and wickedness. Its worship of the goddess Diana (see Acts 19) had spread throughout the world at that time. But the Ephesian church (mother of the Asian churches) stands out as the most spiritual in the sacred record. Yet, as Dr. Campbell Morgan reminds us, "The beginnings of the church there are recorded in Acts 18–20, the eloquent but partial ministry of Apollos being supplemented and amplified by that of Paul. The letter to Ephesus describes the condition of the church thirty-five years later."

Ephesus was given over to idolatry, and they held to a prevailing heresy that Christians could freely participate in the immoralities of heathen festivals. In this way, many Christians left their first love.

Are we as ardent for Christ today as we were in the early days of our witness, when our all was on the altar? Though we are perhaps still theologically sound, can it be that our heart is no longer pulsating with the love of Jesus that we manifested in the first years of our Christian life?

2. SMYRNA (REVELATION 2:8–11)
PERSECUTED CHURCH (A.D. 92–315)

This last stronghold of Christianity before the Mohammedan conquest was a serious rival of Ephesus, some forty miles to the north of Smyrna. Smyrna became one of the largest and most important cities of Asia Minor. Attractively built in John's day, it was also known as "Smyrna the Beautiful." Smyrna is also famous as the birthplace of the Greek poet Homer and as the home of Polycarp, Bishop of Smyrna. It was here that Polycarp was martyred in his ninetieth year, in 168 A.D.

Because Smyrna is not mentioned elsewhere in the New Testament, nothing is known of the founding of the church there. Idolatry was rife in the city, and the fierce persecution of Christians that raged at the time had its center in Smyrna.

The word *Smyrna* is a reference to myrrh, a word used three times in the Gospels. (See Matthew 2:11; Mark 15:23; John 19:39.) Myrrh was also one of the ingredients of the holy ointment (see Exodus 30:23–25) and was likewise used in embalming the dead. As Seiss remarks in his valuable commentary, "The name well describes a church persecuted unto death and lying embalmed in the previous spices of its sufferings, such as the church of Smyrna was. It was the church of myrrh, or bitterness, and yet was agreeable and precious unto the Lord."

As myrrh must be crushed in order to release its fragrance, so the testimony of this church, crushed by persecution, produced a sweet fragrance that was well-pleasing to God. The blood of martyrs in this period became the seed of succeeding churches. The two hundred fifty years from Nero to Constantine are also known as "the martyr period" under Imperial Rome. The ten days of persecution mentioned in Revelation 2:10 may represent the ten distinct attempts by imperial edict to destroy the infant church. The last persecution was just ten years long. Ten can also signify that God will see to it that even suffering has its limit. The ten great persecutions can be listed by the presiding emperor:

- Nero (A.D. 64–68)
- Domitian (A.D. 90–95)
- Trajan (A.D. 104–117)
- Aurelius (A.D. 161–180)
- Severus (A.D. 200–211)
- Maximus (A.D. 235–237)
- Decius (A.D. 250–253)
- Valerian (A.D. 257–260)
- Aurelian (A.D. 270–275)
- Diocletian (A.D. 303–312)

3. PERGAMOS (REVELATION 2:12–17)
STATE CHURCH (A.D. 315–500)

This city was the political capital of Asia, famous for its education in philosophy, culture, and science. It also boasted the largest library outside of Alexandria. Walter Scott reminds us, "It was here that the art of preparing skins of animals for writing upon was perfected, and from which our word *parchment* is derived. Thus, the name of this scripturally ill-omened city (see Revelation 2:12–17) has been handed down through the Christian ages, and, no doubt, many a literary *pergamena* manuscript of value has been prepared in Pergamos."

The city was the seat of emperor worship and was preeminent for its idolatry—hence, the biblical allusions to *"Satan's seat"* and *"where Satan dwelleth"* (Revelation 2:13). Pergamos is now an insignificant town of imposing ruins. Like many another historic city, its glory has departed. Because it was given up to nature worship, which always leads to corruption and extinction, Pergamos—or Pergamum—exists no more as an inhabited city.

The New Testament does not record the founding of a church there by any of the apostles. By the time of the third century, the church had passed the martyr stage and was receiving imperial favors. Emperor Constantine united the church and state by making Christianity the state religion of Rome, in place of paganism. Evidently, the emperor thought the Christian religion would greatly advance his kingdom, so he and his entire family were baptized. It was at this time that infant baptism was first practiced.

The Council of Nicea (A.D. 325) fixed the official creed as Trinitarian. The Nicolaitans (see Revelation 2:15), a Gnostic sect meaning "conquerors of the people," gained power within the church in Pergamos and Ephesus through the rise of the priesthood. It was at this time that the Babylonian system crept into the church.

Pergamos means "thoroughly married," a fitting description for this problematic union between the church and the world. Since this fatal marriage, the church and the world system have never been truly separated. Decreasing spirituality has resulted in an increase of worldly favor. This type of unholy union cripples the spiritual effectiveness of the church in many parts of the world even today.

4. THYATIRA (REVELATION 2:18–29)
THE PAPAL CHURCH (A.D. 500–1500)

Travelers have asserted that the road from Thyatira to Pergamos is one of the most beautiful in the world. This military post of Pergamos was famed for its dyeing of bright scarlet cloth, which was used extensively throughout Asia and Europe. Within the city was a magnificent temple to the goddess Diana. It was also the home of Jezebel, the notorious and influential woman teacher who openly and militantly endorsed immoral living.

G. Campbell Morgan suggests that "the history of the church at Thyatira might be traced back to the riverside prayer meeting recorded in Acts 16, for Lydia, whose heart the Lord opened on that occasion, was a native of Thyatira. What is more likely than that she was instrumental in founding the church on her return home?"

Thyatira means "a continual sacrifice." The word implies a sacrifice whose transcendent luster is dimmed by repetition. This is a foreshadowing of the rise of papacy, with its introduction of Mariolatry, the veneration of the Virgin Mary. During the seventh century, the bishop of Rome came into ascendance as the figurehead of the entire church. The worship of the Virgin Mary as "Queen of Heaven" was introduced into the church from heathen Babylon, and almost every heathen temple was transformed into a Christian church simply by the painting of the names of the apostles on the old idols and the priest's being given a cross to carry. Priestcraft appeared, along with altar and sacrifice. A steady development of apostasy also characterized this period.

5. SARDIS (REVELATION 3:1–6)
THE REFORMATION CHURCH (A.D. 1500–1700)

In the sixth century, Sardis was one of the most powerful cities in the Old World. It was the capital of the kingdom of Lydia. The present name of this once proud and wealthy capital is Sart, and today, it is deserted.

Sardis means "remnant," "precious stone," or "things remaining." Sardius, a precious ruby stone, comes from the same word.

In the Sardis church, the majority of its members were completely given over to heathen practices. "*I know thy works, that thou hast a name that thou livest, and art dead*" (Revelation 3:1). The members of the church at Sardis had a reputation of living for Christ, but inside they were dead to the Spirit of God, although a few managed to remain true to the Lord and His Word. (See Revelation 3:4.)

This is reminiscent of places when the Reformation tried to breathe new life into the state church. Satan denied this effort, unfortunately, and the Church of Rome relapsed into the cold formalism of old. Today, in many quarters of the world, the church looks alive on the outside but carries a dead orthodoxy within. She is like a well-dressed corpse, with vital life lacking.

6. PHILADELPHIA (REVELATION 3:7–13)
THE MISSIONARY CHURCH (A.D. 1700–1900)

It was of this influential city that the skeptic Gibbon wrote, "Among the Greek colonies and churches of Asia, Philadelphia is still erect, a column in a scene of ruins, a pleasing example that the paths of honor and safety may sometimes be the same." This city derived its name from its founder, Attalus Philadelphus, king of Pergamos. Today, the Turks call it Allah Shehr, or "the City of God," although Muslims do not regard the city, which contains many Greek Christians, with any degree of veneration.

In John's day, the church there was a faithful one, with many opportunities for living a spiritual life. Says Walter Scott, "Its freedom from blame in the message to its angel is worthy of note in connection with the fact that it had the longest duration of any of the seven cities named." Here, we have a true church within the professing church.

The word *Philadelphia* means "brotherly love" and is so used in the Greek of the book of Hebrews: "*Let brotherly love continue*" (Hebrews 13:1). In Philadelphia, we see a model for the evangelizing missionary church of the nineteenth century. Out of the great Wesley revivals came the foreign missions movement, followed by the appearance of powerful evangelistic agencies.

7. LAODICEA (REVELATION 3:14–22) THE REJECTED CHURCH OF THE TWENTIETH CENTURY

Laodicea received its name from Laodice, wife of Antiochus II, a Syrian monarch. Laodicea was near Colosse, and the Christians there received a letter from Paul. Four references in Colossians (see Colossians 2:1–3; 4:13, 15–16) prove that the apostle Paul was familiar with the church there. The city itself was a great banking center, noted for its garments of black, its glossy wool, and its great medical school, famous for a powder used to cure the eye disease ophthalmia. However, the fame and splendor of Laodicea have been laid in the dust, for the city is now the scene of ruin and desolation.

The name *Laodicea* means "people's rights," "rulership by the people," or even "democracy." Colossians 4:16 calls it the *"the church of the Laodiceans,"* not the church *at* Laodicea. It was *their* church and no longer that of the Lord. Christ's authority over the' church had been set aside by the laity of an unregenerate membership, suggesting the state of the professing church prior to the rapture.

Here is a summary of the broader meaning of the seven churches.

+ Ephesus: Indicates ecclesiastical pretension and a departure from a first love, characterizing the close of the apostolic period

+ Smyrna: Brings us to the martyr period, concluding with the last persecution under Diocletian

+ Pergamos: Reveals the decreasing spirituality and increasing worldliness common during and after the reign of Constantine, stemming from his public patronage of the church.

+ Thyatira: Covers the Middle Ages, with their cruel persecution of the saints of God by the papal church

+ Sardis: God's intervention by means of the Reformation, the light of which is still burning

+ Philadelphia: Related to the nineteenth century with its vast expansion of missionary activities

+ Laodicea: Portrays the present general state of the professing church, which, because of its lukewarm nature, is nauseous to Christ (See Revelation 3:16.)

It has been suggested that the histories of the first three churches are consecutive, while the histories of the remaining four overlap, running concurrently to the rapture. The *divine* element, suggested by the number three, is dominant in the first group of churches, while the *human* element, suggested by the number four, dominates the second group.

In his introduction to Cosmades' valuable work *The Seven Churches*, W. Stuart Harris remarks:

How saddened we are to learn that there is no Christian believer in Ephesus today, and that this applies to all the other areas of the seven churches, with the exception of the church at Smyrna, where there are now a few believers. The candlestick has been removed, as Christ warned it would be.

CONSTRUCTION OF THE LETTERS

A remarkable and impressive feature of these seven letters is their similarity of format. Addressed by Christ from heaven to His church, each letter has the same form, although certain details vary to fit each church. The headings of all the letters correspond. The framework of each letter appears to be of a sevenfold nature:

1. DESCRIPTION OF CHRIST

In the majority of these letters, there is the repetition of one or more of the titles or designations of Christ found in the first chapter—a title fitting the state of the church in question, and presenting Christ with all power as the authoritative Judge.

2. REVELATION OF CONDITION

The reiterated phrases *"I know"* and *"I will"* imply Christ's complete knowledge and governmental authority, as well as His power to lay bare the inner heart of the churches. Christ reveals His intimate insight into the life and labor of each assembly. Nothing is hidden from Him, the omniscient Lord.

3. COMMENDATION OF VIRTUES

All that is pleasing is generously extolled by the Master. He is careful to praise before He reproves. Christ commends each church, except the last one, for their works and other virtuous characteristics.

4. CONDEMNATION OF FAILURES

Christ would be both unjust and unkind if He did not speak of that which displeases Him, as well as that which pleases. Thus, these letters carry with them a faithful exposure of faults. Each church, except the second and the sixth, is more corrupt than its predecessor; the last is the most corrupt of all, having no virtue to commend it whatsoever.

5. EXHORTATION TO REPENT

We are greatly encouraged as we read these priceless gems of literature because they are fragrant with the grace of Christ. He presents Himself as One willing to restore. It should be noted that the first, third, fifth, and seventh churches are commanded to repent. The second and sixth had nothing to repent of, having been purged by persecution. The fourth was reprobate and past repenting.

6. DECLARATION OF JUDGMENT

Because He is always faithful in the declaration of truth, Christ warns of the peril of continuing disobedience. Happy indeed is the church or Christian who heeds Christ's warning voice! The warning of judgment was given to every church except the second and the sixth.

7. THE PROCLAMATION OF REWARD

Each reward is in keeping with an attribute of Christ. Blessings of personal victory and a call to the individual conclude each letter. There is a promise to the overcomer in each letter. For our enlightenment and edification, let us briefly examine these letters in the light of their sevenfold plan.

THE LETTER TO EPHESUS (REVELATION 2:1–7)

We have already seen that by the angels, we can understand the spiritual representatives of each church. Walter Scott regards *"the angel of the church of…"* as "symbolically representative of the assembly in its actual moral state. Representation is the thought…. We could emphasize the remark that not official but moral representation is the idea conveyed in the word 'angel' as used in connection with the seven churches."

In each of the letters, the speaker is the risen Lord, and the revelation of Himself is adapted to the need of each church. As we have indicated, Christ introduces Himself in symbolic terms taken from chapter 1. Thus, we connect verse 1 here with Revelation 1:20: *"The seven stars are the angels of the seven churches."* Christ is seen walking judicially among the churches. Every act is witnessed by Him who never slumbers or sleeps. And as the One holding the seven golden candlesticks, He is able to remove any one of them out of its place. Surely, it is extremely sobering to realize that the Lord knows exactly what each of us is doing. He knew that the Ephesians could not bear those who were evil. Can we bear them? Do we abhor that which is evil?

There was much to commend in this almost flawless church. Patience was highly commended—the word occurs twice. In Revelation 2:2, it is patience in service; in verse 3, it is patience in suffering. Altogether, our Lord had an eightfold commendation for this Ephesian church.

But there is a sad "nevertheless" in Christ's message to this church. The first love of betrothal to Christ had been forsaken. There was pure doctrine and perfect church order but a lamentable lack of love. Love of Christ is the motive of all acceptable service. (See John 21:15–17.) Did not Paul affirm in 1 Corinthians 13 that the very best in service is of little value if love is lacking? Other loves had crept in, and the Ephesian church was in danger of slipping.

This church was bidden to remember from whence it had fallen and to return to its first love. With the first love went the first works. Love yearns for love, for where there is true love, there is also true labor.

The exhortation *"He that hath an ear, let him hear"* ends each letter. In the first three churches, the call comes *before* Christ's message to the overcomer. In the last four churches, the call is found *after* the promise to the overcomer.

The Holy Spirit is the Administrator of the affairs of the church throughout this age, as indicated by the sevenfold repetition of "*The Spirit saith to the churches.*" To the overcomer in this church, Christ promises the provision of the tree of life, which can mean exemption from bodily deterioration. The "*tree of life*" (Revelation 2:7) was significant to the Greeks as a symbol of life-giving divine power. "*The paradise of God*" meant "a pleasure garden" and represented the sum of all spiritual enjoyment.

THE LETTER TO SMYRNA (REVELATION 2:8-11)

This letter shares with the letter to Philadelphia the distinction of containing no blame. These two churches were also alike in their experience of tribulation at the hands of pagans, instigated by Jews who "*say they are Jews, and are not, but are the synagogue of Satan*" (Revelation 2:9). Likewise, there are many today who say they are Christians but are not!

There are some interesting features to be noted in this shortest letter of the seven. First, how fitting is the title of Christ as the One "*which was dead, and is alive*" (Revelation 2:8). Many in this church were going to die for their Lord. Terrible and cruel martyrdom awaited, but Christ, as the One who had conquered death, could promise them a glorious resurrection. (See verses 10–11.)

Then, there is that brief but rewarding parenthetical "*(but thou art rich)*" (Revelation 2:9). Heartless persecutors had reduced the saints to beggary. But though they were materially poor, they were rich in faith.

Amid gathering darkness, there was a gracious and strengthening "Fear not." (See Revelation 2:10.) They needed to be courageous, for tribulation would have its limits, and the "binder" would ultimately be "bound up himself." (See Revelation 20:1–3.)

For this heroic church, there was no condemnation, nor were there words of censure or reproach. Persecution has a way of keeping saints close to the heart of God. No repentance was urged of the people of Smyrna, who had remained true. No judgment against them is recorded.

Cicero described Smyrna as "the city of our most faithful ally," and it is interesting to observe that the only letter of the seven in which Christ uses the term "*faithful*" (Revelation 2:10) is addressed to a church situated in a place so commended for its patriotic faithfulness. As Smyrna was loyal to its monarch, so the church there was loyal to her Lord, in spite of intense suffering. Smyrna was called "the gateway of the martyrs" because many of them passed through the ports there on their way to Rome and martyrdom. Polycarp, Bishop of Smyrna, was martyred there in A.D. 155, at the age of eighty-six.

For their reward, the people of Smyrna would receive a crown of life, the emblem of royalty and victory. The phrase "*He that overcometh shall not be hurt of the second death*" (Revelation 2:11)—implying a death beyond physical death—might have been a message to the wicked men of Smyrna who were bent on destroying the saints. Perhaps they were warned so that they would take heed and repent. The Smyrnians' reward is contained in verses 8 and 10. There is the interplay of life and death throughout the letter. To encourage the sufferers, the Lord reminds them that there is something more terrible than physical death. But there is "*the second death*," which would not be theirs because they had earned the crown of life.

THE LETTER TO PERGAMOS (REVELATION 2:12–17)

Christ is introduced to the church at Pergamos as having a sharp sword with two edges—symbols of judgment and execution of truth. A comparison of Revelation 2:12 with verse 16 shows how applicable this title was to the Pergamum church:

> *And to the angel of the church in Pergamos write; These things saith he which hath the sharp sword with two edges.*
>
> (Revelation 2:12)

> *Repent; or else I will come unto thee quickly, and will fight against them with the sword of my mouth.*   (verse 16)

The sharp sword penetrates, divides, separates, commands, lays bare, searches out, and conquers. How apt is Isaiah's prophecy of Christ at this point: *"He hath made my mouth like a sharp sword"* (Isaiah 49:2). The Roman envoy in Pergamum wore a sword as the symbol of his office and military power. He had *"the power of the sword"* (Job 5:20)—the authority to pronounce a death sentence. But the sword of the Lord is greater than all the swords of the Caesars, and, when He ultimately wields it (see Revelation 19:15), He will dominate the empires of earth.

Evidently, Satan had his base of operations in this city, a fact that would make the position of believers somewhat perilous. The actual "throne" of Satan is in the air, while his center of activity can change from time to time. Note that he has been described as one who *"walketh about, seeking whom he may devour"* (1 Peter 5:8).

> *I know thy works and where thou dwellest, even where Satan's seat is: and thou holdest fast my name, and hast not denied my faith, even in those days wherein Antipas was my faithful martyr, who was slain among you, where Satan dwelleth.*
>
> (Revelation 2:13)

In spite of satanic antagonism, the saints at Pergamos are commended for their loyalty to *"my name,"* which signifies the character and Person of Christ, and to *"my faith,"* which signifies the teachings and work of Christ. The fidelity of these saints, even with martyrdom before them, is illustrated in faithful Antipas, who died for the Lord, whom he dearly loved. Pergamum was one of the great centers of emperor worship, and the temptation to compromise by misdirecting the worship that belongs to God alone was particularly great. When the Christians compromised, Satan triumphed. When they remained firm, often, martyrdom was the price they paid for loyalty to Christ.

Though hidden and unknown among the thousands at Pergamum, with no grave to mark his ashes, Christ draws out the name of Antipas, in an intimacy of love and a blaze of glory unique even in Revelation. *Antipas* means "one against many." Indeed, this courageous Christian dared to stand alone and seal his witness with his life's blood.

> *But I have a few things against thee, because thou hast there them that hold the doctrine of Balaam, who taught Balac to cast a stumblingblock before the children of Israel, to eat things sacrificed unto idols, and to commit fornication.*
>
> (Revelation 2:14)

Unfortunately, while the Pergamum church was sound in general, there had been the toleration of error among its members. A lack of discipline was clearly evident as we think of those who followed Balaam and the Nicolaitans. This sad complaint is given three times. (See Revelation 2:4, 14, 20.) Has the Lord anything against you? Dr. Campbell Morgan said that Balaamism and Nicolaitanism "appear to describe what came to be known as 'Antinomianism,' the deadly teaching that God's covenant purposes are sure of realization, and that, therefore, it matters not how the subjects of them conducted themselves."

Balaam was the hireling who loved the wages of unrighteousness. He represents the union of the church and the world, which is tantamount to spiritual defilement. The doctrine of the Nicolaitans would indicate those who tried to dominate the laity.

In the call to repentance, we have what one might call "Christ's blitzkrieg": *"Repent; or else I will come unto thee quickly, and will fight against them with the sword of my mouth"* (Revelation 2:16). And when He comes, His Word will be the basis of judgment. For the overcomers, there would be the manna of divine supply and the white stone of acquittal or victory. (See verse 17.)

Many interpretations have been given of the white stone. It is said that a white stone was given to a conqueror in the Olympic Games, carrying with it certain distinctions and privileges. Such a stone was also evidence of acquittal from charges, bearing the name of the one acquitted. Scholars have written of pebbles used in courts of justice at that time—a black pebble for a guilty sentence and a white pebble for acquittal.

A white stone also suggested friendship. The stone would be split in two, and each party would retain the half with the other's name, in token of abiding union and communion.

The message to the Pergamos church is sorely needed today: "The carelessness and compromise in belief and, therefore, in conduct, called for discipline in the churches," said G. Campbell Morgan. "It might be that enrichment would come in some cases by way of subtractions rather than additions."

THE LETTER TO THYATIRA (REVELATION 2:18-29)

It is more than likely that this church originated from that riverside prayer meeting at which Lydia, a native of Thyatira, had her heart opened by the Lord. (See Acts 16.) Perhaps she was instrumental in founding the church there upon her return home. In

Revelation 1, John saw Christ as the Son of Man, a man invested with all the attributes and activities of deity. Here, the divine Speaker introduces Himself as the Son of God, revealing all His omniscience and authority. Christ's eyes of fire and glowing feet from Revelation 1:14–15 illustrate the terrible aspect of judgment He assumes toward this church.

> *I will kill her children with death; and all the churches shall know that I am he which searcheth the reins and hearts: and I will give unto every one of you according to your works.*
>
> (Revelation 2:23)

> *He that overcometh...SHALL RULE THEM WITH A ROD OF IRON; AS THE VESSELS OF A POTTER SHALL THEY BE BROKEN TO SHIVERS: EVEN AS I RECEIVED OF MY FATHER.*
>
> (verses 26–27)

Here, we have Christ's most searching, crushing powers before us. Graciously, this One who *"searcheth...hearts"* thinks of excellence first. If only those who are guilty of misjudging us would follow such a divine example, how different the world would be! Service, love, faith, and patience are justly praised.

Then there comes the complaint regarding evil that is permitted in the church—in this case, personified in an actual woman. In the previous letter, our Lord compared false teachers to Balaam, who taught the Israelites to take part in idolatrous festivals. Now, He compares them to Jezebel, the heathen wife of Ahab, who established idolatry in Israel. The Old Testament name of Jezebel is used as her prototype of sin. This is the only letter in which a woman is mentioned. Jezebel means "chaste," but how untrue she was to her own name! The Old-Testament Jezebel was a brilliant, daring, and unscrupulous woman, recognizing God but actually serving Baal. (See, for example, 1 Kings 19:1–3.) Thyatira's particular form of evil was that of "spiritism"—this woman Jezebel claimed divine revelation about occult activities. (See Revelation 2:20.) Her evil influence was multiplied in that she taught and seduced the servants of Christ to follow her.

In this longest letter of the seven, a solemn warning is given to those who persistently indulge in spiritual harlotry. If they refuse to repent, they must share the condemnation of Jezebel. But the Lord is gracious, even to the worst of evildoers, for *"I gave her space to repent of her fornication; and she repented not"* (Revelation 2:21). Repentance is always God's way out.

To those in Thyatira who had not been influenced by Jezebel and her fornications was promised a share in the rule of Christ. (See Revelation 2:26.) Works based on love play a prominent part in this letter. (See also verse 19.) The *"morning star"* (verse 28) is Christ Himself, and all overcomers are to fully possess Him. What a future awaits all those who have Christ in their hearts as the harbinger of the coming glorious day, and who *"hold fast"* (Revelation 2:25)! If we are faithful, we shall know the heights of sharing in the reign of our Lord.

Ephesians 2:6 reminds us that God *"hath raised us up together, and made us sit together in heavenly places in Christ Jesus."* Therefore, we share in the power of His ascended reign. But Psalm 2:8–9, quoted in Revelation 2 by the risen Lord, has yet to be fulfilled:

> *Ask of me, and I shall give thee the heathen for thine inheritance, and the uttermost parts of the earth for thy possession. Thou shalt break them with a rod of iron; thou shalt dash them in pieces like a potter's vessel.*

The readers of this message, tempted to sink to the depths of Satan, might remember how Satan is spoken of in Isaiah 14:12— as the daystar fallen from heaven:

How art thou fallen from heaven, O Lucifer, son of the morning! how art thou cut down to the ground, which didst weaken the nations!

We, too, must choose between the heights and the depths. Authority over the nations is reserved for all true overcomers, who will share Christ's reign over the nations. As Alexander Maclaren put it, "The life molded according to Christ's pattern is the life capable of being granted participation with Him in His dominion."

THE LETTER TO SARDIS (REVELATION 3:1-6)

And unto the angel of the church in Sardis write; These things saith he that hath the seven Spirits of God, and the seven stars; I know thy works, that thou hast a name that thou livest, and art dead. Be watchful, and strengthen the things which remain, that are ready to die: for I have not found thy works perfect before God. Remember therefore how thou hast received and heard, and hold fast, and repent. If therefore thou shalt not watch, I will come on thee as a thief, and thou shalt not know what hour I will come upon thee. Thou hast a few names even in Sardis which have not defiled their garments; and they shall walk with me in white: for they are worthy. He that overcometh, the same shall be clothed in white raiment; and I will not blot out his name out of the book of life, but I will confess his name before my Father, and before his angels. He that hath an ear, let him hear what the Spirit saith unto the churches.

With this fifth letter, it would seem as though Christ was making a new beginning, And Sardis does indeed mark a change in the series. In the previous letters, "good" was the rule and "evil" the exception. But in Sardis, the reverse is the case—only a small remnant can be commended by Christ.

Both the Spirit and spiritual leaders are under Christ's control and have become avenues of His operation. All the plenitude of power and wisdom that Sardis lacked was His. Though perfect before men, the church here was not perfect before God. It had a name and reputation for organization and orthodoxy but was destitute of life. It had labor without life!

"There was, in all probability," said G. Campbell Morgan, "conformity to the model of the church found in Acts 2:41–42, so far as the ordinances and adherence to doctrine were concerned. The worship and giving were apparently beyond reproach. But in the eyes of the Lord, all was a scaffolding to the structure, as a whited sepulchre, as flowers of wax."

In view of the second advent, the church was exhorted to repent. Like a thief, Christ would rob them of all they had if they failed to turn from their dead, barren orthodoxy. Twice over, as a city, Sardis had been conquered because of failure to watch. Christ tells the church of what would result from its failure to watch for Him.

There were a few in Sardis who had not defiled their garments but instead manifested victorious righteousness. The word *Sardis* means "a remnant," coming from a Hebrew root implying "those who are escaping or escaped." In the church at Sardis, a few believers were found who had escaped the pollution surrounding them and who had lived courageously for Christ.

Are we numbered among the few who are separated unto the Lord, perfect in fidelity to Him? If so, then we, too, will share in the rewards that the Lord has for those who are worthy. Sardis was a church of dead puppets going through the motions of Christianity but producing works that were dead because they were not animated by the life that flows from God. So, the Lord spoke to them as the One in whom revival is to be found.

Sardis is given a similar chance to repent that was given to the church at Ephesus: *"But God, who is rich in mercy, for his great love wherewith he loved us, even when we were dead in sins, hath quickened us together with Christ, (by grace ye are saved;)"* (Ephesians 2:4–5). Sardis must go back to those things that were precious in the old days, and, in the light of what once was life, she must stop the things that she is now doing, lest the spark of life that remains should die out altogether. The condition of maintained life is watchfulness, or wakefulness; the alternative is the sleep of death and a sudden and unexpected judgment from the Lord.

Every saint has the assurance that his name is written in heaven and that it can never be erased from the sacred Book of Life. (See Luke 10:20.) Those who tamper with the authority and veracity of Revelation will see their part removed from the book. (See Revelation 22:19.) Here, *"part"* means "inheritance." All have an inheritance or reward that *can* be lost or taken away.

The wonder of wonders is that Christ is going to confess His victorious saints before the Father and His angels. And what a day that will be for us if we are found *"clothed in white raiment...the righteousness of saints"* (Revelation 3:5, 19:8).

THE LETTER TO PHILADELPHIA (REVELATION 3:7–13)

And to the angel of the church in Philadelphia write; These things saith he that is holy, he that is true, he that hath the key of David, he that openeth, and no man shutteth; and shutteth, and no man openeth; I know thy works: behold, I have set before thee an open door, and no man can shut it: for thou hast a little strength, and hast kept my word, and hast not denied my name. Behold, I will make them of the synagogue of Satan, which say they are Jews, and are not, but do lie; behold, I will make them to come and worship before thy feet, and to know that I have loved thee. Because thou hast kept the word of my patience, I also will keep thee from the hour of temptation, which shall come upon all the world, to try them that dwell upon the earth. Behold, I come quickly: hold that fast which thou hast, that no man take thy crown. Him that overcometh will I make a pillar in the temple of my God, and he shall go no more out: and I will write upon him the name of my God, and the name of the city of my God, which is new Jerusalem, which cometh down out of heaven from my God: and I will write upon him my new name. He that hath an ear, let him hear what the Spirit saith unto the churches.

(Revelation 3:7–13)

This letter shares the distinction of blamelessness with that of the church of Smyrna. Here, the divine Speaker is described as having *"the key of David."* If one is given the key to a city, it means that freedom and privileges are bestowed on him. Here, the key is the symbol of the undisputed right to enter and exercise all needful authority. Because Revelation as a whole looks toward the kingdom, Christ emphasizes His royal claims as the Lord and Head of David's house. All Davidic promises will be fulfilled by Him.

The church of Philadelphia is commended for its faithfulness according to its ability. It had been faithful with little. Though it was unimportant in the eyes of the world, in spite of its obedience and faith, the divine Administrator, who opens and shuts doors, is unstinted in His praise for the way the Philadelphia church had entered the door of opportunity that He had opened.

Philadelphia is one of the two churches that receive only praise and encouragement in these letters. Because its members were faithful, they were given fresh work to do. While we are on earth, the reward of faithfulness is not idleness but greater responsibility. Those who are already idle must be brought back to devotion to God before they can be used by Him. Thus, the Lord speaks to Philadelphia as the One who opens doors of opportunity.

It is in no condemnatory sense that Christ speaks of their *"little strength."* Humanly speaking, their strength was little because they were only a tiny minority among Jews and pagans. Yet, because their strength was based on naming the name of Christ, they could go forward through the open door. It is not said what this door was, and, consequently, this verse has been precious to many generations of Christians in all spheres of service in which a new door has been opened.

Exemption was promised from a special trial, which can mean deliverance from the great tribulation. The word *"from"* signifies "out of" and carries with it the idea of being kept away from tribulation—not merely kept through it, as some assert. Not until the time that this trial overtakes the earth will the full importance of the message of preservation be fully understood or experienced.

Also in this letter, Christ's second coming is used as an incentive to hold fast. May we be determined to retain our crown! Overcomers are to be made pillars in God's temple. Though of little strength on earth, they are to be fashioned into massive, glorious pillars in heaven, where they will share Christ's ultimate victory. Then, identification with the King will be complete. Even if they have no name here, they are to have a new, secret name in heaven. Complete freedom of the New Jerusalem is also theirs: *"He shall go no more out."* Why? Because Christ is the key, and, as such, He keeps His own saints in eternal safety. All who are truly saved by grace are in the register of the living because they have eternal life.

THE LETTER TO LAODICEA (REVELATION 3:14-22)

And unto the angel of the church of the Laodiceans write;
These things saith the Amen, the faithful and true witness,
the beginning of the creation of God; I know thy works, that
thou art neither cold nor hot: I would thou wert cold or hot.
So then because thou art lukewarm, and neither cold nor hot,
I will spue thee out of my mouth. Because thou sayest, I am
rich, and increased with goods, and have need of nothing; and
knowest not that thou art wretched, and miserable, and poor,
and blind, and naked: I counsel thee to buy of me gold tried
in the fire, that thou mayest be rich; and white raiment, that
thou mayest be clothed, and that the shame of thy nakedness
do not appear; and anoint thine eyes with eyesalve, that thou
mayest see. As many as I love, I rebuke and chasten: be zeal-
ous therefore, and repent. Behold, I stand at the door, and
knock: if any man hear my voice, and open the door, I will
come in to him, and will sup with him, and he with me. To
him that overcometh will I grant to sit with me in my throne,
even as I also overcame, and am set down with my Father in
his throne. He that hath an ear, let him hear what the Spirit
saith unto the churches. (Revelation 3:14–22)

This last letter is the saddest of the seven. Containing the severe disapproval of Christ over an apostate church, the letter nevertheless brings us a revelation of the heart of the Lord as is not found in any of the other letters. In describing Himself, Christ does not use any symbol. He declares Himself to be *"the Amen,"* a title as expressive of His glory as *"the way, the truth, and the life"* (John 14:6). As the faithful and true Witness, He is revealed as being in harmony with Himself. *"The beginning of the creation of*

God" indicates Christ's authoritative message, which is interpreted in Colossians 1:15: "[Christ] *is the image of the invisible God, the firstborn* [preeminent One] *of every creature.*" Everything implied by these titles was denied by the Laodiceans, who consequently earned His displeasure and condemnation.

The word *Laodicea* is from two Greek words meaning "people" and "judgment," or "custom." Indeed, the church there was governed by the decisions, judgments, and customs of the people instead of being governed directly by the Word of God.

The condition of this church was completely unfavorable; there was no commendation of any virtue. How tragic it is when there are no good works to commend in a church! Of course, the Laodiceans had plenty of good things to say about themselves. They were self-confident, proud, and self-satisfied. But to their Lord, they were spiritually lukewarm and therefore nauseating. The first church left its love, but this last church was lukewarm.

The Laodicean church was not burdened with debt—it had an abundance of material wealth—yet Christ declared it to be pitiable and bankrupt. We have the *"thou art"* of lukewarmness, the *"thou sayest"* of complacency, and the *"thou art"* of the Lord's infallible and terrible indictment. Like many a church, Laodicea was correct but conscienceless. Christ's contempt for such a condition is seen in His drastic treatment of the church: *"I will spue thee out of my mouth."* Such a travesty of His church was loathsome to Christ.

Even to the most casual reader of Revelation, it must be obvious that its basic theme is the second coming of Christ. In his valuable work *Interpreting Revelation*, Merrill C. Tenney has this enlightening observation:

> The increasing imminence of the Lord's coming is reflected
> in His utterances of correction of these churches:

Ephesus: *"Else I will come unto thee quickly, and will remove thy candlestick"* (Revelation 2:5).

Pergamum: *"Else I will come unto thee quickly"* (Revelation 2:16).

Thyatira: *"Hold fast till I come"* (Revelation 2:25).

Sardis: *"I will come on thee as a thief, and thou shalt not know what hour I will come upon thee"* (Revelation 3:3).

Philadelphia: *"I come quickly"* (Revelation 3:11).

Laodicea: *"I stand at the door, and knock"* (Revelation 3:20).

The vision of the Seven Letters is built around the concept of His coming and of the effect which that coming will have upon the churches.

But grace also shines forth in the judgment, for judgment is the result of Christ's love. As He urges the church to a new zeal, He looks for a man who, though possibly excluded by the church, is willing to welcome the Lord. For such a person, there is the great reward of sharing Christ's provision and throne. The divine Guest becomes the divine Host and lavishes glorious gifts upon those who willingly entertain Him. (See Revelation 3:20.)

In the *"gold,"* the *"white raiment,"* and the *"eyesalve,"* which Christ counseled the church to secure from Him, we have illustrations and symbols that would appear to the Laodiceans, whose city was famous for such commodities.

At the close of chapter 3, we have the saints caught up and the professors spewed out. While John does not record the actual rapture, he takes it for granted, since he does not mention the word *church* again until he finishes the Revelation. (See Revelation 22:16–17.) In these letters to the seven churches, the Lord divides the members into two classes—those who are overcomers and those who are not. In each letter, there is an appeal, a warning, and a promise:

- An *appeal* to come back to the Lord as He represents Himself to each church.
- A *warning* if the appeal is unheeded.
- A *promise* if it is obeyed.

In Revelation 22:6–21, John will pick up the themes he dwells upon in the first three chapters of the book. After Revelation 3, however, it is no longer Christ among the candlesticks but Christ as Priest-Judge on a throne, operating from heaven until He returns to earth.

10

THE SEVEN SEALS

REVELATION 4:1–8:5

Revelation is one of the most dramatic parts of the Bible. As symbolic literature, and as a demonstration of the ultimate triumph of good over evil, the chapters of the Bible's last book are unparalleled. At last we see Christ overturning, overturning, overturning, until He takes to Himself His rightful power and reigns supreme over all.

When considering the seven seals, it is necessary to consider the atmosphere and unfolding of truth in chapters 4 and 5. With the completion of the judgments of the sixth seal, the terrified multitudes cry out in Revelation 6:16, *"Fall on us, and hide us from the face of him that sitteth on the throne, and from the wrath of the Lamb."*

THE THRONE ROOM (REVELATION 4:1–11)

Revelation 4 opens with John being raptured to heaven to receive God's blueprint for the future. At the end of Revelation 3, man is invited to open a door for Christ; in chapter 4, a door is opened in heaven for man to enter. With this open door, the truly prophetic part of the book commences, even though definite prophetic action does not begin until chapter 6. Chapters 4 and 5, with their heavenly scenes, appear to be introductory to the first series of judgments detailed in chapter 6.

The opening phrase *"After this"*—or *"After these things"* (NKJV)—refers to what has just been considered in chapters 2 and 3. Now, we have a new beginning. John passes from church matters to an entirely different subject. The scene is also different, for now John is in heaven. From the heights, he is made to understand what is to transpire below. Because prophecy has its source in heaven, above the mists and clouds, John must receive the mind of God concerning future events. When standing on the earth, we cannot see very far, but what a panorama is spread out before us when we climb some lofty height! This is also true with the things of God. Heavenly matters, even when they concern the earth, can be understood only from the heavenly standpoint.

Twelve times in this chapter the word *"throne"* is mentioned. Altogether, it appears thirty-eight times throughout Revelation; some call it the "throne room" of the Bible. And the *"thrones"* of Revelation make a profitable Bible study. Indeed, Revelation opens and closes with a throne. (See Revelation 1:4; 22:3.) The throne of Revelation 4:2 is preparatory to the judgments beginning in chapter 6 and ending with chapter 20. And so, we travel from the judgment of the wicked living to the judgment of the wicked dead. The throne before us was *"set in heaven"* (Revelation 4:2), speaking of judgments that are righteous and holy. *"The LORD hath prepared his throne in the heavens"* (Psalm 103:19). Nothing but perfect, unbiased judgment emanates from this throne room.

By the *"first voice"* (Revelation 4:1), we acknowledge the voice of the Lord we already heard in Revelation 1:10. It now speaks from heaven, trumpet-like. There are six references to trumpets in Revelation, instruments associated with thrones and judgments. In the Old Testament, trumpets were used to call assemblies. Here in Revelation, they seem to prepare the way for judgment. The divine Occupant of the throne, without shape or form, and who has not been seen at any time, is named as *"Lord God Almighty"* (Revelation 4:8). Two precious stones, jasper and sardius, are used to describe the qualities of this awesome throne-Sitter. Taken together, the stones are emblematic of the excellence of God's character and perfection. The jasper, or diamond, is translucent and the emblem of light; the sardius, or ruby, is a carnation color and the emblem of love. Thus, the One on the throne is characterized by both principle and passion.

That *"there was a rainbow round about the throne, in sight like unto an emerald"* (Revelation 4:3) reminds us that God will be true to His covenants and that a gathering storm is about to break. We have here a complete circular rainbow, not the semicircular ones that we are accustomed to seeing. And instead of the manifold colors of the rainbow, this perfect one carries the beautiful green of the emerald. The color green never tires the eye and can symbolize our never-tiring gaze on the manifested glory of God. The complete rainbow is the symbol of hope.

The identification of the twenty-four elders (see Revelation 4:4) is a matter of dispute among theologians. Some assert that these elders are the heads of an angelic priesthood. Having crowns and white raiment, they must be kingly and priestly beings of a governmental order. Other writers identify the elders as Old-Testament and New-Testament saints, made up of the twelve tribes of Israel and the twelve apostles.

Walter Scott says that it is incongruous to "imagine spirits sitting clothed and crowned, and, therefore, they must represent the general body of the redeemed there in heaven." It will be noticed that the "seats" or "thrones" are subordinate to *the* throne of Revelation 4:2. The number twenty-four is associated with heavenly government and worship. Twelve is the governmental number of the earth. If the elders are the redeemed—and John says they are (see Revelation 5:9)—then the golden crowns intimate the royal dignity and authority that every saint is to share.

A throne is the center of action and interest, and it intimates the unleashing of natural forces as the precursors of coming judgment. The perfect, searching ministry of the Spirit is symbolized by the seven lamps of fire. (See Revelation 4:5.) As the seven Spirits of God, the Holy Spirit is brought before us in the perfection of His being, intelligence, and activity. Identified with the righteous judgment of the throne, the Spirit will expose all that is alien to the absolute purity of the throne. The *"sea of glass like unto crystal"* (Revelation 4:6) declares the eternal holiness and purity of the divine Occupant of the throne.

The *"four beasts ["living creatures"* NKJV]" (Revelation 4:6) are equivalent to the Old Testament cherubim. These living ones symbolize the judicial attributes and authority of the throne-Sitter and are connected with Christ, the living One. They are also represented as having perfect wisdom and rendering unceasing worship and service. They likewise ascribe holiness and eternity to Him who sits upon the throne. As representatives of the throne and as court attendants, they stand ready to do the will of the Judge. They are real, literal beings, vibrant with life. Four is the number of man and of creation, and thus the four living ones are representative of the creation of the world. They are described as having fullness of intelligence; they are *"full of eyes before and behind"* (Revelation 4:6). Both foresight and hindsight are theirs. The past and future are open to them as a scroll.

In the symbolism of the faces of the beasts, Christ is presented as King, Servant, Man, and God.

> *And the first beast was like a lion, and the second beast like a calf, and the third beast had a face as a man, and the fourth beast was like a flying eagle.*   (Revelation 4:7)

The lion suggests omnipotence and majesty; the calf, patient labor on behalf of men; the man, intelligence and sympathy; and the eagle, remarkable vision and rapidity of action. These wonderful creatures also render unceasing service and undying praise. In activity and adoration, they do not rest day or night. This throne chapter closes with the anthem of the elders:

> *The four and twenty elders fall down before him that sat on the throne, and worship him that liveth for ever and ever, and cast their crowns before the throne, saying, Thou art worthy, O Lord, to receive glory and honor and power: for thou hast created all things, and for thy pleasure they are and were created.*   (Revelation 4:10–11)

Praise ascends to the Lord, the Creator of all things. In the next chapter, as the Redeemer, He receives His due. In casting their crowns before the throne, the elders indicate that the Lord alone is worthy to reign.

THE SEVEN-SEALED BOOK (REVELATION 5:1–14)

In our modern times, this last book of the Bible ought to be in our hands continually. The events of today, so heavy with prophetic significance, must be placed alongside God's divine program. Totalitarian governments, with their passions for world mastery, take on a deeper meaning as we enter this section of Revelation, with its manifestation of the One who alone has the right to world rulership.

In Revelation 5, we have the unfolding of the earthly administration of heavenly government. The main feature is a sealed book containing the divine program. This does not mean that it cannot be read, but simply that no one could be found to carry out the heavenly order of reading it.

Regarding this seven-sealed book, it was first of all *"in the right hand of him that sat on the throne"* (Revelation 5:1). The Bible has much to say about that *"right hand"*—the position of authority and power. Also, the book was *"sealed"* (verse 1). Why was it sealed? A seal implies finality and privacy. Breaking a seal often requires legal authority. Who could possibly be authorized to open this book? Must the drama of history fail at this crucial point? There is something very human in the reference to John's tears. *"And I wept much, because no man was found worthy to open and to read the book, neither to look thereon"* (Revelation 5:3). No one above, below, or underneath was worthy or able to break the seals and set in motion those forces liberating the long-awaited kingdom. And so, John burst into tears of anguish, for it seemed as if Satan and sin were to continue their control over world affairs.

The book was sealed with *"seven seals"* (Revelation 5:1), implying the perfect purpose of God in respect to the world. Each portion was individually sealed, with the seventh seal fastening the outside of the entire scroll. John's tears, however, were quickly dried, for one of the elders called, *"Weep not: behold, the Lion of the tribe of Judah, the Root of David, hath prevailed to open the book, and to loose the seven seals thereof"* (Revelation 5:5). With unbounded joy, John looks upon One who can and will open the book. The seals of divine judgment, which man could not break, are broken by Him in whose pierced hands rest the title deeds of world dominion. The breaking of the seals is the Lamb's prerogative, and nothing can happen apart from His governmental will.

In response to the summons, John turned to behold the Lion described by the elder but saw a Lamb instead. (See Revelation 5:6.) The Lion and the Lamb! Christ was both. As to His humanity, He is the Lion of the tribe of Judah, the Root of David. The Lamb is His dominant designation in Revelation, mentioned more than twenty times. John uses a word whose literal meaning is "the little lamb," suggesting Christ's innocence and gentleness; it is used in contrast to the malevolent beast. Notice also that when John looked for the Lion, there only *"stood a Lamb as it had been slain"* (Revelation 5:6). Christ is portrayed as living and risen. The Lion overcomes in the slain Lamb. Sovereignty is based on sacrifice. From the cross comes the crown. The centrality of Christ reappears in the phrase *"in the midst of the elders"* (verse 6). In the Lamb's *"seven horns and seven eyes"* (verse 6) we have perfect power and perfect intelligence as attributes both of the Lamb and of the Holy Spirit.

A dramatic scene is enacted, taking of the book from the hand of God. (See Revelation 5:7.) Christ is taking over prophesied governmental power.

> *I saw in the night visions, and, behold, one like the Son of man came with the clouds of heaven, and came to the Ancient of days, and they brought him near before him. And there was given him dominion, and glory, and a kingdom, that all people, nations, and languages, should serve him: his dominion is an everlasting dominion, which shall not pass away, and his kingdom that which shall not be destroyed.*
>
> (Daniel 7:13–14)

As we shall soon see, the breaking of each seal reveals the accomplishment of a divine purpose in and through Christ.

The taking of the book is followed by the worship by the twenty-four elders, each with a harp of thanksgiving and golden bowls of intercession. (See Revelation 5:8.) Their worship is based on redemption. (See verse 9.) Christ was the only One who could die as Savior, because He needed no savior Himself and is now extolled as the Redeemer. *"No man in heaven, nor in earth, neither under the earth, was able to open the book, neither to look thereon"* (Revelation 5:3) No kinsman-redeemer could be found among angels or men or in the underworld of death. The use of harps speaks of the celebration of victory. Used forty-three times in the Old Testament, the harp, one of the sweetest instruments known to man, is always connected with song. The harps on the willows meant captivity. (See Psalm 137:2–3.) Here, John refers to *"the prayers of saints"* (Revelation 5:8) because they helped to bring about the investiture of Jesus as Judge and Lord of all. Think of the millions of prayers stored up, all centering around the prayer that multitudes have prayed: "Thy kingdom come!"

The redemption song is called *"new"* (Revelation 5:9) because there had never been anything like it before. The whole group of worshippers renders homage to the Lamb and blesses His sacred name. What a hallelujah chorus!

This song of the glorified has three themes to it:

1. Redemption: *"Thou...hast redeemed us to God by thy blood"* (Revelation 5:9).

2. Royalty: *"Thou...hast made us unto our God kings"* (verse 10).

3. Consecration: *"Thou...hast made us unto our God...priests"* (verse 10).

The saints are to reign over and on the earth. The Lamb is the center of the mystic and glowing book of Revelation, as emphasized in the sevenfold note of triumph. (See Revelation 5:12.)

In this chapter we have the divine setting for judgment. All judgments now begin with this universal anthem. The patience of God is exhausted, and the punishment of the seals is about to begin. Divine patience reaches its end, and God's hour has come. Thus, chapters 4 and 5 form an impressive approach to the seals. Tremendous events are about to take place. The chapter concludes with the singing of the new song, myriads of angels joining in the adoring ascription of praise. The whole creation unites to adore the Lamb, this being the consummation of her groaning and anguish.

THE SEVEN SEALS (REVELATION 6:1–8:5)

As we enter this strictly prophetic part of Revelation, we find what has been called "procedure preceding victory." One feature of Revelation 6 is that John writes as an intensely observant eyewitness. "I saw" and "I heard" are expressions of personal experience that we cannot afford to overlook as we study the book as a whole. In Revelation 4 and 5, everything takes place in heaven, where we are privileged to glance into the secret of God's presence and witness the preparation of the coming Judge. But from Revelation 6 onward, the focus is on earth, with the commencement of its judgments. Christ, as the Lamb by right of purchase and power of redemption, takes full control. Sovereignty based on sacrifice is to be manifested.

Because the entire judgment period stretches from Revelation 6 to 20, it is important to note the connection between the seals, trumpets, and vials. The judgments of the seals and trumpets are not contemporaneous but successive. The seals cover a larger area than the trumpets, but the vials are more severe and searching in character. The Lamb opens the seals, the angels blow the trumpets, and God empties the vials. The seven seals, then, include the entire judgment period.

Out of the seals, the trumpets issue, and out of the trumpets, the vials issue. The trumpets and the vials display in detail what the seals denote in general. One might use the illustration of a telescope made of three sections, with the outer section containing the inner two, the middle section extending out of outer section, and the innermost section extending even further out of the middle section, as in the following diagram:

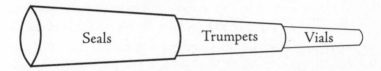

As we have previously indicated, some expositors take a historical view of chapters 6 through 20, that the judgments described cover only the opening of the Christian era to the present time. But my position is that the church is not on earth during these apocalyptic judgments, which are related to the Jews as a nation, and to the Gentiles as nations. Because the church is neither Jew nor Gentile but *"one in Christ Jesus"* (Galatians 3:28) and, therefore, not the object of judgment, she is away from the earth as its divine visitation begins. With this sixth chapter, the divine ministration of the Lamb commences, and it will not end until He has made all His enemies His footstool. (See Psalm 2.)

Here is a common complaint today: Why does God not intervene and do something about the sinful, chaotic condition of the world? If only the people who ask this would read the book of Revelation, their questions would quickly be answered, and their problems of divine nonintervention would be solved. Here, the Lord is about to show His hand.

And what action there is! In Revelation 4 and 5, the throne is set. In chapter 6, Daniel's last week begins. (See Daniel 9:26–27.) Daniel had not been invited to heaven, as John was. Daniel saw everything in night visions, but the full understanding of his visions was withheld. Thus, Revelation complements the book of Daniel. Right now, a usurper controls the world, but Christ's day is coming. This corrupt earth is ready and ripe for judgment. The evil forces that have gone unchallenged are about to meet their Master. Human and material instruments of vengeance are about to execute their divinely appointed task.

God sometimes may appear to be slow in settling accounts, but He always pays at last! If, to us, His mills appear to grind slowly, we are assured that they do grind exceedingly surely. In this age, He extends grace to the inhabitants of earth. He is slow to chide, but, once the rod falls, woe be to the hordes of earth!

1. THE SEAL OF THE WHITE HORSE

And I saw when the Lamb opened one of the seals, and I heard, as it were the noise of thunder, one of the four beasts saying, Come and see. And I saw, and behold a white horse: and he that sat on him had a bow; and a crown was given unto him: and he went forth conquering, and to conquer.

(Revelation 6:1–2)

In the loud summons introducing the seals, there is a significant point to consider. John heard *"the noise of thunder."* The phrase *"as it were"* indicates that John is using symbolic language. What *he* heard was a loud, thunderous voice, calling attention to the opening of the seals. The phrase *"Come and see"* (Revelation 6:1, 3, 5, 7) is rightly deleted in the Revised Version. Retention of the phrase makes it a call to John to come and see the horses. But to whom was the summons addressed? Who is bidden to come? Surely not John, who would not require the noise of thunder, for he was near and had witnessed the opening of the seals. It was the horsemen who came in obedience to the cry of the living one, *"Come and see."* This was the summons to appear and act. And the imperative command of the living creature was instantly obeyed.

The "four horsemen of the apocalypse" are symbolic of divine power in judgment. Almost every symbol in Revelation is interpreted for us in some other part of Scripture. We should keep in mind a golden principle enunciated by Walter Scott: "On no account seek the interpretation of any part of the Apocalypse outside the covers of your Bible. The meaning of every symbol must be sought for in the Word itself." Horses, for instance, are used figuratively in Zechariah 1 and 6. Comparing Scripture with Scripture, we are led to the conclusion that horses are prophetic of the final phases of world dominion by man, and also prophetic of human instruments used by God in His providential judgment of earth.

Two other thoughts are important as we approach the seals: first, the Lamb opens the seals while He is still in heaven in the midst of the throne. Officially and governmentally, Christ is about to exercise the dominion that His death, resurrection, and ascension gave Him. The breaking of the seals is the Lamb's prerogative, for nothing can happen outside His governmental will. Second, the four beasts are here found connected with the execution of divine judgment. Because of their full knowledge of the divine will, they are qualified to assist in this judgment.

The identity of the rider of the white horse is a matter of contradictory exposition. Some say that this is a vision of the armies of heaven, with the rider symbolizing the whole heavenly host, antagonistic to a godless earth. Others see in the riders as impersonal agencies riding forth to their tasks. Other writers affirm that the rider is Christ Himself, and link Revelation 6:1–2 with Revelation 19:11: *"I saw heaven opened, and behold a white horse; and he that sat upon him was called Faithful and True, and in righteousness he doth judge and make war."*

I believe that the rider in this first seal is not the same person who appears as King of Kings and Lord of Lords in Revelation 19:11–16. These two riders have nothing in common beyond a white horse. That fact that both horses are white is no more proof that they are symbolic of Christ than are the white horses which Zechariah mentions in Zechariah 1:8 and Zechariah 6:3–6. Without doubt, a white horse has always been deemed a symbol of victorious power and kingship—Napoleon always rode on a white horse—and this feature is true both of the rider in the first seal and of Christ in Revelation 19. The rider here is not named and has no title, but the rider in chapter 19 is named *"Faithful and True"* (verse 11) and *"the Word of God"* (verse 13) and bears the title *"KING OF KINGS, AND LORD OF LORDS"* (verse 16). Christ as the Lamb is the One opening the seals—therefore, He cannot be the rider in any of the first four seals. The white horse rider has a crown given unto him—by whom we are not told. His possession of a crown merely indicates his rise to power as a king among the ten kings, through the operation of satanic powers. (See Daniel 8:25; 11:36–39; 2 Thessalonians 2:8–12; Revelation 13:1–4.) Christ is not *given* any crown; many diadems adorn His brow by divine right and conquest. (See Revelation 19:12.)

There are other contrasts, as well. The rider in the first seal comes out of the earth, but Christ descends from the opened heavens. (See Revelation 13:1; 19:11.) The first rider causes, and is followed by, war, famine, pestilence, death, and hell—horrors accompanying the rule of an ambitious conqueror as cruel as he is cultured. But Christ is followed by the armies of heaven, clothed in fine linen, white and pure. We also read that the first rider is to go forth conquering and to conquer. Dictators conquer and acquire territory and possession by wars of conquest. But Christ is not coming to conquer. When He appears, He will take to Himself His rightful power and reign. He will not ride on *to* victory but *from* victory, which He accomplished at Calvary when He cried, *"It is finished"* (John 19:30). His judicial authority and reign, set forth in Revelation, are the fruits of His finished work at the cross.

We have no hesitation in affirming that the rider of the white horse is the antichrist. Throughout the ages, the spirit of antichrist has manifested itself in an individual with tremendous power.

Now the persistent conflict comes to a climax. Christ and Satan's masterpiece meet. In the first rider, we have the first manifestation of the Man of Sin, the accepted head of the ten confederated nations. In the crown given him, we have his acknowledgment as head of the revived empire.

White, the color of the horse, denotes the victorious power of the rider. Sacred white horses accompanied every Persian army. The antichrist, a great political leader and military strategist, will be able to produce a series of successive bloodless conflicts. With his genius for conflict and conquest, this universal dictator will have wisdom to settle all national and international unrest and disorder. Then, men will cry, "Peace and safety!" But terrible destruction will be just around the corner, as the second rider indicates. *"And in his estate shall stand up a vile person, to whom they shall not give the honor of the kingdom: but he shall come in peaceably, and obtain the kingdom by flatteries"* (Daniel 11:21). False authority characterizes all that is related to this white horse rider.

Halfway through the seven years, this brilliant figure becomes the beast, who will be responsible for much that will be bestial in character. Beasts are already with us, destroying the very foundations of human society. Increasing drunkenness, widespread drug addiction, legalized sodomy and abortions, sexual promiscuity, and fleshly indulgences are all precursors of the time to come, when iniquity will burst forth uncontrolled.

2. THE SEAL OF THE RED HORSE

And when he had opened the second seal, I heard the second beast say, Come and see. And there went out another horse that was red: and power was given to him that sat thereon to take peace from the earth, and that they should kill one another: and there was given unto him a great sword.

(Revelation 6:3–4)

The various colored horses symbolize the different agencies employed in the execution of divine judgment. The living creatures and horses are related to the first four seals only. Forfeiture of life is figuratively represented by the red, black, and pale colors.

As the white horse indicated bloodless victories, the red horse brings in bloody victories. With the second rider comes a global war, a grim shadow of which was experienced in World War II. Red, being a bloodlike color, is a symbol of strife, violence, and war. The bow gives way to a great sword. All past and present wars are only the forerunners of the terrible carnage under the second seal. At present, there is a "hinderer" holding human restraints in check, but with this red horse comes unparalleled bloodshed. Now, the word is unsheathed for vengeance, and not merely for victory.

The phrase *"power was given to him"* brings us to the permissive will of God. This grim rider has a divine mandate to remove peace from the earth—especially the false peace, which he himself instituted. God promised peace to Israel if they were obedient but a sword if disobedient. War (the sword) is one of God's four sore judgments. (See Ezekiel 14:21.) The devastation of modern wars is appalling, and if the world should experience a nuclear war, the destruction of life and property would be colossal. Treaties, pacts, and covenants will be torn up as scraps of paper. Life will be terribly cheap, for men will be but dung or manure for the earth, fit only for fertilizer.

3. THE SEAL OF THE BLACK HORSE

And when he had opened the third seal, I heard the third beast say, Come and see. And I beheld, and lo a black horse; and he that sat on him had a pair of balances in his hand. And I heard a voice in the midst of the four beasts say, A measure of wheat for a penny, and three measures of barley for a penny; and see thou hurt not the oil and the wine.

(Revelation 6:5–6)

This black-horse rider with scales in his hand is a symbol of famine. In Lamentations 4:8 and 5:10, we discover that black is the Old Testament description of famine and destitution. Terrible attrition and desolation follow the conquests of the prince. War is no time for sowing, and, thus, black follows red.

Famine is the natural result of ambitious conquerors who take peace from the earth. The scorched-earth policy introduced by retreating armies during recent years is another forerunner of ravages of famine yet to be experienced. This condition foreshadows the lamentation and mourning of those who will have to pay famine prices for the staff of life in the great tribulation, when a quart of wheat will be sold for one day's wages of a laborer.

Many of the rich, it would seem, are to be temporarily protected. Chastisement here is particularly for the majority, who will have just enough to live on, hence the mention of *wheat*, the barest staple of the poor. The rank and file suffer first when revolution comes; the more affluent are the last to suffer: *"Hurt not the oil and the wine."* Oil and wine, as luxuries, are found on the tables of the rich. Corn, wine, and oil are often grouped together to give the idea of plenty. (See Proverbs 21:17; Jeremiah 31:12; Psalm 104:15.) The sorrows of the rich come later. (See James 5:1–5.)

None is to escape the retribution he deserves. Prince and pauper alike must share in judgment. (See Matthew 24:6–7.) God often used famine as an instrument of judgment. Thus, we read of a famine in Egypt (see Genesis 41), another when the Babylonians besieged Jerusalem (see Jeremiah 32), and yet another when Titus conquered Jerusalem, in 70 A.D. Ezekiel 14:13 reminds us that famine is judgment upon flagrant sin.

By way of contrast, note the difference in Ezekiel 36:

I will also save you from all your uncleannesses: and I will call for the corn, and will increase it, and lay no famine upon you.

And I will multiply the fruit of the tree, and the increase of the field, that ye shall receive no more reproach of famine among the heathen. (Ezekiel 36:29–30)

If coming events case their shadow before, then the terrible condition in famine-stricken areas of the world, where thousands die daily for lack of food, portend the tragic tribulation events, when the black horse will be conspicuous, and vast multitudes will perish from hunger.

4. THE SEAL OF THE PALE HORSE

And when he had opened the fourth seal, I heard the voice of the fourth beast say, Come and see. And I looked, and behold a pale horse: and his name that sat on him was Death, and Hell followed with him. And power was given unto them over the fourth part of the earth, to kill with sword, and with hunger, and with death, and with the beasts of the earth.

(Revelation 6:7–8)

These initial judgments increase in severity, as the description of this new harbinger of judgment implies. Here, for the first time, the rider is named. And what a dreadful name it is—*"Death,"* with *"Hell"* acting as "death's hearse," as Bengel expresses it. In a literal sense, *pale* is colorless, even though we describe a sickly face as being "deathly pale." Such an unearthly green-yellow color implies a cadaverous hue or corpse-like aspect.

Death and Hell—or hades—are the respective custodians of the bodies and souls of men. Death claims the body, while Hell takes the spirit. Under this seal, all four sore judgments predicted in Ezekiel 14:21 are unleashed:

For thus saith the Lord GOD; How much more when I send my four sore judgments upon Jerusalem, the sword, and the famine, and the noisome beast, and the pestilence, to cut off from it man and beast?

The days of Israel's greatest sorrow, long foretold, have arrived.

One of the horrors of the tribulation will be that of the ghastly trail of death. War, famines, persecutions, pestilences, and earthquakes will all add their quotes to the reign of the king of terrors. The pale horse and its rider will be an all-too-common sight as the shadows of final judgment encircle around a condemned world. The plague of the Middle Ages was called "black death." Every judgment sent upon Israel for disobedience will be repeated in the tribulation, and recognized as sent by God. (See Leviticus 26:22.) In this death seal, the wild beasts of the earth also become an instrument of death.

D. M. Panton would have us remember that "even in the day of grace, animals are only held in leash by the dread of man, which God put upon them in the Noahic Covenant. What will happen in the tribulation is obvious. Famine, with the scarcity of food for both man and beast, will drive beasts mad with hunger; depopulation will embolden them, for wherever men die out, savage beasts multiply; and God, increasing their number and unchaining their ferocity, will seek to reason with carnal men by the only arguments the carnal understand. What the removal of animal dread of man will be, even from the ox or the dog, is unimaginable. God has foreshown, once for all in Israel's history, how He can use this sore weapon."

Thus, the corpse-like color of the horse is in keeping with the rider. Death and Hell are inseparable companions, and they now act together in judgment, dividing the spoil. Hell, as a consort and companion, receives those whom Death cuts off.

The *"beasts of the earth"* are the wild beasts who will complete the destruction. All such beasts have the culmination of their cruelty in *the beast*. In wrath, God remembers mercy, so the rider's authority is limited. The rider of the pale horse, with Hell as his companion, is limited to *"the fourth part of the earth"*—that is, the political realm. The fourth world empire was the Roman Empire, and it covered a large area of the earth. *"Sword," "hunger," "death,"* and *"beasts"*—what terrifying avenues of judgment! Would that the Christless could be aroused to the terrible days awaiting them! Finally, Death and Hell are to be cast into the lake of fire forever, which is truly a fitting and deserved end for this horseman and his companion. (See Revelation 20:14.)

5. THE SEAL OF THE MARTYRS

And when he had opened the fifth seal, I saw under the altar the souls of them that were slain for the word of God, and for the testimony which they held: and they cried with a loud voice, saying, How long, O Lord, holy and true, dost thou not judge and avenge our blood on them that dwell on the earth? And white robes were given unto every one of them; and it was said unto them, that they should rest yet for a little season, until their fellowservants also and their brethren, that should be killed as they were, should be fulfilled. (Revelation 6:9–11)

Now we turn from horses to heroes, from steeds to saints. The scene darkens, and the public intervention of God in the affairs of men becomes more obvious. In the last three seals, we have the full expression of God's wrath on guilty Christendom.

Who are these martyred saints? Some expositors affirm that they are made up of two classes: Jews and Christians. But the church can hardly be included, since all believers are with the Lord by this time, having received their new bodies at the rapture. These martyrs will be mainly Jews, although there will be Gentile martyrs, as well. With the exclamation *"How long, O Lord?"* we have the cry of tribulation martyrs for the avenging of their blood.

This plea for judgment upon murderers proves that the martyred were recently slain and that their murderers are still alive. Cries for vengeance that are not consistent now, in an age of grace, will be proper then. What we have here is the remnant pleading for vengeance. The martyrs are told to restfully wait for the right time of judgment, as many other martyrs are to be added to their number. God accepts their attitude and stamps approval upon it.

"*Souls*" is sometimes used as a figure for "people," as in Acts 7:14: "*Then sent Joseph, and called his father Jacob to him, and all his kindred, threescore and fifteen souls.*" The color "*white*" has been called "the livery of heaven" and figures prominently in Revelation.

The slain souls were seen "*under the altar,*" the place of sacrifice. This signifies being covered by the sacrifice. The ancient cry "*How long shall the wicked triumph?*" (Psalm 94:3) remained unanswered until John was given the vision of those under the altar. He heard the question "How long?" and received the answer in the "*white robes.*" In days of military triumph, Roman citizens walked through the streets dressed in white following a victorious general who had returned with trophies from battle. Did not Christ promise that His overcomers should walk with Him in white? "*White robes*" takes us back to the Old Testament, in which we find robes associated with honor and reward.

The persecution that is prophesied in Matthew 24:9–14 will reach a terrible severity under the beast, just as millions of Jews were massacred by Adolf Hitler. Yet, even with this seal, there is exhibited the patience of God.

This fifth seal closes the first three-and-a-half years of the tribulation. The most severe forms of tribulation still lie ahead, when multitudes who refuse to worship the beast will be killed, and, with them, the list of martyrs will be complete.

6. THE SEAL OF WRATH

And I beheld when he had opened the sixth seal, and, lo, there was a great earthquake; and the sun became black as sackcloth of hair, and the moon became as blood; and the stars of heaven fell unto the earth, even as a fig tree casteth her untimely figs, when she is shaken of a mighty wind. And the heaven departed as a scroll when it is rolled together; and every mountain and island were moved out of their places. And the kings of the earth, and the great men, and the rich men, and the chief captains, and the mighty men, and every bondman, and every free man, hid themselves in the dens and in the rocks of the mountains; and said to the mountains and rocks, Fall on us, and hide us from the face of him that sitteth on the throne, and from the wrath of the Lamb: for the great day of his wrath is come; and who shall be able to stand?

(Revelation 6:12–17)

This scene is both terrible and exalted. As the sixth seal opens, we have the premonitions of coming events: convulsions in nature and consternation among men. For a picture of social chaos in which nature shares the violent disruption, general catastrophe, and universal terror, these verses are unparalleled. Is the language literal or symbolic? Perhaps both are interwoven in John's description of governmental and moral collapse, of disasters and disturbances in social and material realms.

In this awful picture of the terrible results of apostasy, kings are found leading the agonizing hosts of earth. We have now reached the wrath of the Lamb, as it produces unlimited terror among men. A disturbed heaven and earth bring about the destruction and complete overthrow of all civil and moral order. The whole structure falls. Thunder and earthquakes symbolize the upheaval within the social, ecclesiastical, and political spheres. Black mourning clothing represents the darkening power of Satan. *"The sun"* stands for complete authority of government, *"the moon"* symbolizes dependent authority, and *"the stars"* depict still lesser authorities. How men's hearts will fail them for fear!

"He reserveth wrath for his enemies" (Nahum 1:2). The days of revolution and slaughter are the forerunner of the tragic time of the tribulation. Men will pray, but not to God, from whose face the horrified multitudes will flee. Instead, people will pray *"to the mountains and rocks."* Their only refuge is in hiding *in* the Lamb, not *from* Him, but He will offer no protection for the unrepentant, for the time of grace has now passed. There is no cry of repentance on the part of these fear-driven multitudes, no entreaty to be delivered from their sin and from coming eternal woe—only an urgent plea for their physical safety.

Seven classes of people are named in Revelation 6:15, and these include...

1. kings (the rulers)

2. the great (the inspirational)

3. the rich (the influential)

4. chief captains (the authorities)

5. the mighty (the soldiers)

6. bondmen (the oppressed)

7. freemen (all the rest)

Hiding from God was the result of the first disobedience, and Adam tried to hide from God behind the trees and shrubs in the garden of Eden. As with Adam, so it will be with a guilty world when the Lord prepares to come in glory. Note how this sixth seal corresponds to the prophecy of Isaiah 2:12, 17–22; 13:6–13; and 24:1–6:

Who can stand before his indignation? and who can abide in
the fierceness of his anger? his fury is poured out like fire, and
the rocks are thrown down by him.   (Nahum 1:6)

The prayers of the martyred (see Revelation 6:10) are now partially answered. At last, the Warrior-King is drenched in blood. No wonder Walter Scott concludes this chapter by saying that every reader must feel awed at the "almost unparalleled magnificence and sublimity" of the scene about to be enacted, which is revealed in terms so clear that their meaning can hardly be misunderstood.

⚯

Revelation 7 is a "parenthesis of grace." In this chapter, there are two separate visions: the first, concerning Israel (see verses 1–8); the second, concerning the Gentiles (see verses 9–17). There are two groups of redeemed saints. It is not all judgment in these days of tribulation. John gives us a deeply interesting episode of blessing for both Jews and Gentiles. The course of judgment is suspended, and the veil is drawn aside, so that we may witness the heart of our God. Just when this visitation of blessing takes place, we are not told. But we do know that Christ's return for His church will create a profound impression in the world and that, after this translation of the saints, God will work in grace among His ancient people, the Jews and the Gentiles. Many people will be saved after the rapture, and they will incur the active and cruel hostility of the unsaved people around them. Many of these converts will be among the first group of witnesses preaching the gospel of the coming kingdom throughout the Roman world. (See Matthew 24:14.) They will also become the first martyrs.

This break in God's judgments is provided so that there might be an outflowing of God's grace. Four angels come into view. They are related to the four directions of the compass. (See Isaiah 11:12.) They control the four winds, which implies that, through them,

God is able to control or release judgment. The number four signifies the completeness and universality of judgment. The fifth, or sealing, angel of Revelation 7:2 cannot be Christ, as some have suggested. The angel-priest of Revelation 8:3–5 and the strong angel of Revelation 10:1–10 refer to Christ, because the terms used and the actions described could not be applied to any created being, however exalted. The sealing angel is evidently a distinguished spiritual being who is authorized to seal the servants of God. He appears from the east, which is the direction from which God manifests Himself.

In Revelation 7:4–8, the sealed Jews (unlike the Gentile throng) are numbered, and the tribes are carefully distinguished. In precise figures, there are 144,000 sealed Jews. They are saved *before* the great tribulation and are sealed to go through it. Any tampering of an official seal carries the liability of punishment Thus, the seal here speaks of freedom from molestation. Twelve is Israel's number, and we have, in this sealing, a complete yet limited number of Israel—the Jewish remnant preserved from martyrdom. This group of 144,000 is not identical with the equal number of people mentioned in Revelation 14. Here we have 144,000 representing all of Israel. In chapter 14, we have the 144,000 of Judah only, who emerge out of the horrors of the coming hour of trial

We are not told when the sealing of the specific number out of the twelve tribes of Israel takes place.

But because the seal is in the name of the Lamb and the name of the Father, the numbered Jews who are described must have accepted the Lamb as their Messiah, and they are now protected because of the choice they made. Those Israelites who were faithful to God in spite of the abominations committed by others among their nation were protected by a mark on their foreheads. (See Ezekiel 9:4.) The 144,000 are among those Daniel referred to as "*found written in the book*" (Daniel 12:1).

A seal represents official recognition and possession, and any tampering with it is subject to the penalty of the law and government. God will have a sealed people whom He will protect and deliver through the tragic times overtaking the earth. This seal will also shield those who possess it from the demons released from the pit. (See Revelation 9:4.)

The *"great multitude [of Gentiles], which no man could number, of all nations, and kindreds, and people, and tongues"* (Revelation 7:9) is in sharp contrast to the more limited and exactly defined number of Israel. This palm-bearing Gentile multitude must not be confused with either the church or Israel. This is the mighty ingathering of souls that Joel predicted when he said that in the day of the Lord, *"whosoever shall call on the name of the LORD shall be delivered"* (Joel 2:32). The innumerable company represents the fruit of an extensive work of grace begun immediately, or soon after the translation of the church, and continued through the future prophetic week of seven years. Previously, John had described the ascription of praise as being *"out of every kindred, and tongue, and people, and nation"* (Revelation 5:9.)

Three questions emerge in connection with this extensive work of grace:

1. *What about the heathen?* The fate of millions of unevangelized people is a matter of serious concern. Will all these people be damned once the church has gone to heaven at the time of the rapture? It is encouraging to find that vast numbers will be saved—the *"great multitude"* that will come out of *"all nations, and kindreds, and people, and tongues."* Thus, although the church has failed seriously in its missionary work in this dispensation, the ends of the earth will yet be reached by the message of the precious blood of Christ.

2. *Will souls be saved after the rapture?* When the true church has gone, will all opportunity for the lost be cut off? Are we

warranted in holding out to the unsaved any hope of salvation once the day of grace, as we presently understand it, has ended? For those of us who have unsaved dear ones when Christ returns at the rapture, they may be among the number who will come out of the great tribulation, washed through the blood of the Lamb. Passages like Revelation 5:8 and Revelation 8:3, which have to do with our stored-up prayers, may mean that our current unanswered prayers for dear ones may be answered in that day. Such a hope, however, should not create indifference about the lost. If it is hard for the lost to respond to the Savior in these days of light and liberty, it will be more difficult for them to believe when the antichrist is abroad. Because of the multitudes who are to be destroyed by war, famine, pestilence, and anarchy in the days of the Man of Sin, it is imperative to call upon the lost to repent and be saved while the door of mercy stands open and while conditions are still conducive for decision.

3. *Will the Spirit go with the church?* Some people teach that the Holy Spirit will be completely withdrawn from the earth once the church is caught up to meet the Lord in the air. But because the Spirit is always vitally connected with human salvation, He must be the active Agent in the great revival among those on the earth after the rapture. John is recording not a past act but a present action, and those who keep coming are blood-washed, so the Spirit must be near, since He is always the One to apply the efficacious blood of the Lamb. The phrase *"in the blood of the Lamb"* should read as *"through* the blood of the Lamb," implying the thought "because of." Nothing can ever be made white by being washed in blood. All who stand before the throne of God are covered with Christ's righteousness and are eternally secure because of all He accomplished on their behalf and their acceptance of Him as their Substitute.

This great saved multitude will not form part of the church but will have their place before the throne. C. I. Scofield remarked, "They are not of the priesthood, the church, to which they seem to stand somewhat in the relation of the Levites to the priests under the Mosaic covenant." We cannot regard this saved company as a heavenly one, for what is presented is an earthly scene. All the people of earth who pass into the millennium must be those who acknowledge the Lamb as their Lord. Millennial blessings, however, are to be shared by this white-robed throng. For these tribulation saints, there are manifold rewards, as John so clearly indicates. They include...

+ to be *"before the throne of God"* (Revelation 7:15).

+ to *"serve him day and night in his temple"* (Revelation 7:15).

+ to have God *"dwell among them"* (Revelation 7:15).

+ to *"hunger no more, neither thirst any more"* (Revelation 7:16).

+ to not have *"the sun light on them, nor any heat"* (Revelation 7:16).

+ to have the Lamb *"feed them, and...lead them"* (Revelation 7:17).

+ to have God *"wipe away all tears from their eyes"* (Revelation 7:17).

+ to experience *"rest from their labors"* (Revelation 14:13).

+ to have seven angels *"stand on the sea of glass, having the harps of God"* (Revelation 15:2).

+ to reign *"with Christ a thousand years"* (Revelation 20:4).

7. THE SEAL OF SILENCE

And when he had opened the seventh seal, there was silence in heaven about the space of half an hour.   (Revelation 8:1)

Why does one whole chapter intervene between the sixth and seventh seals? Why does a parenthesis break the orderly sequence of events? One answer is that the sixth seal announced such appalling judgment that people will think this horror is the great day of the wrath of the Lamb. But it is not. So, when the seventh seal is opened, which is preparatory to the infliction of still further and more severe judgments, the veil is drawn aside to permit two great groups of redeemed people to be introduced into the scene as the result of an extensive work of grace carried on, even as judgment is desolating the earth.

When this seventh seal is opened, and when all the contents of the previous six seals are completed, there is silence in heaven, but not elsewhere. This seal of silence is somewhat startling since we have little silence in the book as a whole. Revelation is a book of speech, thunder, voices, and fast-moving action.

What is the significance of this silence, the only content of the seal? It represents a brief pause, during which the course of divine judgment is suspended. God is reluctant to smite, for He has no pleasure in the death of the wicked. The silence also indicates a pause between two series. This seventh seal is a unique conclusion of all the terrible judgments of the other seals and a fitting interlude between them and the terrible events of the seven trumpets to follow. It is stillness before the storm, calm before catastrophe. It is a solemn sign that the Lord is about to leave His holy realm to punish the earth. It foreshadows the terrible nature of coming anguish.

This silence is in heaven, seeing that the source of earth judgments is the throne set in heaven. As to the *"half an hour,"* some expositors wonder whether this period of time is literal or symbolic. It is sufficient to say that it simply signifies a brief period during which judicial action is suspended. Half an hour will be long enough. It will seem like centuries to those who wait breathlessly for the Lord to smite! When the silence is over, His work of judgment will be a short one. *"The Lord is slow to anger"* (Nahum 1:3).

11

THE SEVEN TRUMPETS

REVELATION 8:6–11:19

The fact that the word *angel* occurs more than seventy times in Revelation proves how prominent angelic ministry is in the unfolding of God's final purposes for the world. His angels are the media of His manifold operations. In this church age, we are not dependent on angels, since the Holy Spirit is the Administrator of the affairs of the church and acts as the Executor of the Godhead, the true Vicar of Christ. After the rapture of the church, angels are again conspicuous in the execution of divine edicts. The more we read Revelation, the more we are impressed and awed at the obedience, dignity, and authority of these angelic beings, who are mentioned more often in Revelation than in any other book of the Bible.

The Greek word for *angel* simply means simply "messenger" and is used of human as well as of heavenly heralds. The seven stars of Revelation 1:20 are used to symbolize the angels of the seven churches. These angels describe not the *nature* but the *office* of the spiritual rulers in the churches, who were responsible for maintaining the light of the glorious gospel during the dark night of church history.

The context where the word *angel* is used determines its application either to human or heavenly beings. In many passages, the word *"messengers"*—the same word as used for *"angels"*—is used to describe human messengers of various kinds. (See Luke 7:24; 9:52; 2 Corinthians 12:7; James 2:25.) When the term is specifically used of heavenly beings, it also implies the great characteristic of service. (See Psalm 103:20–21; Hebrews 1:13–14.) There are other references where *"angel"* carries the idea of "representations" or "guardianship," as in our Lord's announcement about His little ones having their angels in heaven to represent them. *"His angel"* in Acts 12:15 and Revelation 1:1 was a heavenly being prominent in the hierarchy of heaven, who, in his ministry, represented the Lord of angels.

In this gospel age, angels are *"ministering spirits"* (Hebrews 1:14), sent forth to minister for those who shall be heirs of salvation. In Revelation, particularly in that majority of the book dealing with the preparation for and execution of Christ's judicial authority, almost every phrase has its angel or angels, as this brief summary shows:

+ An angel is the intermediary between Christ and John in the conveyance of the book of Revelation. (See Revelation 1:1–4.)

+ Angels are the moral representatives of the seven churches. (See Revelation 1:20; 2; 3.)

+ An angel challenges the universe to bring forth One competent enough to fulfill the righteous counsels of God relating to the world. (See Revelation 5:2.)

+ Angels, as a numberless throng, worship and praise Christ as the slain Lamb. (See Revelation 5:11–12.)

+ Angels are given power to control natural elements. (See Revelation 7:1.)

+ Angels have authority to seal those who are true servants of God. (See Revelation 7:2–3.)

+ Angels are trumpeters, each of the seven trumpets having its own angel. (See Revelation 8.)

+ Angels are identified with the seven vials of divine wrath. (See Revelation 16.)

+ Angels are allies of God in the heavenly war against hellish forces. (See Revelation 12.)

+ An angel proclaims the everlasting gospel. (See Revelation 14:6.)

+ An angel announces the news of the fall of Babylon. (See Revelation 14:8.)

+ An angel thunders forth the terrible doom of the worshippers of the beast. (See Revelation 14:9.)

+ An angel comes out of the temple (see Revelation 14:15), and another angel comes out of the altar (see verse 18).

+ An angel is the guardian of the *"waters"*—a symbol of the peoples of earth. (See Revelation 17:15.)

The term *"another angel"* is used three times in Revelation (see Revelation 8:3; 10:1; 18:1) and deserves special attention when we encounter it in our treatment of these references.

There are two distinct groups of seven angels. There are the seven angels associated with the trumpet judgments (see Revelation 8–14) and the seven angels related to divine wrath, or the last plagues (see Revelation 15:1; 16:1). Two other numbered groups of angels include *"four angels"* (Revelation 7:1) and *"twelve angels"* (Revelation 21:12).

THE SEVEN TRUMPET ANGELS

And the seven angels which had the seven trumpets prepared themselves to sound.　　　　　　　　　(Revelation 8:6)

While it is true that a numberless host of angels wait upon the throne of God, it would seem that these seven trumpet angels are "presence angels," or "*angel*[s] *of his presence*" (Isaiah 63:9) and are therefore of an exalted order. Gabriel described his position as standing "*in the presence of God*" (Luke 1:19). Can it be that all seven of these angels are archangels?

The number seven implies that these high-ranking angelic beings represent the complete power of God in judicial affairs and are the executors of His will in respect to judgment. Behind their pronouncements and actions is the authority of the throne, before whose divine Occupant they stand. That there are distinctions among the angelic hosts is hinted at by Paul's mention of "*principalities,…powers,…*[and] *rulers*" (Ephesians 6:12). But while various orders and ranks are distributed among the angels of God, none of them ever usurps its position. Rather, all of them are united as they offer God unquestioning obedience and activity in service.

THE SEVEN TRUMPETS

In Joshua 6, seven rams' horns sounded by the seven priests on seven successive days announced and achieved the overthrow of Jericho. Those seven priests blew their trumpets together, but the seven angels do not blow in unison. They blow their trumpets one by one. Thus, one might argue that one angel is the equivalent of seven priests and is therefore "*greater in power and might*" (2 Peter 2:11).

Trumpets served many purposes in Old Testament times. They were used for journeys, alarms, public notices, and preparation of God's hosts against His enemies. Walter Scott remarked, "The seven trumpets signify a complete and full announcement. The mystic trumpets of Revelation are not to be confounded with the literal trumpets of Old Testament times." Once these trumpet blasts are heard by men, they will not be confused as to their significance and dreaded message. Is there not something majestic yet solemn about these angelic trumpeters as they prepare to sound? There they stand in rank, trumpet in hand, waiting to blast forth their respective judgments.

Out of the womb of the impressive silence of the seventh seal, the seven trumpets emerge with their mission of a judicial character, and the series of seven increases in severity. As to the seven seals, the seven trumpets, and the seven vials, these are not identical judgments executed concurrently. They present three different series of judgments experienced during the great tribulation. The judgments under the seals, trumpets, and vials are not contemporaneous but successive.

The first four trumpets describe the civil and ecclesiastical condition of the revived Western Roman Empire; the fifth trumpet of first woe is related to apostate Judaism; the sixth trumpet, or second woe, is associated with the guilty, godless inhabitants of the Roman world; the seventh trumpet, or third woe, suggests the universal effects of God's judgments.

Before we examine the announcements of the seven angels, we must identify the separate angel—*"another angel"* (Revelation 8:3)—who appears in their company. Is this just another angel, or is he someone in particular? Whenever the phrase "another angel" appears in Revelation, the Greek word *allos* is always used, meaning "another of the same kind." Most expositors believe the expression "the angel of the Lord" implies the presence of deity in angelic form, and sometimes even in human form. (See, for example, Genesis 18:1–14.) These are referred to as the "theophanic appearances of Christ" before His incarnation. Christ is similar to the angels in respect to His heavenly, spiritual being, but He is infinitely better than angels because He is the Son of God and Lord of the angels; in order to save mankind, He was made *"a little lower than the angels"* (Psalm 8:5; Hebrews 2:7).

Some expositors of Revelation affirm that the special angel functioning at the altar is only one of the angelic host, and not the Lord Jesus Christ. They maintain that Jesus is the Lamb opening the seals and directing the processes of judgment and that His mission in the tribulation is not one of intercession but of condemnation. It is further explained that the incense mentioned is given to this prominent angel, while Christ would have needed no one to hand Him the censer.

I am convinced that no angel, whatever his high rank, is qualified to stand at the celestial altar before God on behalf of man, nor is given priestly functions to exercise.

> No Cherub's heart or hand for us might ache,
> No Seraph's heart of fire had half sufficed;
> Thine own were pierced and broken for our sake,
> O Jesus Christ![6]

As there is only one Mediator between God and men, the Man Christ Jesus, who gave Himself as a ransom for all, we are convinced that this Angel-Priest whose action is at the altar is Christ, our great High Priest.

The glory of the descending Angel of Jehovah is seen in a threefold way:

1. As the Angel-Priest, on behalf of His suffering remnant. (See Revelation 8.)

2. As the Angel-Redeemer, taking possession of His inheritance. (See Revelation 10.)

3. As the Angel-Avenger of His people, taking vengeance on Babylon. (See Revelation 18.)

That the description of the Angel-Redeemer is not that of an ordinary angel is proven by the fact that He refers to the two

6. Christina Georgina Rossetti, "Good Friday Evening," 1893.

martyred prophets as *"my two witnesses"* (Revelation 11:3), which could not be written of any angel. Furthermore, a rainbow is never used in the Bible apart from God. (See Revelation 10:1.) Therefore, the angel here must be the Son of God. The description *"as when a lion roareth"* (Revelation 10:3) speaks of Him who is also *"the Lion of the tribe of Judah"* (Revelation 5:5).

This Angel-Priest must surely be the Mediator Jesus Christ, for no other can add efficacy to the prayers of saints. In the heavenly scene that John received and recorded, discernible features appear beneath Jewish imagery. For example, priests alone served at both the brazen and golden altars. The altar of burnt offering, standing in the court of the tabernacle, is recalled by the language John used.

The Spirit-inspired prayers of saints are never forgotten. If these prayers are not answered in the lifetime of those offering them, they are often answered after the intercessors have gone to heaven. The Lord never forgets any of His own. They are always in remembrance before Him.

Incense represents the Savior's life and labors. His sweet savor is the incense, and His efficacious death and resurrection give acceptance by God to our Spirit-inspired prayers. The altar is the place of substitutionary atonement, while fire speaks of divine judgment on sin, and judgment on the earth is what the angel-trumpeters announce. (See Revelation 8:6–7.) It must be noted that the angels only *announce* judgment; they do not *execute* or *dispense* it. It is the Angel-Priest who *metes out* judgment. (See Revelation 8:5.)

THE FIRST TRUMPET

The first angel sounded, and there followed hail and fire mingled with blood, and they were cast upon the earth: and the third part of trees was burnt up, and all green grass was burnt up. (Revelation 8:7)

The tribulation days will witness a recurrence of the plagues of Egypt that Pharaoh and his host experienced. Destructive agencies are about to overtake the earth, and what happens after the first trumpet has sounded corresponds to the seventh plague in Israel's time. (See Exodus 9:18–26.) Scripture is not silent as to the symbolic significance of the figures used. A. T. Robertson, the eminent Greek scholar, wrote, "In the visions and all through the book there is constant use of symbols....These symbols probably were understood by the first readers of the book, though the key to them is lost to us." But with all deference to this learned expositor, such a key has not been lost to us, for Scripture interprets Scripture.

Hail, coming from above, proves God to be the Executor of severe judgment in a sudden, sharp, and overwhelming calamity. (See Joshua 10:11; Isaiah 28:2, 17; 30:30; Ezekiel 13:13.)

Fire, symbolically used of God, of Christ, and of the Holy Spirit, is often employed as an expression of God's wrath upon man because of his sin. (See Deuteronomy 32:22; Isaiah 33:14; Matthew 25:41.) It also indicates the purifying influence of the Word of God. (See Jeremiah 23:29; Malachi 3:2.)

Blood signifies dreadful slaughter, life forfeited by sin but claimed by a holy God, and complete apostasy from God and truth. (See Leviticus 3:17; 17:10–14; Revelation 14:20; 16:3.)

Hail and fire mingled with blood present a fearful combination. Such a trinity expresses a terrible manifestation of divine wrath upon the earth and its inhabitants. As for the seven trumpet judgments, the first four are on places, material things, and the accessories of life. The last three judgments are on people and life itself.

Under the first judgment, a third of the trees are burned up. Different parts of the world have experienced devastating forest fires, but history records no such event as a third of all the trees in the world being destroyed by fire. Therefore, a historical interpretation of Revelation can be ruled out. The twelvefold repetition of the phrase *"third part"* is impressive. As used by John, it is equivalent to the revised power of Rome. Walter Scott affirmed, "The Western part of the prophetic earth is here designated as the *'third part.'"*

We must not forget that the shadow of Rome, past and future, is cast over Revelation. The twelve uses of *"third part"* can represent God's vengeance upon Rome, since twelve is God's governmental number concerning the most guilty part of the earth.

Trees symbolize human greatness and pride. (See Ezekiel 31; Daniel 4.) Our righteous God hates the pride of man and will overtake the high and mighty of the earth with judgment.

Grass, symbolic of prosperity of a temporary character—and, likewise, human frailty—describes the desolation of so many people, even though the *"green grass"* of a highly prosperous condition was theirs.

THE SECOND TRUMPET

> *And the second angel sounded, and as it were a great mountain burning with fire was cast into the sea: and the third part of the sea became blood; and the third part of the creatures which were in the sea, and had life, died; and the third part of the ships were destroyed.*　　　(Revelation 8:8–9)

Comparing Scripture with Scripture, we find that the *sea* is used for the restlessness of human nature, and also of peoples in a state of anarchy and confusion. (See Isaiah 57:20.)

Ships represent travel and commerce. Phrases like *"as it were"* occur often in Revelation and indicate the use of symbolic language. Here, *"a great mountain"* is the symbol of a kingdom. All the Gentile world is to suffer God's righteous vengeance.

"The sea became blood" corresponds to the plague that overtook the Nile in Exodus 7:17–21. As the ever-restless sea symbolizes the masses of earth's population in rebellion because of the absence of a strong hand to rule them, the blood-like sea describes the fearful destruction about to overtake them. Make the sea impassable, and the world's main highway of trade is blighted. But the uses and products of the sea are indelibly stamped with the sign of death. The symbol of a burning mountain cast into the sea denotes that this destruction is not caused by anything within the power of man but comes directly from God as a judgment warning.

The destruction of *"the third part of the ships"* reveals how commerce and communication will also feel the weight of divine judgment. Exports and imports will be seriously curtailed. In World War II, there was a colossal toll of ships sinking—about a third of all the naval ships of the nations involved in the war went to the bottom of the sea! A tremendous shipbuilding program replaced this dreadful toll of sunken ships. In the tribulation days, however, with men and materials destroyed, such replacement of losses will not be possible.

THE THIRD TRUMPET

And the third angel sounded, and there fell a great star from heaven, burning as it were a lamp, and it fell upon the third part of the rivers, and upon the fountains of waters; and the name of the star is called Wormwood: and the third part of the waters became wormwood; and many men died of the waters, because they were made bitter. (Revelation 8:10–11)

"Rivers" and *"fountains of waters"* suggest sources of profitable pleasure, or of nations acting under turbulent influences. But as the third angel sounds, the call goes out to earth's pleasure-producing sources, calling them to go to war against rebellious man. The *"great star"*—a meteor with its gaseous vapors covering

the freshwater supply—will be absorbed by a third of the waters, rivers, and fountains, an event that recalls what happened in the first Egyptian plague. This symbolizes the instrument of God's power. This particular *"star"* is not to be confused with the falling star under the fifth trumpet. (See Revelation 9:1.) These two distinct stars are spiritual rulers, however, and both are viewed as morally fallen from their high position. Heaven is the center and source of divine authority. *"The heavens do rule"* (Daniel 4:26). The apostate distinguished rulers are subject to such dominion. Who the one of exalted rank is, we are not told.

The term *"Wormwood"* is not so much the name of the person referred to as it is descriptive of his evil influence. Some writers identify the great star as Satan or the antichrist. Wormwood is related to sagebrush and is the source of an essential oil obtained from the dried leaves and tops of the plant. As such, it symbolizes bitterness. (See Deuteronomy 29:18; Jeremiah 23:15.) The continuous use of this liquor produces mental deterioration and even death. Solomon spoke of the end of an evil woman as being *"bitter as wormwood"* (Proverbs 5:4).

Earth is to reap the bitter fruits of sin, as essential supplies are contaminated by this plant. In times of war, nations experience how detrimental it is to have their natural and communal supply of water polluted or cut off. As Sir William Ramsey expressed it, "When you look out at these bitter ingredients infused into the water by the fall of this great star, the wonder is not that many died, but that any lived."

Every earthborn pleasure has *"wormwood"* bitterness in it, and in the tribulation judgment, a third part of the earth, instead of finding life in fountains of life-giving water, will find death. Conversely, God is able to make bitter waters sweet. (See Exodus 15:25–27.) The geographical area affected by the blight of bitterness is *"the third part,"* suggesting that, as someone once said, "the steps of God from mercy to judgment are always slow, reluctant, and measured."

THE FOURTH TRUMPET

*And the fourth angel sounded, and the third part of the sun
was smitten, and the third part of the moon, and the third part
of the stars; so as the third part of them was darkened, and
the day shone not for a third part of it, and the night likewise.
And I beheld, and heard an angel flying through the midst of
heaven, saying with a loud voice, Woe, woe, woe, to the inhabiters of the earth by reason of the other voices of the trumpet of
the three angels, which are yet to sound!*

(Revelation 8:12–13)

The judgment of the fourth trumpet will be hard on those
lovers of astrology who believe that their life is regulated by the
movement of the sun, moon, and stars. The declarations of horo-
scopes as to their association with the events of our present or
future life are pure nonsense. Our times are not wrapped up in the
stars but are in the hands of Him who made the stars! *Astronomy* is
a most fascinating and legitimate study; *astrology* is simply guess-
work on the part of money-inspired necromancers.

Man speaks about the fixity of the laws of nature, but God's
command of the luminaries in the heavens declares Him to be the
Lord of the universe. When it comes to light or darkness, He can
do as He pleases, as the Egyptians discovered when they suffered
a terrible blackout but saw that the Israelites had light in their
dwellings. When first created, the sun, moon, and stars were commissioned to give light to the earth, and their power for good has
always been great. Now, however, the benefit received from them
is diminished by one-third, for God's edict goes forth to destroy a
third part of them.

During World War II, the British people were accustomed to
blackouts during terrifying air raids at the hands of German bomb-
ers. But all man can do is extinguish *artificial* lights. He cannot stop

the heavenly lights from shining. During a blackout, it seemed ironic to hear an air warden shout to a householder, "Put out that light!" while, above, a most brilliant moon was sending out its light as usual, making visible so much for the raiders to see. But a divine blackout is coming, and when God withdraws the rays of the sun, moon, and stars, the earth will experience a darkness it will dread.

The last verse of this chapter contains a loud and universal announcement of three woes that usher in the last three trumpets. These solemn woes indicate the severity of further judgments and their terrifying effects. These last three trumpets will result in a new quality and degree of divine displeasure and con-sequent disaster. The woe is threefold because the three worst judgments are yet to come. Under the sounding of the first four trumpets, man is revealed in his earthly relationships. Men may look where they will on the things ministering to their pleasure or their sustenance, but they must see everywhere the mark of God's judgment brought down by their own sin.

THE FIFTH TRUMPET

And the fifth angel sounded, and I saw a star fall from heaven unto the earth: and to him was given the key of the bottom-less pit. And he opened the bottomless pit; and there arose a smoke out of the pit, as the smoke of a great furnace; and the sun and the air were darkened by reason of the smoke of the pit. And there came out of the smoke locusts upon the earth: and unto them was given power, as the scorpions of the earth have power. And it was commanded them that they should not hurt the grass of the earth, neither any green thing, neither any tree; but only those men which have not the seal of God in their foreheads. (Revelation 9:1–4)

With the sounding of the last three trumpets, we pass from the *visible* to the *invisible*. With the previous trumpets, man was seen in his material surroundings—things seen by the human eye—but now, we are no longer in the material realm but in the spiritual realm. A sad sight is presented under this judgment, but worse sights are yet to come. In these verses, we have one of the most fearful descriptions of devastation ever penned, as the fifth angel goes forth to exercise his frightful mission.

Here, again, a star falling to earth has been identified. Some say it is descriptive of Satan being cast out of heaven, or of the antichrist, the false prophet, or a religious or political system. I feel that the fallen star may be the antichrist, Satan's chosen instrument to inflict such scenes of cruelty and bloodshed as depicted by John. To this expelled one is committed *"the key of the bottomless pit"*— the prison house of demons. Possession of *"the key"* means doleful power and authority to execute death. The smoke arising out of the abyss results in a most devastating army of locusts. By smoke, we can understand the blinding and withering effect of satanic delusion. Paul's portrait of demon imitation in 2 Thessalonians 2:9–12 corresponds to the power that Satan makes possible for the locust army.

The locusts with *"power, as the scorpions of the earth"* symbolize those hordes of devilish agencies bringing vengeance on the guilty, described as those *"which have not the seal of God in their foreheads."* As 144,000 people of Israel are sealed and therefore secure from judgment, it is the unsealed Gentile multitudes who must drink the cup of vengeance. As Sweete put it, "As Israel in Egypt escaped the plagues which punished their neighbors, so the new Israel is exempted from the attack of the locusts out of the abyss."

The description of these locusts is heavy with meaning. This locust plague is based on similar plagues in Exodus and Joel, where we are reminded of the fearful nature of the havoc produced by locusts upon the vegetable kingdom. Under the fifth trumpet, they are the symbol of the terrible nature of the judgment to overtake men. The literal locusts devastated Egypt under the hand of Moses, and here, we have a picture of the judgment of these abyss locusts upon unsealed men.

Travelers in areas where scorpions are common are wary of this creature, which is often found under loose stones and in ruins. When disturbed, this creature's sting is sharp and severe. Lobster-like in appearance, scorpions have poison secreted in their tails. This striking weapon is an instrument of excruciating pain, mental distress, and, sometimes, even death. Our Lord connected serpents and scorpions with the power of Satan. (See Luke 10:19.)

In Revelation 9:4, the locusts are commanded not to hurt the grass. Why this specific prohibition? God, as the Creator, disrupts the natural eating habits of locusts, which normally feed on plants and trees. This sparing of the vegetable world suggests a temporary preservation of the most necessary commodities. Under the eighth Egyptian plague, the locusts destroyed every green thing. (See Exodus 10:12–15.) Here, their consumption of green things is in abeyance, and they hurt only men who do not belong to God.

> And to them it was given that they should not kill them, but that they should be tormented five months: and their torment was as the torment of a scorpion, when he striketh a man. And in those days shall men seek death, and shall not find it; and shall desire to die, and death shall flee from them. And the shapes of the locusts were like unto horses prepared unto battle; and on their heads were as it were crowns like gold, and their faces were as the faces of men. And they had hair as the hair of women, and their teeth were as the teeth of lions.
> (Revelation 9:5–8)

The locusts were given power to torment men five months. Why only five months? Such a limited time implies that this trumpet judgment will not separate the guilty from God forever and is meant only to warn sinners of the final doom awaiting them unless they repent. The specified months are likewise related the locusts themselves because this is the natural lifespan of the locust—usually from May to September. Their entire lifespan is taken up with the anguish of men. Here, we have a brief but determinate period of woe for those marked for torture. How relieved the tormented will be that the locusts do not live longer than five months! During the activity of these creatures, the human anguish will be both indescribable and without relief, a gnawing and horrible plague that is dreadful in the extreme.

In these days *"shall men seek death, and shall not find it."* Sin produces torment, takes away all pleasure of living, and often causes the sinner to long for death. But the permitted powers of physical distress are not allowed to kill men outright, and therein lies the warning to *repent*. Death would be a welcome relief to those so grievously afflicted, but death eludes them. Suicide will not be possible, and the power to kill is withheld from the locusts themselves, for the commission is only to *torture*. What despair will possess those who desire to end their anguish by taking their life but are not able to die!

The locusts here are shaped *"like unto horses prepared for battle."* Sin brings its own punishment, and there are forces always ready to assail the sinner as he sins, as is emphasized by this further description of the locusts. Like war horses, the locust army stands arrayed and ready to carry out the commands of their king. Hostile armies, especially cavalry, are symbolized by a locust invasion in Jeremiah 51:27 and Joel 2. In Italy, locusts are called "little horses" because of the resemblance of their heads to those of horses. *"The appearance of them is as the appearance of horses; and as horsemen, so shall they run"* (Joel 2:4).

These locusts wear *"crowns like gold."* The characteristic phrase *"as it were"* suggests a make-believe sovereignty. *Crowns* represent victory and dominion, while *gold* denotes deity. Man will never be able to sin without suffering, because, by divine decree, the penalty of sin will always be exacted. A divinely conferred crown of gold rests upon the head of Christ (see Revelation 14:14), but, here, the dignity and pretension of royal authority are spurious. Satan has always been an *imitator* of that which is real.

Also, the locusts had *"the faces of men."* Here again, the words *"were as"* imply that the locusts did not have *real* human faces but imitation ones. Implied by this description is the thought that the pain of the locusts is not inflicted indiscriminately but is intelligently regulated according to the sin committed. The human-looking faces of these demonic hordes, suggesting the intelligence and capacity of men, give them an added sense of terror. But, lacking human intelligence, they are not able to appeal to human reason; they act mechanically as commanded.

The locusts' *"teeth were as the teeth of lions."* What is more suggestive of destruction than the teeth of lions? Sin, when eagerly pursued, ultimately destroys the sinner, as if his or her head were literally crushed between the massive teeth of a lion's jaw. The implication of this symbolism is that the smoke-born, fearful locusts will be cruel, savage, and unrelenting in the torment they cause.

> *And they had breastplates, as it were breastplates of iron; and the sound of their wings was as the sound of chariots of many horses running to battle. And they had tails like unto scorpions, and there were stings in their tails: and their power was to hurt men five months. And they had a king over them, which is the angel of the bottomless pit, whose name in the Hebrew tongue is Abaddon, but in the Greek tongue hath his name Apollyon. One woe is past; and, behold, there come two woes more hereafter.* (Revelation 9:9–12)

With their *"breastplates of iron,"* these hellish agents of torture are immune from personal destruction. Destitute of all feeling, on they come, showing no pity. Man is helpless to pierce their defense. Any effort to drive them back is useless. No weapon that man can build will be strong enough to keep them back. But, for the child of God, there is always protection against all the forces of darkness. Paul called it *"the breastplate of righteousness"* (Ephesians 6:14).

The locusts' wings make a sound like chariots in battle. How vivid is the symbol at this point! *"The sound of their wings was as the sound of chariots of many horses running to battle."* Man will not be able to overcome or repel his deserved judgment by the might of his own armaments, nor will he be able to evade or escape the judgment, for the armies of terror will march upon him from all sides. Joel employs a similar description of the utter hopelessness of resistance against the oncoming armies of destruction. (See Joel 2:5.)

The locusts have stingers in their tails, like scorpions. Naturalists tell us that the scorpion constantly shakes its tail to strike, and that the torment caused by its sting is very severe. Another reading of Revelation 9:10 is, *"They had tails and stings like scorpions, and in their tails they had power to torment people for five months"* (NIV). The one who follows after sin is sure to receive its scorpion-like sting, charmed into sin but destroyed by lion-like teeth.

The locusts even have their own king. Solomon, one of the greatest naturalists in history, made it clear that ordinary locusts have no king. (See Proverbs 30:27). But the horrible scorpions that John describes have a cruel leader. From Joel, we learn that the invading host does not wander aimlessly around, but that each one walks in his designated route. The destructive forces that John depicts are under the devil, who is the king of the infernal powers of hell. While the antichrist will be the personification of Satan's malignant influence, the commander of the locust army is Satan himself, spoken of as *"Abaddon"* and *"Apollyon"*—names that are similar in meaning.

Abaddon means "perdition or destruction." *"Destruction [Abaddon] hath no covering"* (Job 26:6)—that is, before God. (See also Proverbs 15:11.)

Apollyon, the Greek form of the Hebrew name, means "destroyer." Satan is the king of these locust hordes and is the spirit of destruction inspiring these dreadful hosts. This vivid picture reveals Satan as *"the destroyer of the Gentiles"* (Jeremiah 4:7)—not only of corrupt Christendom but also of apostate Judaism.

How significant is the statement *"One woe is past."* What a relief to come out of a midnight of terror and torment! But those who reject God will have no respite; the worst is yet to come: *"Behold, there come two woes more hereafter."*

THE SIXTH TRUMPET

And the sixth angel sounded, and I heard a voice from the four horns of the golden altar which is before God, saying to the sixth angel which had the trumpet, Loose the four angels which are bound in the great river Euphrates. And the four angels were loosed, which were prepared for an hour, and a day, and a month, and a year, for to slay the third part of men. And the number of the army of the horsemen were two hundred thousand thousand: and I heard the number of them. And thus I saw the horses in the vision, and them that sat on them, having breastplates of fire, and of jacinth, and brimstone: and the heads of the horses were as the heads of lions; and out of their mouths issued fire and smoke and brimstone. By these three was the third part of men killed, by the fire, and by the smoke, and by the brimstone, which issued out of their mouths. (Revelation 9:13–18)

The judgment of this *second woe trumpet*, while resembling the judgment of the previous trumpet, is of much more aggravated nature. To the vast hosts, to the powers of the horse, to the lion, and to the scorpion are added new desolating forces. The multitudes are more numerous and the horses' heads are more lion-like. As the sixth angel sounds, John hears *"a voice from the four horns of the golden altar which is before God."* The golden altar stands in the immediate presence of God and receives the offered incense, symbolizing the accepted prayers and worship of God's people. Here, the golden altar reminds us that the judgments to follow come in response to the cry of persecuted and martyred saints.

The separate quartet of angels has an ominous mission to perform, and their united authoritative voice carries God's answer to the cries of His suffering children. Finally, they are to be avenged. The number *four* is significant, for it is the number of earth and suggests universality. We have the four seasons of the year and the four quarters of the earth.

Horn symbolizes strength and power (see Psalm 132:17), and the *golden altar* speaks of the privilege of worship and communion made possible by the blood, which was shed at the *brazen altar*. Chained in loving obedience to the altar until needed, the four angels are liberated to accomplish their deadly task. This angelic quartet is different from the four restraining angels of Revelation 7:1–3, where their mission was to hold in check evil forces. Here the four angels liberate destructive powers and operate in the circumscribed region of the Euphrates River.

The Euphrates River is worthy of being called *"great"* because it is some 1,780 miles in length and is the longest and most important river in Western Asia. On the northeast boundary of Palestine, this famous river formed a line of defense against the powerful enemies of Israel, the Assyrians. Sometimes its waters overflowed, sweeping away everything before it. This is why Isaiah used the river as a symbol of the destructive onrush of the Assyrians to execute divine judgments upon Israel. (See Isaiah 8:5–8.)

As used by John, this same river is the site of God's judgment on the unsaved world. The Euphrates is where it is believed that human sin began and where Satan held dominion for so long. Now, it endures the divine scourge.

The angelic ministers of retribution cannot act without God's signal. They are held in check for *"an hour, and a day, and a month, and a year."* These periods of time refer to the restraint of the angels, not to the duration of the ministry of destruction. Why they were held in check so long, we are not told. All we know is that they could not strike until the set time on God's clock. They were always ready to perform their task but were not let loose until the exact moment appointed in the counsels of God had arrived. God's judgments are held in His divine limitations.

That this sixth judgment will be sharp and overwhelming is seen in that a *"third part of men"* are slain. Under the third seal, a *fourth* part were slain (see Revelation 6:8), and now, a third of the remaining three-fourths are slain. What a bloodbath awaits the inhabitants of all the territory associated with the Euphrates!

John describes *"two hundred thousand thousand"*—two hundred million—horsemen. For the terrible slaughter of the godless, God orders out His reserves, and such an invading and avenging host are not human beings but demon incarnations. Global wars accustom us to speak and act in millions, and to see millions die. Think of the millions upon millions of deaths associated with World War II!

In the time that John envisions, God is to permit a vast and overwhelming army to rid the earth of those who have long held Him in contempt. One out of every three humans will succumb to these horsemen of hell, whose defensive armor is a combination of *"fire, and of jacinth, and brimstone"*—symbols of everlasting torment. As J. Stafford Wright wrote,

John now sees all the horrors of war. In his day armed cavalry were some of the most terrible forces, and he sees these first. But as he looks, he is aware that these are no ordinary horses, but strange monsters that destroy with smoke that comes from their mouths, and from other mouths at the end of serpent-like tails. There is no doubt that John was allowed to see the destroying instruments in the form of artillery. Under the inspiration of Satan, man turns everything to his own destruction, and war succeeds war.

Scripture references to the qualities of the horses are numerous, but little is said of their use as a beast of burden for agricultural purposes. Jews were forbidden to breed horses because of the risk of them returning to Egypt. (See Deuteronomy 17:16.) Egypt was most famous for its cavalry horses, and, in Scripture, a horse is regarded as a symbol of war, just as an ass symbolizes peace. Successful power in war and conquest is associated with the horses that John describes. Under this sixth trumpet, the locusts, with their destruction and agony, give way to horses—fearful and hideous, the aggressive and military agents of rapine and slaughter.

They had *"the heads of lions."* Have you ever paused to study the head of a lion in a zoo or a photograph? What majesty, courage, strength, and fearlessness its features portray! No wonder the lion is spoken of as the king of the forest. These judgment horses, with lion-like heads, are invested with all the fearsome qualities of lions.

They were known *"by the smoke, and by the brimstone, which issued out of their mouths."* Satan is to arm his four-legged host with a trinity of *offensive* destructive forces: fire, smoke, and brimstone. These elements out of the mouths of the horses will give the godless a foretaste of the agony of the lake of fire. Belching forth hellish fumes, the horses will manifest diabolic pleasure in their task.

> *For their power is in their mouth, and in their tails: for their tails were like unto serpents, and had heads, and with them they do hurt. And the rest of the men which were not killed by these plagues yet repented not of the works of their hands, that they should not worship devils, and idols of gold, and silver, and brass, and stone, and of wood: which neither can see, nor hear, nor walk: neither repented they of their murders, nor of their sorceries, nor of their fornication, nor of their thefts.*
> (Revelation 9:19–21)

The horses also had *"tails...like unto serpents."* In Scripture, a *tail* is the symbol of false prophets and false teaching. (See Isaiah 9:14–15.) As used here, *"tail"* expresses Satan's malignant influence, falsehood, and mischief. They *"had heads, and with them they do hurt,"* which shows that Satan's craftiness is intelligently directed. *Head* is emblematic of the seat of moral government, and of intelligence or power. What hope has a sinner in himself against such a combination of satanic subtlety and misdirected wisdom?

The fact that a third of the men are killed by the fire, smoke, and brimstone out of the mouths of the horses has no sobering effect on the rest of men. The limit of divine forbearance has been reached, and so God permits those deserving of His wrath to reap what they have sown. Persistent forgetfulness—or blatant defiance—of God ends in abandonment to merited fate. The spared apostates persist in their hardness of heart, in spite of the fearful terrors of the horsemen of hell. Twice, we read that they *"repented not"* (Revelation 9:20; 16:9). Because of this, sin is allowed to work out its inevitable doom.

Describing the end-time period of the Gentile age, Jesus declared that *"iniquity shall abound"* (Matthew 24:12). Here, we have summarized some of the gross forms of iniquity during those last days.

They worship devils. Demonism, Satan worship, and black magic are widespread today. We live in a demonized world. John predicted a time when the demonic host would be worshipped openly and universally.

They worship idols. Mankind has lifeless idols, according to their stations in life. The rich have gods of gold and silver, the middle class have idols of brass and stone, and the poor have idols of wood. Out of this twofold form of idolatry—Satan and idols— evil deeds appear.

They are murderers. "*Neither repented they of their murders*" (Revelation 9:21). Our Lord said that Satan has been a murderer from the beginning, as the instigator of Cain's murder of his brother Abel. (See John 8:44.) Since that first murder, countless millions of people have been murdered, including a vast host of believers as martyrs for their faith. In our time, the daily toll of murder is frightening, but in the time that John described, men are satanically energized, and murder will be practiced habitually.

They are sorcerers. Witchcraft and illicit dealings with spirits, an integral part of spiritism or spiritualism, have made rapid strides over the last fifty years. Strongly condemned in Scripture, sorcery meets its doom when judgment descends on all who traffic with "*familiar spirits*" (see, for example, Isaiah 8:19; 19:3). An interesting fact to observe is that our English word *sorcerer* is *pharmahos* in Greek, from which we get the word *pharmacy*.

A. T. Robertson, in his *Word Pictures in the New Testament*, wrote, "Our word *pharmacy* as applied to drugs and medicine has certainly come a long way out of a bad environment, but there is still a bad odor about patent medicines." We have certainly come to a drugged age, when various drugs are warping the minds of multitudes, especially the youth. Repentance will be far from the narcotic addicts of the tribulation era.

They are fornicators. When God and justice are rejected, and when general wickedness prevails, what else can be expected but indulgence in the wildest forms of unbridled lust? Easy divorces make a mockery of the safeguard and bulwark of the marriage tie. Unions are broken almost as quickly as they are made. Our low moral standards are a shadow of the corrupt condition of the world when the sixth trumpet is to sound.

They are thieves. Thefts from stores, banks, and other businesses have reached an appalling number. The mass numbers of men not killed by hell's horsemen will have little respect for each other's rights. The gospel of the day will be, "Each for himself and the devil take the hindmost." A man will live to enrich himself at the expense of his neighbor. International criminals, with no regard for the property of others, will become more common as the age deteriorates, but their doom is assured.

Before we approach the parenthesis between the sixth and seventh trumpets, let us review the meanings of the first six trumpets.

The first four trumpets show us man as a citizen of a sin-blighted world; everything above and around him tells of the curse brought about by the fall of man.

The fifth trumpet presents man as the actual sinner and shows us that *"the whole world lies under the sway of the wicked one"* (1 John 5:19 NKJV). Man sins and is therefore of the devil. His sins bring hell-sent torments.

The sixth trumpet makes it clear that judgments come upon sinners by virtue of the fixed law that sin must inevitably bring suffering. The divinely inflicted judgments remind us of the truth that *"God is angry with the wicked every day"* (Psalm 7:11). Under the sounding of this trumpet, the positive infliction of God's judgments on man is symbolized. Because man is left without excuse, his escape from punishment is impossible.

THE INTERLUDE (REVELATION 10:1–11:14)

Between the sixth and seventh trumpets, we have an impressive and significant parenthesis, containing one of the most profound yet simple sections of Revelation, in which John saw the mighty angel, the little book, the measuring rod, the two witnesses, and the earthquake.

Things are drawing to a close. We see a world in' open rebellion against God and His people, upon whom the beast and the antichrist pour out their fury. But before the last dregs of the Lord's vengeance are drunk by the Gentile and Jewish apostates and their followers, this consoling vision breaks through the dark clouds of judgment. It is a stern reminder to the world that, in spite of the raging of the wicked, the government of the earth is the just claim of the Creator, and a claim that will now be made good in power. But the vision is also designed to strengthen and console believers, especially suffering believers, for the same power that will crush the enemy will exalt the sufferers to honor.

THE MIGHTY ANGEL

And I saw another mighty angel come down from heaven, clothed with a cloud: and a rainbow was upon his head, and his face was as it were the sun, and his feet as pillars of fire: and he had in his hand a little book open: and he set his right foot upon the sea, and his left foot on the earth, and cried with a loud voice, as when a lion roareth: and when he had cried, seven thunders uttered their voices. And when the seven

*thunders had uttered their voices, I was about to write: and I
heard a voice from heaven saying unto me, Seal up those things
which the seven thunders uttered, and write them not.*

(Revelation 10:1–4)

Who is this glorious angel who occupies heaven, earth, and
the sea? God's chariot is in the clouds (see Psalm 104:3) and sends
forth this angel who comes with glory. Some writers see in him the
herald angel, announcing the solemn crisis under the third woe, or
seventh trumpet of Revelation 11. Because the word *"angel"* does
not necessarily mean an individual member of the angelic race but
often denotes a thing or person in active service, can it be that this
"mighty angel" is Christ Himself, coming forth to act on behalf of
His faithful people?

Christ not only leaves heaven as a point and place of departure,
but He comes *"down from heaven,"* His native home. Providential
dealings with earth are about to cease, so the Lord leaves His
abode to establish His worldwide kingdom once His judgment
work is finished. How the angelic and redeemed hosts in heaven
will praise Him as He leaves their presence to take to Himself His
power to reign!

Christ is *"clothed with a cloud."* The cloud is a symbol that
requires little interpretation, for clouds in Scripture are an indication of the presence and majesty of Jehovah. How dependent Israel
was upon the cloud of *shekinah* glory! (See, for example, Exodus
24:16–18.) The cloud is a visible, public indication of our Lord's
majesty.

Christ has *"a rainbow...upon his head."* The rainbow, already
seen in Revelation 4:3 as *"round about the throne,"* encircles the
head of the mighty angel. The rainbow symbolizes a fulfilled covenant, and, by it, His faithful remnant are assured that even amidst
the fiercest conflict, they are secure and need feel no fear. Christ

is coming as the Messenger of the covenant-keeping God, and He will call the earth as witness, since, because of the climax of man's rejection, He is about to break His covenant with the world. What a glorious sight He will present with His head diademed with a magnificent rainbow!

Christ's *"face was as it were the sun, and his feet as pillars of fire."* Here, we have a repetition of what we saw in the Patmos vision. (See Revelation 1:15–16.) The double metaphor of sun and fire speaks of the supreme, searching, and fixed character of the message about to be given. Taken together, the sun-like face and pillar-like feet of fire suggest Christ's supreme majesty and His eternal stability, as earth experiences the unbending holiness of His judicial mission.

Christ has *"in his hand a little book open."* The word for *"book"* comes from the Greek word *biblos*, from which we also get *Bible*. Here is a "little bible," a larger version of which is the seven-sealed book of Revelation 5. The "little" book is open, but the larger book was sealed until opened by the Lamb. This smaller book is open for all who read its unmistakable message.

Christ *"set his right foot upon the sea, and his left foot on the earth."* In this bold and graphic picture that John gives us of the mighty angel, he is presented as a colossal figure standing astride both land and sea. As the Lord of creation, He dominates the scene entirely. It has been asked whether there is any special significance in the position of the feet. There certainly is!

+ *The sea*—turbulent, agitated, and restless—represents the chaotic, revolutionary condition of the nations.

+ *The earth*, which has been partially harnessed by man, symbolizes the orderly government of civilized and educated people. Three times over, the angel is depicted as standing on sea and earth (see Revelation 10:2, 5, 8), and this repetition denotes divine emphasis. The strong and sure tread of Christ's feet of fine brass signifies the complete subjugation to Him of all people and forces in the world. Men everywhere will acknowledge His dominion as He exercises both His *right* and His *might*.

Christ's voice is *"as when a lion roareth."* Here, we have another feature of *"his voice as the sound of many waters"* (Revelation 1:15). No voice is more feared by both man and beast in the jungle than the roar of the lion. Loud, roaring voices are not always intelligible, but there will be no mistaking the meaning of the roar of the Lion of the Tribe of Judah as it causes intense terror and despair among men. (See Hosea 11:10; Joel 3:16). In Psalm 29, we are given a sevenfold description of the Lord's majestic voice.

If the lion's roar is suggestive of irresistible power, the *"seven thunders"* speak of the terror of the Lord in all its completeness as He comes in judgment. Just what the nature of this judgment is, we are not told, as John was commanded to *"seal up those things… and write them not."* Ten times over, thunder occurs in Revelation, and because the thunder proceeds out of the throne, it has a divine message and mission. Job spoke of *"the thunder of his power"* (Job 26:14), and while Jesus was here on earth, the voice of God seemed like thunder to those who heard it. (See John 12:28–29.) As Walter Scott wrote, "Thunder is God's voice in judgment, the expression of His authority therein."

Like Daniel's visions, the contents of these seven thunders had to be closed and sealed. John understood them and knew that they were the perfection of God's intervention in judgment, but the divine command as to their nature was to *"write them not."* Much of the prophetic section of Revelation will only be fully understood as the predicted events actually take place.

And the angel which I saw stand upon the sea and upon the earth lifted up his hand to heaven, and sware by him that liveth for ever and ever, who created heaven, and the things that therein are, and the earth, and the things that therein are, and the sea, and the things which are therein, that there should be time no longer: but in the days of the voice of the seventh angel, when he shall begin to sound, the mystery of God should be finished, as he hath declared to his servants the prophets.

(Revelation 10:5–7)

When Jesus ascended to heaven, He lifted up His hands in priestly benediction on His own people. Now, as He descends, His hand is lifted up to heaven, as if, through an oath, He will fulfill the righteous judgment of God's holy throne. A hand lifted up to heaven was a customary gesture in taking an oath. We have here one of the most sublime visions in Revelation. Try to visualize the scene: the mighty angel of Jehovah, with the sea and earth under His feet, the small book of closing prophecy in His left hand, and His right hand lifted up to heaven, swearing by the ever-living God and Creator that judgment upon the godless will be immediate.

How are we to understand the phrase *"that there should be time no longer,"* or, as some versions put it, *"delay no longer"* (NKJV)? Can it be that the age-old cry for retribution, *"How long, O Lord?"* (Psalm 13:1–2; Revelation 6:10) is about to be answered, and man's day will now end in sharp and severe judgment? As we have seen, seven suggests perfection. The seven trumpets and seven thunders signify the perfect completeness of God's warning judgments. No space is left for anything else to transpire before the *final* judgment, of which all previous judgments have been previews. In virtue of His native right and His redemptive work, Christ returns to consummate the judgment committed to Him by the Father. (See John 5:22, 27.)

The word *Revelation* implies the unveiling of a mystery, and in this act of the drama, the mystery of God that was foretold by the prophets and apostles is about to be finished. (See, for example, Romans 16:25–26; Ephesians 1:9–10.). Now we see so many things in a glass darkly—for example, the mystery of God's apparent silence when His saints are crushed and cruelly persecuted. As a God of justice, why does He allow the terrible sins of men to go unpunished, and why does He not intervene to right the wrongs of earth?

The mystery John spoke of may be the brutal martyrdom of the tribulation saints and the silence of heaven as to this terrible wrong that was perpetrated. But the mystery is about to end. Christ appears to wrest world-government from the grasp of Satan, to expel him as the usurper, and to end his tyranny on earth. The mystery of divine patience for over six millennia is about to cease. The judgment hour has come for God to fully and finally avenge His own elect who have cried out to Him day and night.

How moving is James Hervey's eloquent tribute to John's unrivalled description of the *"mighty angel"*:

> Observe the aspect of this august Personage. All the brightness of the sun shines in His countenance, and all the rage of fire burns in His feet. See His apparel! The clouds compose His robe, and the drapery of the sky floats upon His shoulders; the rainbow forms His diadem, and that which compasses heaven with a glorious circle is the ornament of His head. Behold His attitude! One foot stands on the ocean, and the other rests on the land. The wide extended earth and the world of waters serve as pedestals of those mighty columns. Consider His action! His hand is lifted up to the height of the stars; He speaks, and the regions of the firmament echo with the mighty accents as the midnight desert resounds with the lion's roar. The artillery of the skies is discharged as a signal; a peal of sevenfold thunder spreads the alarm, and prepares

the universe to receive His orders. To finish all, and give the highest grandeur, as well as the utmost solemnity to the representation, He swears by Him who lives forever and ever.[7]

THE BITTERSWEET BOOK

And the voice which I heard from heaven spake unto me again, and said, Go and take the little book which is open in the hand of the angel which standeth upon the sea and upon the earth. And I went unto the angel, and said unto him, Give me the little book. And he said unto me, Take it, and eat it up; and it shall make thy belly bitter, but it shall be in thy mouth sweet as honey. And I took the little book out of the angel's hand, and ate it up; and it was in my mouth sweet as honey: and as soon as I had eaten it, my belly was bitter. And he said unto me, Thou must prophesy again before many peoples, and nations, and tongues, and kings.   (Revelation 10:8–11)

John is now commanded to eat the little book that he saw in the hand of the mighty angel. We can safely assume that the contents of this volume were the counsels and prophecies of the rest of Scripture, from Genesis to Jude. The time has now come to declare the divine counsel to peoples, nations, tongues, and rulers. John must mentally digest the message of the book and then declare it.

Several times in Scripture, God's Word is compared to food that must be consumed. Ezekiel, like John, experienced a bittersweet prophecy. (See Ezekiel 2:8; 3:1–3). Jeremiah likewise had to consume the divine Word. (See Jeremiah 15:16.) The first effect of the prophetic communication was as sweet as honey to the mouth, and it brought John unbounded delight as he saw how past

---

7. James Hervey, *Meditations and Contemplations, Volume 2* (London: John Rivington, Jr., 1779), 22–23.

predictions were about to be fulfilled. It was sweet to his taste to realize that, at last, earth's rule was to pass from Satan to Christ, that an evil age was about to end and a new era was beginning.

But then the apostle meditated on the effect of judgment upon the multitudes without God, the final wrath under the seven vials, and the terrors of the Lord about to overtake the godless. As John pondered the final doom of the lost, anguish gripped his heart. What was sweet to his taste would have a bitter effect on rebellious earth dwellers. His commission was renewed, and out John was sent, prophesying to the multitudes about judgment to come.

For all preachers in this age of grace, the same principle holds. A God-given message must be received and absorbed into the soul. Secondhand truth is never dynamic. Both the sweetness and the bitterness of a God-revealed gospel must be part of the spiritual training of heralds.

THE MEASURING REED

And there was given me a reed like unto a rod: and the angel stood, saying, Rise, and measure the temple of God, and the altar, and them that worship therein. But the court which is without the temple leave out, and measure it not; for it is given unto the Gentiles: and the holy city shall they tread under foot forty and two months. (Revelation 11:1–2)

The reed, a measuring instrument about ten feet in length, was frequently mentioned by the prophets of the Old Testament. Ezekiel spoke of the measuring rod being applied to the temple. (See Ezekiel 40:3; 42:16–20.) In the New Jerusalem, an angel measures the glorified church with a golden reed (see Revelation 21:15); here, John uses a wooden reed to measure the temple. Such a measurement suggests the appropriation, preservation, and acceptance by God of the temple, altar, and worshipper. *"Unto a rod"* signifies the strength and stability of the action referred to.

What is measured *belongs* to God and will be *preserved* by Him. The command was to measure not only the temple but also those who worship Him there. What does this extraordinary expression imply? Surely it was not meant to be a measurement of the height and girth of these persons. The word translated as *"temple"* is *naos*, meaning "the holy of holies," or "the inner sanctuary." In 1 Corinthians 3:17, Paul said, *"For the temple [naos] of God is holy, which temple [naos] ye are."* Measuring those who *"worship therein"* (Revelation 11:1) refers to those who are God's believing children, His dwelling place. For the godless Gentiles, the command was to *"measure it not."* For them, there is rejection.

John's mentions of the *"court"* and the *"temple"* reveal that we are approaching Jewish ground. In fact, all of Revelation 11 is anticipative in character. The Jews are to be back in their own land, and the temple is to be rebuilt. As a whole, the trumpets are related to the devastation of Gentile, Christianized lands and peoples, but now, judgment is about to be transferred from the Gentile to the Jew.

God's dealings with the apostate part of the Gentile world are about to conclude. The times of the Gentiles have run their course. We now approach the second half of the tribulation era. The Man of Sin makes a covenant with the Jews for seven years, but he turns traitorous halfway through the period. What is depicted here is the agony of Israel's final hour of unbelief during this time.

This period covering the trampling of the Gentiles is divided into four forms. Forty-two months of thirty days each correspond to the 1,260 days—or *"a thousand two hundred and threescore"* (Revelation 11:3) days—of the two witnesses. This period is used of the duration of the blasphemy and power of the beast. Jerusalem's forty-two days of agony, then, will be long enough to drink the cup of the Lord's fury.

THE TWO WITNESSES

And I will give power unto my two witnesses, and they shall prophesy a thousand two hundred and threescore days, clothed in sackcloth. These are the two olive trees, and the two candlesticks standing before the God of the earth. And if any man will hurt them, fire proceedeth out of their mouth, and devoureth their enemies: and if any man will hurt them, he must in this manner be killed. These have power to shut heaven, that it rain not in the days of their prophecy: and have power over waters to turn them to blood, and to smite the earth with all plagues, as often as they will. And when they shall have finished their testimony, the beast that ascendeth out of the bottomless pit shall make war against them, and shall overcome them, and kill them. And their dead bodies shall lie in the street of the great city, which spiritually is called Sodom and Egypt, where also our Lord was crucified.

(Revelation 11:3–8)

In our chapter on the seven spirits of God, we briefly referred to these martyred prophets as being raised by the Spirit of life. We now look at them in more detail, noting that we are passing from worshippers in the sanctuary to witnesses in the city, and that worshippers and witnesses both testify to the priesthood and royalty of the One of whom it was predicted, *"He shall be a priest upon his throne"* (Zechariah 6:13).

As to the number and identity of the two witnesses, many explanations have been advanced. Some expositors believe that we are to understand by these two witnesses a competent number of faithful servants of Christ. Two, it is said, represents testimony: *"In the mouth of two or three witnesses shall every word be established"* (2 Corinthians 13:1). Therefore, a full and adequate testimony is the thought supposedly intended in the number of witnesses. However, I reject this supposition. The language that is used points to two well-known characters. The article is emphatic: *"My two witnesses."* Furthermore, the words *witness* and *prophesy* were usually applied to individuals, not to abstractions.

The two inspired witnesses who are to be raised up to minister encouragement to the afflicted have been variously identified as Moses and Elijah, Enoch and Elijah, the Old and New testaments, the law and the gospel, and Jew and Gentile. If the two witnesses are Enoch and Elijah, this would avoid the difficulty of dying a *second* time, for these two Old Testament saints have never yet died and therefore could perhaps be the witnesses slain.

John does not give us any clue to their identity but simply describes them as witnesses, olive trees, candlesticks, prophets. *"The two olive trees"* takes us back to Joshua and Zerubbabel (see Zechariah 4:3, 12), who ministered to the Jewish people just as the two olive trees emptied oil out of themselves and into the bowl of the candlestick. The two witnesses in the tribulation period are to be channels of the oil feeding the remnant, as well as symbols of coming peace. The Holy Spirit will be their oil, making their ministry of encouragement possible. As candlesticks, or lamps, these witnesses are to give a sure and clear testimony. Their ministry will be exercised in the clear light of God, because they stand before the Lord of the earth.

As representative light-bearers, they will testify that the One who was so widely disowned on earth is now about to be recognized openly as the rightful King over all. As *"prophets"* (Revelation 11:10), they preached in such a faithful way as to make men conscience-stricken. Sin, with its tragic consequences, is a tormenting subject to even the most hardened and scarred conscience. Thus, these witnesses are to have a tormenting ministry by the plagues they have power to inflict, and also by their testimony against the human environment.

The two witnesses are to prophesy *"clothed in sackcloth"*—that is, dressed in a manner suited to their message. (See Matthew 11:21.) Sackcloth was the garment used by prophets when they called people to repentance of their sins. Their exterior appearance accorded with their words. (See Joel 1:13; 1 Kings 20:31.) It may be that the sackcloth of the witnesses is a catchword, linking this episode under the sixth trumpet, when *"the sun became black as sackcloth of hair"* (Revelation 6:12), in righteous retribution under the sixth seal on the apostates who rejected God's righteousness.

The days of prophecy, or preaching, of the two witnesses, under the inspiration of the Spirit, are to be *"a thousand two hundred and threescore,"* or 1,260 days. In those days, they will execute their prophetic office. Their length of service is set. They are not to give an intermittent testimony. Daily they will testify, until the allotted period is exhausted—a period which we believe covers the last half of the great tribulation proper.

It is also evident that these witnesses are to be delegated power without limit. They will be empowered to perform miracles *"as often as they will"* (Revelation 11:6) and to vindicate in stern judgment their mission to the rebellious. (See Psalm 68:18.) These witnesses are to repeat the miracles that Moses and Elijah performed against slavery and apostasy. As with Elijah, rain is to be withheld. (See 1 Kings 17:1.) As with Moses, waters are to turn to blood. (See Exodus 7:17.)

But the two preachers in sackcloth are immortal until their work is done. The immediate certainty of the accomplishment of their mission is indicated by the phrases *"if any man will hurt them"* (repeated twice in Revelation 11:5) and *"they shall have finished their testimony"* (verse 7) Prophesying in Jerusalem, the center of prophetic and political interest during the final three-and-a-half years of the tribulation, they are invincible until their dynamic and spectacular task is completed.

The conclusion of the prophecy of the two witnesses is to be marked by a violent death. *"The beast that ascendeth out of the bottomless pit"* (Revelation 11:7) is nothing less than the Antichrist, who is here mentioned for the first time in Revelation. This beast is also fully described in Daniel 7:8, 11, and in Revelation 13:1, a further proof of the unity of Scripture. The triumph of this beast, who in cruelty and blasphemy exceeds any previous wickedness that has appeared on the earth, is evidently complete, for the witnesses are silenced and slain. All martyrdom and massacres of the saints, throughout the ages, find their climax here. With the killing of the divinely empowered witnesses, brute force appears to have triumphed over truth and righteousness.

To add to the humiliation and scornful treatment of the two witnesses, *"their dead bodies shall lie in the street of the great city"* (Revelation 11:8) for the same number of days as the years of their ministry. For three-and-a-half days, the spectators gloat over the dead bodies, with a delight that is both fiendish and childish.

"Sodom and Egypt," as applied to Jerusalem, stands as a symbol of oppression and slavery. *"Sodom"* represents filthiness and wickedness; *"Egypt"* is the nation in which Israel found herself oppressed.

> *And they of the people and kindreds and tongues and nations shall see their dead bodies three days and an half, and shall not suffer their dead bodies to be put in graves. And they that dwell upon the earth shall rejoice over them, and make merry, and shall send gifts one to another; because these two prophets tormented them that dwelt on the earth. And after three days*

and an half the Spirit of life from God entered into them, and
they stood upon their feet; and great fear fell upon them which
saw them. And they heard a great voice from heaven saying
unto them, Come up hither. And they ascended up to heaven
in a cloud; and their enemies beheld them. And the same hour
was there a great earthquake, and the tenth part of the city
fell, and in the earthquake were slain of men seven thousand:
and the remnant were affrighted, and gave glory to the God
of heaven. The second woe is past; and, behold, the third woe
cometh quickly.   (Revelation 11:9–14)

The jubilant celebration over the cessation of the activities of
the two prophets is universal; *"the people and kindreds and tongues
and nations"* indicates the fourfold distribution of the human
family. Gifts are distributed as at a joyous festival. The death of
truth is a cause of public rejoicing, but divine vindication is just
around the corner. Remorse is about to replace rejoicing. God's
day to laugh is coming.

Public vilification now gives way to public vindication. *"The
Spirit of life from God"* causes the dead bones of the witnesses to live,
and the spectators are panic stricken. Similarities can be drawn
between Israel's dry bones (see Ezekiel 37:10–11; Hosea 6:2) and
our Lord's resurrection after three days.

Christ's ascension was in the presence of His friends (see
Acts 1:9), as it was with Elijah (see 2 Kings 2:11). But the ascension of these two raised witnesses is in full view of their enemies. Now, retributive justice on the people and the city for the
wanton shedding of the blood of the witnesses quickly falls. An
earthquake, called *"great"* because of its appalling destruction,
causes a *"tenth part of the city"* to fall, and seven thousand men
perish. In the *"tenth,"* we have complete judgment, for *ten* signifies perfection of divine order. In the seven thousand slain, we
have God's "blacklist." These men were marked out as deserving

of God's righteous judgments. By way of contrast, there were the seven thousand people in Israel, whom God reserved for Himself. (See 1 Kings 19:18). In this fixed number of men doomed to death, we have the two perfect and comprehensive numbers *seven* and *thousand*, implying the full and complete destruction of the impenitent.

Summarizing the courageous ministry of the two witnesses, we have them declaring Christ, the rejected One, as the Lord of the whole earth. They testify unsparingly of human wickedness, thereby incurring the hatred of the godless. They proclaim the just character of the Judge, warning the people of righteous retribution in the days to come, decrying the blasphemous claims of the wild beast, and preaching against a corrupted Jerusalem.

Of *"the remnant"*—the spared Israelite inhabitants—it is said that they were *"affrighted, and gave glory to the God of heaven,"* into which the two witnesses had gone. At long last, the God of heaven is also acknowledged as the God of the earth.

THE SEVENTH TRUMPET

And the seventh angel sounded; and there were great voices in heaven, saying, THE KINGDOMS OF THIS WORLD ARE BECOME THE KINGDOMS OF OUR LORD, AND OF HIS CHRIST; AND HE SHALL REIGN FOR EVER AND EVER. And the four and twenty elders, which sat before God on their seats, fell upon their faces, and worshipped God, saying, We give thee thanks, O Lord God Almighty, which art, and wast, and art to come; because thou hast taken to thee thy great power, and hast reigned. And the nations were angry, and thy wrath is come, and the time of the dead, that they should be judged, and that thou shouldest give reward unto thy servants the prophets, and to the saints, and them that fear thy name, small and great; and shouldest destroy them which destroy the earth. And the temple of God was opened in heaven, and there was seen in his temple the ark of his testament: and there were lightnings, and voices, and thunderings, and an earthquake, and great hail. (Revelation 11:15–19)

We now reach the third woe, which is the final trumpet. *Six* is close to *seven* but does not reach it. World judgments are complete in six, but, by the fulfillment of seven, the world kingdoms become Christ's. *Six* is the number of a world given over to judgment. It is half of *twelve*, the number of tribes and apostles, even as *three-and-a-half* is half of *seven*, the divine number for completeness.

Expositors who affirm that we must follow the church as far as we dare link this last trumpet with the one Paul refers to in 1 Thessalonians 4:16 and 1 Corinthians 15:51–52. Thus, the rapture of the church is said to coincide with Christ's return at this time. But Donald G. Barnhouse has ably answered such an interpretation.

Dr. _____ is well known for his deeply spiritual meditations…and has now written a book seeking to interpret the apocalypse. He has, of course, seen the utter fallacy in the post-tribulation-rapture theory, but we believe he errs greatly and that his book loses most of its value because of the placing of the rapture in the tenth chapter of Revelation instead of at the beginning of the fourth chapter. [His] error grows out of an attempt to make the last trumpet of 1 Corinthians 15:52 agree with the seventh trumpet of the apocalyptic series. He asks, "What is meant by 'the last trumpet'? 'Last' can mean but one of two things: last in point of time, or last in point of sequence." But Dr. _____ has not seen that "last" can mean a third thing, namely, last in any given series. Both Malachi and the Revelation are "lasts" in the Bible.

Deuteronomy is also a last, and so is the gospel of John. Just as we can see that there may be many "last" books (the meaning of the word to be interpreted by the context), so the last trump with reference to the gathering out of the church and the last of the seven trumpets of judgment are two quite different things.

The beast has ascended out of the abyss to perform his deadly work, and now Christ descends out of heaven to take to Himself His great power as the blessed and only Potentate. What a dramatic scene is presented of God's panorama of future and final events!

In the seventh trumpet-angel, some writers see Gabriel, whose name is a compound of *El* ("God") and *Geber* ("mighty man"), and who appropriately announced to Mary the advent of the "mighty God-man." It would be fitting for this archangel to announce the final triumph of the Christ of God.

The *"voices"* in heaven are in contrast to the *"silence in heaven"* of Revelation 8:1. Exultant praises abound over the setting up of heaven's visible sovereignty over the earth, which, when *invisibly* exercised, had been rejected by the earthly rulers before. It is the *anticipation* of the kingdom, rather than its actual establishment, that is the cause of heavenly joy in this passage.

This seventh trumpet is akin to the seventh seal in that no immediate judgment is announced. Nothing is recorded as immediately resulting from the trumpet being blown. We are simply given a summary of the final phases that bring us to the portal of the new creation.

This, of course, is the crowning lesson of the apocalypse. Christ's absolute sovereignty is the sure and glorious outcome of an agelong struggle. He scorned partnership with Satan in the rulership of the world, and now, He is about to exercise His sovereign right to reign as world emperor. Earth is to enter its last throes of agony, and then will dawn earth's millennial morning with Christ as King over all. His beneficent rule will provide a happy contrast to past and present governmental rule! One universal kingdom will cover the globe, with Christ as the sole reigning Monarch.

Such a sublime prospect demands the adoration of the elders. Profoundest worship on their part is their response to the praise of heavenly voices. A doxology follows, in which the elders magnify God and Christ for uniting in taking the kingdom. Walter Scott draws attention to the fact that there are seven doxologies in the course of these apocalyptic visions, of which this is one.

Heaven's wrath will match that of earth. There is fearful progress in these words, for the unbounded anger of the nations will be destroyed by the divine anger. Note the difference in tenses: "*The nations **were** angry, and thy wrath **is** come.*" How petty man's impotent anger, standing here side by side with that of omnipotent God!

The judgment of Revelation 11:18 is the judgment of the unbelieving. We are now brought to the conclusion of the kingdom, with the great white throne. Among the many judgments, these four must be kept distinct:

1. The judgment of the earth during its whole course of history. (See Acts 17:31.)

2. The judgment of believers at the sacrificial altar. (See 1 Corinthians 3:12–15.)

3. The judgment of the nations at the beginning of Christ's reign. (See Matthew 25:32.)

4. The judgment of the wicked dead at the end of Christ's reign. (See Revelation 20:11–12.)

Rewards are to be bestowed upon all God's saints deserving of them. In the kingdom, there will be varying degrees and positions of honor. While rest and glory will be for all saints, special crowns will be awarded only to those who have earned them. The faithful believers of every era of church history are to be graciously recompensed.

Retribution awaits all destroyers. Satan, the beast, the false prophet, and all who have followed them are to be recompensed for their wickedness. (See Daniel 7:14–18; Luke 19:27; Revelation 16:5–7). Destruction overtakes all destroyers. It is here that we can understand many of the imprecatory psalms.

"The temple of God was opened in heaven, and there was seen in his temple the ark of his testament" (Revelation 11:19). This *"temple"* is the sign that God is taking up the cause and interests of Israel, and it is in heaven that God is occupied with His people then on earth. The ark of His covenant is the token of Jehovah's presence with His earthly people and His unchanging faithfulness toward them. God will remember His covenant with Israel.

It is interesting to observe the seven great "openings" in Revelation:

1. A door is opened in heaven. (See Revelation 4:1.)

2. Seals are opened. (See Revelation 6:1–9.)

3. The abyss is opened. (See Revelation 9:2.)

4. The temple of God is opened. (See Revelation 11:19.)

5. The tabernacle of testimony is opened. (See Revelation 15:5.)

6. Heaven is opened. (See Revelation 19:11.)

7. Books are opened. (See Revelation 20:12.)

The trumpet judgments close with judgment action over the whole earth. Here is the storm of divine wrath that has its origin in heaven. Short, sharp, and decisive judgments are indicated by the combination of destructive elements. Natural forces are unleashed by their Creator to mete out His righteous wrath upon all who persist in resisting His claims. God now operates in terrible might and majesty. By the seventh trumpet, we learn that the warnings of God are perfect and complete, leaving man without excuse when the final and irreversible doom falls upon him.

12

THE SEVEN PERSONAGES

REVELATION 12:1–13:18

The close of Revelation 11 left us with the tragedy and triumph of the two faithful witnesses. Chapters 12 and 13 bring us to the rise and reign of the two foul beasts. It should be noted that almost every verse of these two highly dramatic chapters commences with the conjunction *"And"*—thirty-one in all—showing the unity prevailing throughout this section. Chapters 12, 13, and 14 form one connected prophecy.

We now come to the heart of Revelation. The stage is set. The drama of the ages is about to begin. We are now to witness the clash of heavenly, human, and hellish forces. Christ receives authority and adoration in chapters 4 and 5, where we have the divine setting of judgment. Here, in chapters 12 and 13, *Satan* receives man's adoration, and we have the devilish setting of judgment.

Twice, we see the word *"wonder"* (Revelation 12:1, 3), which, in Greek, means "sign." Signs that were prophesied earlier appear here now. The term signifies momentous truths and events. The same word will appear again in Revelation 13, verses 3 and 13. *"Wonder"* is also associated with the significance and nature of the work wrought. John was given these signs from heaven. (See Revelation 1:1.) Of course, the element of wonder is in the thing itself. The two signs appear in heaven, implying that all of God's purposes are known there. They appear not merely in the sky but also in the heaven beyond. (See Revelation 11:19.) The adjective *"great,"* a characteristic word of Revelation, is used six times in chapter 12, revealing it as a chapter of great subjects.

1. THE SUN WOMAN

And there appeared a great wonder in heaven; a woman clothed with the sun, and the moon under her feet, and upon her head a crown of twelve stars: and she being with child cried, travailing in birth, and pained to be delivered.

(Revelation 12:1–2)

The earliest appearance of a female figure is in Revelation 2:20. Altogether, we have four representative women in the apocalypse, each of whom is the expression of a corporate body of persons in a system.

1. Jezebel (see Revelation 2:20) represents the past corrupt church.

2. The woman invested with the fullness of governmental authority (see Revelation 12:1) represents Israel.

3. The great whore (see Revelation 17:1) represents the future corrupt church.

4. The bride, the Lamb's wife (see Revelation 19:7), represents the church glorified in heaven.

There are different identifications of the *"woman clothed with the sun"* (Revelation 12:1). Some say she is the Virgin Mary—Mary was indeed the Jewish woman who brought forth the Man-Child, Jesus. Others identify the sun-clothed woman as the church, the mother of us all. Still others say that Christendom is meant.

I believe that the woman is *Israel*. The nation of Israel is often referred to as a married woman. (See Isaiah 54:1–6; Jeremiah 3:1–11; Hosea 2:14–23). Jesus came out of the tribe of Judah. It is true that both Israel and the church stand closely related to Christ—Israel as the *mother* and the church as the *wife*. It was Israel, however, who became the mother of the Messiah. (See Isaiah 9:6; Micah 5:2; Romans 9:5.) A passage like Isaiah 54:1 is very expressive:

> *Sing, O barren, thou that didst not bear; break forth into singing, and cry aloud, thou that didst not travail with child: for more are the children of the desolate than the children of the married wife, saith the* Lord.

To hold that the woman is the church would mean that she brought forth Christ. But was it not *His* anguish that produced the church?

> From heaven he came and sought her
> To be his holy bride;
> With his own blood he bought her,
> And for her life he died.[8]

The symbolism of the sun, moon, and stars suggests a summary of Israel's history, as given in Genesis 37:9, where the whole family is represented in similar manner. In the celestial luminaries, we have the presentation of a complete system of government. These luminaries, then, symbolize the twelve tribal heads, as seen in national restoration.

"CLOTHED WITH THE SUN"

Here, we have Israel depicted as the bearer of divine, supernatural light and authority. She will yet be *Israel My Glory*. Or, the

---

8. Samuel J. Stone, "The Church's One Foundation," 1866.

sun can stand for Christ, whom Israel will yet recognize as the Sun of Righteousness.

"THE MOON UNDER HER FEET"

As the moon is subordinate to the sun and derives its light from the sun, all of Israel's glory and influence are derived from the One who brought her into being. The moon shines at night, and Israel is to give her light and her bright witness amid the world's gathering darkness in the tribulation era.

"UPON HER HEAD A CROWN OF TWELVE STARS"

By the twelve stars, we understand the twelve tribes of Israel. In Joseph's dream (see Genesis 37:9), the future glory of these tribes is symbolized in the same way. Israel's future glory and rule, therefore, are portrayed here. She is yet to be invested with the splendor and fullness of governmental authority on earth. *Twelve*, as we know, is the number of government.

"SHE BEING WITH CHILD CRIED, TRAVAILING IN BIRTH"

The metaphor of childbirth is common in Scripture. (See, for example, John 16:21; Galatians 4:19.) The travail, as used by John, is not literal, for the woman is a symbol. With a passage like Isaiah 66:7 before us, we have no difficulty in reconciling maternal anguish as applicable to Israel.

"The travailing and pain refer to Israel's coming hour of trial," said Walter Scott. "But *before* the great tribulation, the Messiah, the Man Child, is born. The prophet Micah confirmed this in a clear and unmistakable passage. After referring to the birth of the Messiah (see Micah 5:2), he added, '*Therefore He shall give them up, until the time that she who is in labor has given birth; then the remnant of His brethren shall return to the children of Israel*' (verse 3 NKJV). The travail of the woman is at least two thousand years subsequent to the birth of the Messiah and refers to her sorrow in the coming tribulation. Before she travailed, she brought forth; before her pain came, she was delivered of a Man Child."

Travails of Israel are numerous in her past and present history, and these will culminate in the worst anguish ever experienced. Terrible sorrow will be hers after the Man of Sin breaks the seven-year covenant guaranteeing her protection.

Why, then, is the travail of the woman linked in this special way with the birth of the Messiah?

First, notice that the present lengthened period of Israel's rejection, coming as it does between the birth and the travail, is passed over in silence in the chapter before us. It is a parenthesis whose history is not given in prophecy but is found elsewhere.

Second, it shows the deep interest that the Messiah takes in His people. He prepared the tribulation and made provision as to enlightening it many centuries prior. (See Matthew 24:15–22).

Third, at the time in which our chapter will take place, the Jewish nation will undergo its awful sorrow, and the object of going back in history to the birth of Christ is to connect Him with them in it. The travail, then, indicates Israel's sufferings during the tribulation. The Jews have been, and are being, cruelly persecuted, but still darker days are ahead for God's chosen people.

2. THE RED DRAGON

And there appeared another wonder in heaven; and behold a great red dragon, having seven heads and ten horns, and seven crowns upon his heads. And his tail drew the third part of the stars of heaven, and did cast them to the earth: and the dragon stood before the woman which was ready to be delivered, for to devour her child as soon as it was born. (Revelation 12:3–4)

Without doubt, this great red dragon represents Satan in his worst character. Later, in Revelation 20:2, John expressly identifies the devil as *"the dragon, that old serpent."* Both Pharaoh and Nebuchadnezzar are referred to as great dragons because of their cruelty and haughty independence. (See Ezekiel 29:3; Jeremiah 51:34.) *"Dragon"* appears ten times in Revelation and is a fitting symbol of God's chief adversary in his role as the relentless persecutor and murderer of multitudes of saints and sinners. Job gives us a most remarkable description of a dragon: *"He is a king over all the children of pride"* (Job 41:34). (See also Isaiah 27:1.) The term is used of Satan only in the book of Revelation, and it suggests the hideousness and horror of his rule. In Psalm 74:13, we have a reference to *"the heads of the dragons,"* for, truly, Satan will head up all the insatiable violence represented by the dragon.

Red, being a blood color, indicates the devil's murderous nature, for he has been a murderer from the beginning. (See John 8:44.) Red can also represent pseudo-sanctity. Once the most beautiful of angelic beings, Satan is now the object of abhorrence. As the ape of Christ, who, as the Conqueror, will wear many diadems, Satan is also adorned with his crowns, or diadems. The seven crowned heads signify the cruel and despotic exercise of earthly power and authority, while the ten horns can stand for the future limits of the empire as distributed into ten kingdoms. Satan delegates power and authority to the first beast, who is similarly described in Revelation 13:1.

The tail, representing the most dangerous part of a dragon, is like a great comet in this monster. As a lying prophet is likened to a tail by Isaiah (see Isaiah 9:15), Satan's malignant power and influence as a liar and deceiver are similarly described. With power and wisdom combined, Satan will bring about the utter moral ruin of a third part of the stars of heaven, which can mean eminent rulers in places of authority. There may also be in John's words a veiled reference to all those angels who rebelled with Satan before creation.

As a dog on a leash, the devil is permitted certain prescribed operations. He can produce moral collapse at this time only among those in the third part of the earth, identified by some writers as the western part of the Roman Empire. His dragging down the stars with his tail, lashed back and forth in fury, implies Satan's persuasion to apostatize.

The terrible spectacle of the dragon standing before the woman, waiting to devour her newborn child, is easily interpreted. It was not the woman but her seed whom the monster was bent on destroying, just as Pharaoh tried to murder all the male children of Israel. (See Exodus 1:15–22.) What a fascinating study it is to trace Satan's efforts to destroy Israel, the royal seed that was to produce Christ, and then to destroy Christ Himself! As soon as Jesus was born, there was a satanic effort to destroy Him during the slaughter of the innocents. (See Matthew 2:16.)

3. THE MAN CHILD

And she brought forth a man child, who was to rule all nations with a rod of iron: and her child was caught up unto God, and to his throne. And the woman fled into the wilderness, where she hath a place prepared of God, that they should feed her there a thousand two hundred and threescore days..

(Revelation 12:5–6)

The *"man child"* ("a son, a male," as the original expressed it) surely represents Christ, who was born to rule. (See Genesis 3:15; Psalm 2:9; Revelation 12:5; 19:15; Psalm 110:1–2, 5; Daniel 4:26.) Yet, there are teachers who see in the Man Child a group out of Israel, the first fruits to God from Israel out of the tribulation. The 144,000 sealed Jews, for example, are identified with Christ in a special way, and because of their relation to persecution, they are sometimes thought to be the "child" here.

But the following prophecy of universal rule nullifies such an interpretation. It was the Virgin who brought forth the promised Man Child, who, concerning the flesh, came of Israel (see Romans 9:4–5; Galatians 4:4–5), whom Herod tried to kill while He was under two years of age. The persistent enemies of Christ—the scribes and Pharisees—also tried to destroy Him. Born as a King, Christ came into the world having universal dominion, which He will yet exercise. (See Psalm 8.)

The iron rule of the nations will be broken by Him who comes to shepherd them with an iron rod. Here, the word *"rule"* means "to tend as a shepherd," and, in this role, Christ will break up the consolidated powers of the earth gathered against Himself and His people. With irresistible might, He will mete out judgment to the guilty kings and peoples in the West (see Revelation 19) and then deal with those of the North and East. (See Isaiah 10.) Furthermore, this ruling with a rod—for long-continued obstinacy, until submission results in obedience—reveals the nature of Christ's reign. The revolt at the end of the millennium manifests what reluctant submission characterized large numbers of the people of the earth during His reign.

The ascension of Christ is expressed in *"her child was caught up unto God, and to his throne"* (Revelation 12:5; see also Mark 16:19; Luke 24:50–51; Acts 1:9; 7:56.) Nothing is said of the death of the Man Child, seeing that He is connected with Israel and the rule of all nations, both of which are dependent on His birth and His ascension to His throne. And yet, in that Shepherd-hand grasping the rod will be the marks of the nails. It is as the slain Lamb that He reigns.

I reject the interpretation that sees in this verse the rapture of those who are sufficiently holy when Jesus comes. Those who hold the "partial rapture" theory sometimes employ the last part of this fifth verse to teach the erroneous doctrine of a selected rapture.

All who are Christ's, irrespective of their state, will be caught up to meet the Lord. If unfit, they will suffer loss in respect to their reward. Between verses 5 and 6, we have the whole stretch of history from Christ's ascension to the tribulation.

By the determined counsel and foreknowledge of God, a place of safety and sustenance is provided for the remnant. There are those who suggest that this place of refuge is Petra, at Mount Seir, in the land of Edom and Moab. Petra, or Sela, means "rock" or "stronghold" and, as such, can accommodate thousands of people. The rapid flight and journey of the persecuted woman is likewise aided by God.

Between the interrupted statement of verse 6 and the resumption of it in verse 14, we have the episode of the war in heaven and the heavenly rejoicing upon its success. The careful numbering of days—1,260 in all—testifies to the Lord's tender interest in His afflicted people. This last half of Israel's week of prophetic sorrow will elicit constant care and provision on the Lord's part. The *wilderness* is sometimes used as a condition that is destitute of natural resources, a place of isolation. In Ezekiel 20:35–36, we find the wilderness employed not literally and locally but spiritually, as a state of discipline and trial among the Gentile people. It was in a wilderness that our Lord was tempted of the devil.

4. THE WAR IN HEAVEN

And there was war in heaven: Michael and his angels fought against the dragon; and the dragon fought and his angels, and prevailed not; neither was their place found any more in heaven. And the great dragon was cast out, that old serpent, called the devil, and Satan, which deceiveth the whole world: he was cast out into the earth, and his angels were cast out with him. And I heard a loud voice saying in heaven, Now is come salvation, and strength, and the kingdom of our God, and the power of his Christ: for the accuser of our brethren is cast down, which accused them before our God day and night. And they overcame him by the blood of the Lamb, and by the word of their testimony; and they loved not their lives unto the death. Therefore rejoice, ye heavens, and ye that dwell in them. Woe to the inhabiters of the earth and of the sea! for the devil is come down unto you, having great wrath, because he knoweth that he hath but a short time. (Revelation 12:7–12)

After the complete picture of the first six verses given under the two signs, we come to the climax of age-old antagonisms. The book of Revelation is a book of wars, and in the war in heaven, we have one of the most dramatic of battles. At last, the prophetic word of Isaiah is about to be fulfilled—*"And it shall come to pass in that day, that the* LORD *shall punish the host of the high ones that are on high, and the kings of the earth upon the earth"* (Isaiah 24:21).

The most significant battle in the history of the world is now to be staged. What a spectacle! Forces, both heavenly and hellish, are to clash in this grim conflict. Opposing ideologies are grouped together in a twofold way. John presents the "allies"—Michael and his angels—and the "enemy"—Satan and his angels. Of the outcome, there is no doubt. The declaration of final victory against Satan was given by Christ in Luke 10:18 and John 12:31. Surely, such a hope should impel us to soul-saving activity!

The phrase *"war in heaven"* (Revelation 12:7) is somewhat startling. After a *"silence in heaven"* (Revelation 8:1), we have a *"war in heaven."* By "heaven," we are not to understand the immediate presence of God but the sphere that Satan has occupied since he was cast out of God's dwelling place because of his rebellion. He is *"the prince of the power of the air"* (Ephesians 2:2), and the atmospheric heavens are populated with multitudes of beings, both heavenly and hellish. Somewhere between earth and heaven, Satan has his seat of operation, and it is here that the battle is to rage, resulting in his expulsion to earth, from which Satan will be consigned to the bottomless pit for a thousand years and then, ultimately, to the lake of fire.

MICHAEL AND HIS ANGELS

Michael is peculiarly the prince, or presiding angel, of the Jewish nation. This grand leader, who is to force the usurper from the heavens, is mentioned five times in Scripture. (See Daniel 10:13, 21; 12:1; Jude 9; Revelation 12:7.) This leader of the angelic hierarchy is always related to Old Testament saints. His name signifies "one who is like God." To Michael is assigned the safety of God's people, and, in the grim conflict described in this chapter of Revelation, he will see to it that Israel shall not perish. Michael and his angels, who excel in strength, overcome the dragon and his angels only by ferocious battle.

THE DRAGON AND HIS ANGELS

Our Lord refers to Satan and the rebellious angels under his command in Matthew 25:41, while Paul reminds us of Satan's ability to appear as an angel. He is the archangel of the fallen angels. (See 2 Corinthians 11:14.) It has been indicated that the movements of nations—their wars, politics, and social policy— are shaped and dictated by higher and spiritual powers. There are good and bad angels who are constantly influencing men and governments. (See Daniel 10.) Wars and strife on earth are merely the reflex of opposing spiritual powers in the lower heavens. Because these heavens are the abode of Satan as *"the prince of the power of the air,"* God has declared that *"the stars are not pure in his sight"* (Job 25:5).

The invisible struggles between the powers of light and the forces of darkness are real and earnest, and by the influence of these spiritual beings, the world is providentially governed. With this *war in heaven,*" the climax is reached in the struggle between invisible and visible forces, and the outcome of this battle is the overthrow of the dragon and his angels. Satan suffers an ignominious defeat and is expelled from the heavens with the suddenness of a flash of lightning. Baffled and beaten, the dragon will then roam this doomed scene and vomit his wrath against the Jewish remnant.

The sixfold description given of Satan and his work is worthy of our special notice. He is referred to by at least six prominent names:

1. The Great Dragon: This diabolical fiend has always been conspicuous for his remorseless cruelty. Legend paints the dragon as a monster in form and appearance outside the limits of the animal kingdom, a combination of superhuman craft and cruelty. What a sad day it will be for the inhabitants of earth when this hellish foe roams unchecked!

2. That Old Serpent: The allusion here is to Genesis 3, verses 1 and 4, where we find the record of Satan's first, successful attempt to destroy God's purposes and mar the happiness of man. "Old" or "ancient" refers to Satan's first historical connection with the human race. The title "serpent" speaks of our enemy's subtlety, deceit, cunning, and craft. (See, for example, 2 Corinthians 11:3.) The degradation of the serpent, even in millennial days, is hinted at in Isaiah 65:25.

3. The Devil: This name is from the Greek word *diabolos,* "one who throws down, slanders, tempts." Such a name represents all that the devil stands for. He throws down, debauches, and destroys, but Christ elevates from the dunghill to a position among princes.

4. Satan: *Devil* is a Greek term, while *Satan* derives from the Hebrew term for "adversary," especially in a court of justice.

This twofold designation, Greek and Hebrew, marks the two-fold objects of his accusation, which include the elect Gentiles and the elect Jews. Both names prove Satan to be an actual, historical being.

5. The Deceiver: *"Which deceiveth the whole world"* (Revelation 12:9) encapsulates the special work of Satan. With the accumulated wisdom and cunning of millennia, he is able to deceive the inhabited earth. To act as the master deceiver is the devil's aim and occupation. Artful in his beguiling, he often succeeds in getting us to deceive ourselves. (See 1 John 1:8.) In tribulation days, he will attempt to deceive the elect by miraculous signs. (See Matthew 24:24; 2 Thessalonians 2:7–12.) The last glimpse of Satan in the Bible is as "the deceiver." (See Revelation 20:7–8.)

6. The Accuser: In some mysterious way, Satan is able to present his accusations against the saints before God. (See Job 1:6; 2:1.) Often, he accuses us to our own conscience, but we have the efficacious blood to plead. (See 1 John 2:1–2.) Our solemn obligation is to live in such a way that we shall never give Satan any cause of complaint or ground of accusation.

> I hear the accuser roar
> Of ills that I have done;
> I know them well, and thousands more;
> Jehovah findeth none.[9]

In the scene described in Revelation 12:9, Satan is completely vanquished and overthrown. Never again will his accusations, just or unjust, be listened to in the courts of heaven. The three elements in victory over Satan are emphasized in verse 11: *"the blood of the Lamb," "the word of their testimony,"* and personal sacrifice in that *"they loved not their lives unto the death."* The precious blood

---

9. Samuel Whitlock Gandy, "I Hear the Accuser Roar," 1838.

of Christ is the grounds and the means of victory. Through His blood, we have boldness before God, which, in turn, produces boldness before men. *"Testimony"* here is of a prophetic nature. The martyr spirit challenges the devil to do his worst, since a glorious resurrection awaits all who are willing to hazard their lives for Christ's sake.

All the redeemed in heaven and all the saints on earth now unite to rejoice over the complete expulsion of Satan. *"Now is come salvation."* Fullest hallelujahs arise because the defeat of the devil has been accomplished, fully and finally.

While the doxology of Revelation 12:10–12 announces that the kingdom has come, it is only in an anticipative sense. A necessary and preliminary step in the setting up of Christ's millennial kingdom is the casting out of Satan from the heavenlies. Now that the power of the kingdom has been so gloriously vindicated in heaven, all is announced there as if it had already come. With the imprisonment of Satan in the abyss, the kingdom will actually be set up on earth. Post-millennialists, those who say that Christians will bring in the kingdom, should remember that there can be no kingdom without the King, and that the kingdom will not be inaugurated until the King appears in all His power and glory and takes His kingdom by force. At present, He is completing His church, which is His mystical body.

The contrast in Satan's defeat is striking: rejoicing in heaven versus misery on earth. *"Rejoice, ye heavens"* versus *"woe to the inhabiters of the earth."* Knowing that his time on earth is short, Satan manifests great rage, exceeding even the wrath of the nations that he himself inspired. (See Revelation 11:18.) *"Wrath"* here means "boiling rage." Great anger is Satan's because of his exile from the heavenly realm and because his permitted time span for doing harm on earth becomes suddenly and severely limited. No wonder the devil hates this book of Revelation that we are considering. His doom is written prominently in its pages!

5. THE REMNANT AND HER SEED

And when the dragon saw that he was cast unto the earth, he persecuted the woman which brought forth the man child. And to the woman were given two wings of a great eagle, that she might fly into the wilderness, into her place, where she is nourished for a time, and times, and half a time, from the face of the serpent. And the serpent cast out of his mouth water as a flood after the woman, that he might cause her to be carried away of the flood. And the earth helped the woman, and the earth opened her mouth, and swallowed up the flood which the dragon cast out of his mouth. And the dragon was wroth with the woman, and went to make war with the remnant of her seed, which keep the commandments of God, and have the testimony of Jesus Christ. (Revelation 12:13–17)

After the episode of the war in heaven, we now resume the thread of the discourse that was interrupted in Revelation 12:6. With his sphere of operation now restricted to earth, Satan gives himself to the destruction of the woman, the line of Judah from which *"the man child"* came. Now that he is confined to the earth, the Dragon seeks to work vengeance on Judah, now restored to the land and representing the whole nation of Israel before God.

Fiercely persecuted, the woman is forced to flee, but she is wonderfully assisted in her flight. She receives *"two wings of a great eagle."* We cannot agree with those who interpret these eagle wings as the world powers of Babylon and Egypt. The eagle symbolizes God's protection of His own people. His past care and deliverance from impending danger are indicated in this way in the following verses:

Ye have seen what I did unto the Egyptians, and how I bare you on eagles' wings, and brought you unto myself.

(Exodus 19:4)

As an eagle stirreth up her nest, fluttereth over her young, spreadeth abroad her wings, taketh them, beareth them on her wings: so the LORD alone did lead him, and there was no strange god with him. (Deuteronomy 32:11–12)

Wings convey the idea of rapid motion and guaranteed protection, things we attribute to God. Two wings can mean help and safety. To suggest that wings express the remote parts of the earth, or that the two wings symbolize the east and west divisions of the Roman Empire, is to destroy the providential aspect of this part of the chapter. Divine protection is afforded for *"a time, and times, and half a time"*—or 1,260 days, the same length of time as forty-two months, or three-and-a-half years. All these expressions cover the last half of the tribulation.

Scholars present differing views regarding *"the wilderness"*— the place prepared by God where He will exercise His care of the woman and her seed. The most sane interpretation is that of the remnant having an earthly destiny and, therefore, being provided with an earthly refuge. Petra, the rock city and one of the wonders of the world, was located southwest of the Dead Sea, as a possible hiding place. With its accommodation for a quarter of a million people, such a marvelous cavern would afford excellent protection.

The crafty nature of Satan is emphasized in the effort of the serpent to destroy the woman by a flood. The earth swallowing the flood may represent those friendly nations willing to befriend the Jews, thereby neutralizing and circumventing Satan's wily method of energizing other nations against the Jews. These nations sheltering the Jewish remnant will be the "sheep nations" in the judgment of the living nations. (See Matthew 25:31–46.)

Such overruling providential frustrations will stir up the anger of the dragon and will cause him, in his frustrated rage, to make war with the godly remnant in Palestine. Keeping the commandments of God and having the testimony of Jesus Christ always excite the wrath of the devil. The phrase *"to make war"* can imply every form of attack upon the saints, whether by persecution or by war. Physical harm and evil of every kind the devil is capable of is referred to under this technical expression. But both *"the man child"* and the God-fearing Jews will be delivered from the murderous hate of the devil.

6. THE SEA BEAST

The whole of Revelation 13 is devoted to a description of the nature and activities of two fearsome and awe-inspiring beasts. The earth is now the scene of satanic operations, as God-fearing Jews and Gentiles become the objects of the devil's murderous intentions. His principal ministers of deceit and cruelty are two beasts, actual men who use their delegated power efficiently on behalf of their hellish master.

The first beast—the sea beast—is apparently a Gentile, and exercises a rule characterized by brute force. The second beast—the earth beast—is probably an apostate Jew, and will be conspicuous because of his subtle religious influence. Later, these blind dupes will stand in battle array against Christ and His heavenly hosts. (See Revelation 19:11, 19.)

And I stood upon the sand of the sea, and saw a beast rise up out of the sea, having seven heads and ten horns, and upon his horns ten crowns, and upon his heads the name of blasphemy. And the beast which I saw was like unto a leopard, and his feet were as the feet of a bear, and his mouth as the mouth of a lion: and the dragon gave him his power, and his seat, and great authority. And I saw one of his heads as it were wounded to death; and his deadly wound was healed: and all the world wondered after the beast. And they worshipped the dragon which gave power unto the beast: and they worshipped the beast, saying, Who is like unto the beast? who is able to make war with him? And there was given unto him a mouth speaking great things and blasphemies; and power was given unto him to continue forty and two months. And he opened his mouth in blasphemy against God, to blaspheme his name, and his tabernacle, and them that dwell in heaven.

(Revelation 13:1–6)

Because the word *"beast"* is used of a power or kingdom—or the personal head of a power or kingdom—the term is sometimes used interchangeably for an empire or its personal head. From Scripture, it would seem as if *beast* carries a double significance: first, the folly of acting without feelings of responsibility toward God (see Daniel 4:16; 1 Corinthians 15:32); and, second, the error of imperial power acting without reference to God (see Daniel 7). In this chapter, the Greek word used for *"beast"* is not *zoon,* "living one" (as in chapter 4), but *therion,* "wild beast," and is therefore descriptive of the bestial, demonic, vengeful reign of terror on the part of the two beasts.

With the appearance of the sea beast, we have Satan's masterpiece and the most awesome personage ever to appear on the earth. He will be the composite of all beasts that have gone before, the embodiment of all misrule and anarchy, and the personification of iniquity. Every feature of his portrait is portrayed in Psalm 10 and Daniel 7, verses 3 and 7. With the appearance of this fierce, wild beast comes the ultimate struggle for world dominion, the final clash of opposite ideologies. Let us try to understand the person and prestige of this satanically inspired superman, as John saw him from his vantage point from *"the sand of the sea."*

First of all, this beast emerges from the sea, which can represent the unsettled condition of mankind. The sea is used in a figurative way of a great multitude and is employed by John as a symbol of the chaotic revolutionary forces at work as the beast appears, which he will command in the interest of brute force. Out of the general collapse of all governing authority—under the sixth seal in Revelation 6:12–17—the beast will emerge. One writer has suggested that this may be the Mediterranean Sea, since the four great empires of the world at that time were located around this body of water. Also, Gentile nations or peoples are symbolized in the Bible by the great waters of the sea. (See Isaiah 57:20; Revelation 17:15.)

We must not lose sight of the fact that this beast is an actual person and not merely a principle or a force. Further proof of this fact will be his presence in the lake of fire. (See Revelation 19:20; 20:10.) This first beast is as definite a personality as Jesus, whom he seeks to counterfeit. Satanically inspired and energized, he is also satanically sustained and controlled, and he will be the last ruler of the last Gentile form of government.

He will be the last world ruler before Christ. As to his course and nation, Daniel's prophetic emphasis on this last ruler of the Gentiles and oppressor of Israel centers in the province of Syria. Arising from this province with Jewish assistance, he will displace three rulers of the "league of ten" and will revive ancient Greece.

Coming to the symbolism of the heads and horns of the beast, the exact identification of these will be simple enough when God, in His providential arrangements, brings them into fulfillment. Ralph A. Brown, in his *Outlines of Bible Prophecy*, wrote that the seven heads represent seven Gentile nations that have ruled, or will rule, the biblical world and Israel. The seven crowns signify pseudo-supremacy, and the ten horns signify pseudo-strength. When it says in Revelation 17:11, "*The beast…is the eighth, and is of the seven,*" it refers to the revival of one of the seven nations, as well as the final Gentile government. As number eight, he usurps authority and forms a government distinct from the ten kings. (Along with Revelation 13:1–8, other Scriptures to study on this matter include Daniel 7:7–8, 23–26; Revelation 17:8–18.)

The form of the first beast is likened to a leopard, a bear, and a lion (reversed in order from Daniel 7). This is because Daniel looks *forward* into the ages, whereas John looks *backward*. The antichrist will unite in himself the God-opposed characteristics of three preceding kingdoms that resemble, respectively, the leopard, the bear, and the lion. The catlike vigilance of the leopard; the slow, crushing power of the bear; and the fearsome strength of the lion were familiar features to shepherds in Palestine.

Combined in this dread creature will be the infamy and ferocity of past empires: *Macedonian* swiftness and brilliancy of conquest, *Persian* tenacity of purpose and massiveness of power, and *Babylonian* voracity, all combined into the most autocratic Gentile dominion ever known. All civil and legal power is to be vested in this despotic head, whose throne will be one of iniquity. (See Psalm 94:20.) Names of blasphemy on his head, or heads, speak of his utter defiance of God. Blasphemous titles assumed by the Roman emperors of the first and second centuries, and of certain succeeding Roman leaders, are the forerunners of names that the beast will proudly display. Nero, for example, was saluted as "the eternal one." Defiant and flagrant opposition of God and His Christ in the eyes of men is presented to us in the beast's blasphemous conduct.

Delegated constitutional rule is committed to the beast by the dragon. Embodying all the strength and brutality of the Babylonian, Median, and Persian empires, the beast is a fitting agent for Satan to use. The sovereignty of the world that was offered to Christ by the prince of the world (see John 12:31) was refused by our Lord (see Luke 4:5–8). Here, it is offered to, and accepted by, the beast.

Death and resurrection are here, and they result in universal adoration of the beast. Though *"wounded to death,"* the deadly wound is healed. The Greek word implies being "slain to death." Brought back from the realm of death, the "resurrection" of the beast proves how tremendous the power of Satan will be and how easily the world will be deceived.

In the healing of the deadly head wound, some writers see the political death and resurrection of the beast. Imperialism, as represented by the worldwide dominion of the caesars, has lain in the iron grip of political death since A.D. 476. But God will permit an empire to rise out of revolutionary passion and conflict. Faber explains the healing of the deadly wound as the revival of the Napoleonic dynasty after its overthrow at Waterloo. But because the bulk of Revelation is prophetic, any historical interpretation must be ruled out, except for that which is used as illustration. Here, John views as an accomplished fact a revived form of the Roman Empire, which vanished over a millennium-and-a-half ago. It is fascinating to watch the trend of present-day events and to trace in the movements of today's nations the preparation of the world for the beast's universal, commanding influence. The lack of ability on the part of present-day rulers to govern adequately is preparing the way for this satanically inspired dictator.

In the worship of the dragon and of the beast, we see another aspect of imitation. Satan wanted Christ to fall down and worship him, but the Master bowed His knee to no one but God. Michael and his angels make war with the devil and his angels, and they overcome them. But here, a deluded people cry out, *"Who is like unto the beast? who is able to make war with him?"* (Revelation 13:4). This beast, with his deadly wound healed, is surely immune to further destruction. Although he will reign over only one of the ten kingdoms during the first half of the tribulation, he will reign over all ten kingdoms throughout the last three-and-a-half years.

The Beast—this superhuman, satanic being, this "willful king" (see Daniel 11:36)—will be cruelly anti-Semitic and will act in the superhuman power of the Dragon. He will manifest a warlike prowess that spares not and knows no pity. The presence of such a terrible dictator, with the destiny of millions in his hands, will be the sign of hastening judgment for all who bear his mark.

The great American Pentecostal minister Finis Jennings Dake summarized the multiplied power of the beast as follows. He has power to...

- blaspheme God. (See Revelation 13:5–6; Daniel 7:8, 11, 20, 25; 11:36.)

- overcome the Jews. (See Revelation 13:7, 15; Daniel 7:21; 12:7.)

- overcome the saints. (See Revelation 14:13)

- conquer many nations and rule them as he wills. (See Ezekiel 38–39; Daniel 7:8, 20–24; 11:36–45.)

- overcome and kill the two witnesses. (See Revelation 11:3, 7.)

- change times and laws. (See Daniel 7:25.)

- understand mysteries. (See Daniel 8:23.)

- protect or punish the Jews as long as he desires. (See Daniel 9:27; 2 Thessalonians 2:4, Revelation 11:1–2.)

- work with signs and wonders. (See Daniel 8:24; 2 Thessalonians 2:8–9.)

- cause craft to prosper. (See Daniel 8:25.)

- control money and riches in his own realm. (See Daniel 11:38–43.)

- cause great deceptions. (See Daniel 8:25; John 5:43; 2 Thessalonians 2:10–12.)

+ do according to his will. (See Daniel 11:36.)

+ control religion and worship. (See Daniel 11:36; 2 Thessalonians 2:4.)

+ control the lives of all men in his realm. (See Revelation 13:12–18.)

+ control kings as he wills. (See Revelation 17:12–17.)

+ make all other nations fear him. (See Revelation 13:4.)

+ cause men to fight against Christ. (See Revelation 17:14; 19:19–21.)

+ continue in full power for forty-two months. (See Daniel 7:25; Revelation 13:5.)

Dake also had this most fitting summary of the beast's character and characteristics:

> He will be a man who will possess the talent and leadership of all previously gifted conquerors and leaders. In addition to these natural gifts, he possess the miraculous power of attracting people of every class, fascinating them with his marvelous personality, successes, superhuman wisdom, administrative and executive ability, and bringing them under his control through well-directed flattery and masterly diplomacy. He will be endued with the power of Satan in the exercise of these gifts until the world will wonder after him and worship him as God.

What follows in Revelation 13:5–7 is an extension of what is implied in *"the name of blasphemy"* (Revelation 13:1) and *"his mouth as the mouth of a lion"* (verse 2). The old Roman Empire was guilty of blasphemy in that it assumed divine right in public documents. The contempt and mockery of anything divine will be openly practiced when devil worship is widely recognized. Boasting and blasphemy are included in the *"great things"* coming from the loud lion-mouth of the beast: *"a mouth speaking great things"* (Daniel 7:8). God Himself, including His name and His dwelling place with all its inhabitants, is cursed by the beast. We can understand the blasphemy against those in heaven since they rejoiced over the dragon's expulsion from heaven in Revelation 12:10.

> *And it was given unto him to make war with the saints, and to overcome them: and power was given him over all kindreds, and tongues, and nations. And all that dwell upon the earth shall worship him, whose names are not written in the book of life of the Lamb slain from the foundation of the world. If any man have an ear, let him hear. He that leadeth into captivity shall go into captivity: he that killeth with the sword must be killed with the sword. Here is the patience and the faith of the saints.*   (Revelation 13:7–10)

The faithful saints on earth are to be given over to the power of the beast, who will be allowed to wreak his vengeance on them and overcome them. His authority to kill or spare will be unlimited in range and extent, as seen in the mention of the three divisions of the human race—*"all kindreds, and tongues, and nations."* The rage of the dragon over his defeat in the war in heaven is now poured out upon the saints on earth.

Beast worshippers are clearly defined as those whose names are not in the divine register belonging to the slain Lamb. The elect *"dwell in heaven"* (Revelation 13:6) and are heavenly; the worshippers of the beast *"dwell upon the earth"* (verse 8) and are earthy. The widely proclaimed humanism today is simply self-worship and is just one step away from devil worship. In the personal exhortation *"If any man have an ear, let him hear"* (Revelation 13:9), we have Christ's own words of admonition, used both in the Gospels and in Revelation. As employed here, it is a call to a full understanding of the apocalyptic judgments about to break loose.

Punishment with retribution in kind is the principle indicated for friends and foes alike. Whether saints or sinners, we reap what we sow. Saints crushed under the rule of the beast are not to resist. Here is the patience, or endurance, of the saints: they must bear their appointed sufferings and thereby triumph. Because their names are written in heaven and they dwell there, the weapons they wield are not carnal but spiritual. They are eternally secure; no hellish or human power can rob them of moral victories. Trusting in the vengeance of God, the saints of the tribulation will use their captivity as a means of grace, knowing that an eternal captivity in the lake of fire is to be the portion of the beast. All who cause God's people to suffer must face retributive justice. *"With what measure ye mete, it shall be measured to you again"* (Matthew 7:2). (See also Jeremiah 15:2.)

We conclude this study of the sea beast with several contrasts suggested by Ralph Brown.

Christ	Antichrist
Son of Man	Son of sin
Son of God	Son of Satan
Son of righteousness	Son of perdition
Superhuman	Superman
Very God	Claims to be God
Redeemer	Destroyer
King of Kings	World dictator
Agent of God	Agent of Satan
Humble	Proud
Sacrificing	Tyrannical

7. THE EARTH BEAST

Let us summarize the teaching of Scripture on this second beast, who, because he is a *religious* beast, is more dangerous than the first beast. Though this second beast is mentioned after the sea beast, it does not follow that he will come into existence after him. The way the earth beast works to enforce the worship of the first beast proves that they appear together and exercise similar powers concurrently. As the sea beast takes the stage, his companion beast quickly follows.

> *And I beheld another beast coming up out of the earth; and he had two horns like a lamb, and he spake as a dragon. And he exerciseth all the power of the first beast before him, and causeth the earth and them which dwell therein to worship the first beast, whose deadly wound was healed. And he doeth great wonders, so that he maketh fire come down from heaven on the earth in the sight of men, and deceiveth them that dwell on the earth by the means of those miracles which he had power to do in the sight of the beast; saying to them that dwell on the earth, that they should make an image to the beast, which had the wound by a sword, and did live.*
>
> (Revelation 13:11–14)

THE ORIGIN OF THE EARTH BEAST

The second beast that John saw came out of chaos and revolution but quickly produced a civilized, consolidated, and ordered condition of society. Troubled agitations are speedily overcome by the rider of the white horse, who is able to achieve bloodless victories among the various peoples. It is out of this established order of civil and political government that this more dangerous executive agent of the devil emerges.

With his appearance, the arrogant imitation of the Holy Trinity is complete, for opposing God, Christ, and the Holy Spirit we have the dragon, the antichrist, and the False Prophet. While both beasts are false prophets, of a kind, the second beast is the executor of the first one. The multiple uses of *"earth"* is symbolic of people on the earth, and, if the part of the earth that this second beast arises from is the land of Israel, then he will probably be an apostate Jew.

"Coming up out of the earth," he will seem akin to ordinary people. The second beast's rise coincides with the healing of the first beast's deadly wound and his resurrection. With the appearance of the lamblike beast, Christ's three offices are perverted. The first beast is the false *kingship*; the harlot represents false *priesthood*; the second beast is the false *prophet*.

> And he had power to give life unto the image of the beast, that the image of the beast should both speak, and cause that as many as would not worship the image of the beast should be killed. And he causeth all, both small and great, rich and poor, free and bond, to receive a mark in their right hand, or in their foreheads: and that no man might buy or sell, save he that had the mark, or the name of the beast, or the number of his name. Here is wisdom. Let him that hath understanding count the number of the beast: for it is the number of a man; and his number is Six hundred threescore and six.
>
> (Revelation 13:15–18)

THE CHARACTERISTICS OF THE EARTH BEAST

"Two horns like a lamb" mark this beast as the false Messiah. Both beasts imitate God's Lamb—the first beast, in that he was mortally wounded and revived; and the second beast, in that he has two lamblike horns. The *lamb* is on the outside, but the *dragon*

is on the inside. Fullness of power belongs to the true Prophet, but limited power belongs to the False Prophet. Primasius of Adrumentum, a writer of the sixth century, said of the false Messiah, "He feigns to be a lamb that he may assail the Lamb— the body of Christ." His activities, however, are confined to the followers of the Lamb *on earth*, for before his appearance the church will have been caught up to heaven.

The *horn* is the symbol of physical, moral, or kingly power, and the earth beast's two horns represent the combination of king and prophet. These two horns can also speak of the combined power of natural and miracle-working religions. This counterfeit Messiah has only two horns, in contrast to the ten horns of the first beast. His authority covers two realms—religious and miraculous— and in both of these, we see his lamblike yet satanically deceiving speech. The horns will also give the false prophet a strong religious appeal, and he will be able to unite all conflicting religious bodies into one universal church.

Specifically mentioned as a "*false prophet*" (Revelation 16:13; 19:20; 20:10), he plays the role of a servant. A prophet is one who comes in the name of another and speaks for that person. Thus, Satan's counterfeit "Christ" will have a counterfeit "Elijah." As Ralph Brown expressed it, the False Prophet will be "the Elijah of the antichrist."

The manifold character of this false prophet is hinted at by our Lord in His description of the last days: "*Many false prophets shall rise, and shall deceive many*" (Matthew 24:11); "*There shall arise false Christs, and false prophets*" (Matthew 24:24). Under his title as False Prophet, he exercises great spiritual authority among the Jews and the people of Christendom in general.

As the False Prophet, he is found only with the Antichrist. The unholy two are inseparable. The dragon gives his external power to the first beast (see Revelation 13:2) and his spirit to the second beast, for he speaks as a dragon (see verse 11). He is to employ the same subtlety and deceit that Satan used when he deceived Eve and that he currently uses to deceive an ungodly world. Lamblike in appearance, he is betrayed by his speech as Satan's minister. Because physical and moral ruin constitutes the aim of the dragon, he uses the beast for political and civil purposes and the False Prophet for spiritual and moral ends. Thus, the two beasts will be Satan's chief lieutenants as the end approaches.

THE ACTIVITIES OF THE EARTH BEAST

Comparing Scripture with Scripture, we find these features in the works of the earth beast:

+ He exercises the power of the beast.

+ He carries out the will of the beast.

+ He empowers an image of the beast.

+ He demands absolute worship of the beast.

+ He shares the doom of the beast.

He exercises the power of the beast. Here is a specific statement, and as dreadful as it is specific: *"He exerciseth **all** the power of the first beast before him"* (Revelation 13:12). He is ministering to and upholding the first beast. He is the active minister of the beast, exercising a subordinate power. The wording here does not imply that the first beast is a mere passive head and that all power is concentrated in the second beast. The first beast is the powerful head of a mighty federation of nations (see Revelation 17:9–13), and, as the imperial ruler, he remains bold and blaspheming until his defeat by Christ, the mightier One.

Exercise of the power of the first beast by the false prophet will lie in employment of the force and prestige of the beast's authority to bring people everywhere into worship of the beast. Of the two, the false prophet is the worse, since he influences men religiously.

He is as a wolf in sheep's clothing, and the deceptiveness of his activities will win him great victories. In his description of the *"little horn"* in Daniel 7:8, Daniel speaks of him as having *"eyes like the eyes of man,"* as well as *"a mouth speaking great things."* The phrase *"the eyes of a man"* symbolizes cunning and intellectual culture, the very characteristics of the false prophet.

With all persuasiveness, he will succeed in claiming exclusive worship for himself in the land of Israel. He will claim divine worship for himself and will sit in the temple built by the unbelieving nation. He will set himself above all authority, whether divine or human, and will take God's place as much as he can. Outside the Holy Land, the false prophet will also exercise authority, forcing worship of his great confederate, the first beast, on all the nations.

He carries out the will of the beast. Raised up to represent the beast, and receiving his commission from this dragon-inspired creature, the false prophet will live, move, and have his being in the will of the beast. He will play the role of a devoted servant. Later, he will inspire the nations to have one mind and to give their power and strength to the beast. (See Revelation 17:13.) The false prophet will have supreme delight in carrying out the wishes of the beast and in forcing those wishes on the world at large.

Christ's devotion to the will of God was rewarded in many ways. His miraculous ministry, for example, attested to His identification of aims and wishes: *"No man can do these miracles that thou doest, except God be with him"* (John 3:2). And here is the false prophet doing great wonders in the sight of men. Miracles of a demonic kind, not merely tricks, are performed. By demonic aid, wonders of "signs" are worked that are designed to deceive the earthly-minded, though not the elect at this time. Followers of the true Lamb will know that a miracle is not enough to warrant belief in a professed revelation, unless that revelation is in harmony with God's already-revealed will.

Publicly, *"in the sight of men"* (Revelation 13:13), he produces fire from heaven and thereby deceives men. Other miracles performed *"in the sight of the beast"* (Revelation 13:14) produce the same delusion. With such usurping of divine prerogatives, retributive judgment should and will begin on those already given up by God. Handed over to the *"strong delusion, that they should believe a lie"* (2 Thessalonians 2:11), those guilty of devil-worship in a triune form are ripe for judgment.

He empowers an image of the beast. In the creation of a remarkable image of the beast, we have the setting up of an actual representation of the beast, by which he will be worshipped. This image will be as real as the one of Nebuchadnezzar set up in the plans of Dura, when, at the beginning of Gentile supremacy, men were compelled under pain of death to worship an image representing the power and majesty of the first major world empire. (See Daniel 3.) Now, we see the end of Gentile dominion, with its rejection of image-worship. The false prophet gives life or breath or spirit to the image of the beast. True life can be given by no one but God, and so the image is energized by a spurious vitality. Breath is given so that the image can speak, producing a ventriloquism effect. Even now, science can imitate the human voice and physical appearance in mechanical robots.

He demands the absolute worship of the beast. In Daniel, three Hebrew youths were cast into the fiery furnace for refusing to worship the image of Nebuchadnezzar. Pliny, an army commander of the early Roman Empire, in a letter to Trojan states, consigned to punish those Christians who would not worship the emperor's image with incense and wine. These, as well as other historical images that have been set up as a test of secular and spiritual allegiance, are merely forerunners of the worship of the beast's image,

208 *Revelation: Drama of the Ages*

which the false prophet will demand under pain of death. Even as the Holy Spirit presently directs our attention to Christ as the Object of worship and adoration, so the false prophet will direct the worship of multitudes to the beast. All who refuse to bow their knee will be murdered.

Universal subjection to the beast will also be forced by the most rigid control of commerce ever practiced. The most stupendous boycott ever instituted of food and trade will operate universally. No one will be able to buy or sell, whether rich or poor, unless he has the official ration mark—the emblem of the kingdom of the Man of Sin. Then, the choice will be idolatry or starvation. And the False Prophet will see to it that there are no black markets or bootleggers. The most fearful secret police force will be created to enforce the economic union for trading and living. The most abject submission to the vilest tyranny ever experienced will be evidenced by a mystic mark on the right hand or the forehead, even as animals and slaves have often been branded with their owner's name or mark.

Absence of the mark of the beast will mean relentless ostracism. Such a mark will be necessary for life and for all social and business relations. In effect, it will be a diabolical trading license. It will be in plain sight, indicating that the branded person is the active slave of the beast. The raised, open hand is a form of the Roman salute; when hands are raised to the image, it will be seen immediately whether those who salute the beast are beast-worshippers and, therefore, qualified to buy and sell. The brand upon their skin will be the public sign of abject submission to the beast.

The name of the beast is another phase of satanic mimicry. Christ has a name that is truly above every name, but the False Prophet will see to it that the beast's name is honored above every other name. A name, as we know, can mean an emblem of allegiance. Faithful believers, however, will refuse to wear such a name.

In stern and solemn protest, they will refuse to be branded with any symbol of submission to the beast. They will die rather than bow to the beast. Sealed by God, they will scorn any imitation. In those days, Psalm 23 will be exceedingly precious, for despite imminent starvation, the Lord will prepare a table for His loyal servants in the presence of their enemies, and, passing through the valley of the shadow of death, they will fear no evil. The ideal Shepherd will preserve His own from the cruel deceptions of the *"idol shepherd"* (Zechariah 11:17).

Spiritual wisdom will be needed to solve the mystery of iniquity, so as not to be deceived by it. What is fully meant by the name and number of the beast will be granted to those saints who are on earth when the beast is here in person. Of this we are certain: no one at present has sufficient wisdom to understand the number of the beast. What is meant by the trinity of sixes has been the subject of much research and debate. Many Greek and Hebrew names have a numeral value of 666. Many ingenious interpretations have been given of this symbolic number.

Ellicott, in his most valuable commentary, devoted much space to the significance of this symbolic number but wisely concluded his treatment of it by saying,

> I am disposed, therefore, to interpret this "six hundred and sixty-six" as a symbolical number, expressing all that it is possible for human wisdom, and human power, when directed by an evil spirit, to achieve, and indicating a state of marvelous earthy perfection, when the beast-power has reached its highest development, when culture, civilization, art, song, science, and reason have combined to produce an age so nearly resembling perfection—an age of gold, if not a golden age—that men will begin to say that

faith in God is an impertinence, and the hope of a future life a libel upon the happiness of the present. Then will the world-power have reached the zenith of his influence; then will only wisdom descended from above be able to detect the infinite difference between a world with faith and a world without faith, and the great gulf which the want of a little heaven-born love can fix between an age and an age.[10]

Expositors have brought skill, learning, and, in some instances, great research to the attempted answer to the question: What is meant by the number 666? There is divine wisdom wrapped up in this symbolic numeral, which occurs only once in Scripture—and it requires spiritual understanding to unlock its mystery. No doubt, its full, precise, and final solution will be apparent to the wise or godly during the tribulation days, when the beast's power, under the craft of Satan, will exhibit the highest human development in pride, impiety, and combined religious and political opposition to God and His anointed. In general, this is the moral significance of 666. The meaning will be obvious to the saints of the tribulation, who will call for prompt repudiation of the beast, the political minister of Satan in blasphemous opposition to God.

The number 666 is man's number, the number 6 being impressed upon him at his creation and in his subsequent history.

+ Man was created on the sixth day.

+ His appointed days of toil are six per week.

+ A Hebrew slave was to serve six years.

+ For six years, the land was to be sown.

Under the sixth seal in the sixth chapter of Revelation, an appalling and universal breakdown of all governmental power and authority takes place, as the days of tribulation approach. The

10. Charles J. Ellicott, D.D., ed., *The New Testament Commentary for Schools* (London: Cassell, Petter, Galpin & Co., 1884), 177.

numeral 7 is God's number, usually denoting perfection or completion. Six falls short of that number, signifying human imperfection and toil.

There is an obvious connection between the first and the last of the four major world powers. In character, they are identical, except that the last is the worst of the four. The image of gold raised up by King Nebuchadnezzar for his own glorification was sixty cubits high and six cubits wide. (See Daniel 3.) No doubt, that idol on the plain of Dura was meant to consolidate and unify the numerous and diversified religions of the mighty Babylonian Empire. Under threats of death, worship of the image was demanded. (See Daniel 3:4–6.) Surely, Daniel points ahead to the deeper and more satanic evil of Revelation 13.

He shares the doom of the beast. Both beasts share the same doom at the same time. Existing together in their terrible reign, they are consigned to hell together and, ultimately, to the lake of fire. Defeated together at Armageddon, when Christ appears in power, they leave this earth to endure the torment their crimes deserve. (See Revelation 17:13–14; 19:19–21.) When we come to the seven dooms, we will have more to say about the final destination of the trinity of evil. What a purge this will be when Christ takes to Himself His power and reigns! If Christ's return for His own is not far away, then these very beasts may be alive on earth today. But, before they are fully revealed to the world, we shall be caught up to meet the Lord in the air.

Praise God, the church will not witness the beast-worship and agony of the great tribulation! Our present obligation is to seek and save the lost around us in order to spare them from the horrors of the age to come and from a more terrible fate forever.

13

THE SEVEN
DIVINE INTERVENTIONS

This parenthetical chapter in Revelation is largely anticipative. Chapters 14 through 16 describe preparations for messianic judgment and offer a mingling of songs and sobs, music and misery, joy and judgment, glory and gloom, heaven and hell. Chapter 14 contains a sevenfold divine intervention in grace and judgment, and it constitutes an answer to the cry of the remnant, *"Why standest thou afar off, O LORD? why hidest thou thyself in times of trouble?"* (Psalm 10:1). The oft-repeated cry *"O LORD, how long?"* (Psalm 6:3; 90:13; Habakkuk 1:2) finds an answer, a responsible chord in our own hearts, as we think of the slaughter, misery, and anguish of our sin-laden, war-torn days. Will God never show His hand? Are the forces of iniquity to be forever victorious? Has God abandoned His saints to the will of the enemy? When will He intervene?

This chapter proves that God will have His day. The mills of God's justice may appear to grind slowly, but they grind exceedingly surely. This chapter is well-placed, since it serves as a necessary prelude to the fearful providential judgments of God. Chapters 12 through 14 form an episode of dramatic interest—a single, connected prophecy. Chapters 12 and 13 describe the doings of the dragon and the beasts. Truth has fallen on the streets; the blood of the saints flows freely as water; open defiance of God is the order of the day. Good is almost banished from the earth (see Psalm 4:6), and faith has gone (see Luke 18:8). The entire prophetic scene has become Satan's playground.

But we breathe more freely in chapter 14. The divine reaper is at hand. Earth's horrible iniquity is about to end. Coming between the trumpets and the vials, this fourteenth chapter sounds the death knell of arrogant, blasphemous, cruel men. The accumulated load of anguish and distress will now vanish from the hearts of God's persecuted people.

As a whole, this chapter contains a contrast between the Lamb and the 144,000 sealed Jews, between the nations and the antichrist, between the six angels and their announcements, and between the two sickles and their vintage.

1. THE SINGERS AND THEIR SONG

And I looked, and, lo, a Lamb stood on the mount Sion, and with him an hundred forty and four thousand, having his Father's name written in their foreheads. And I heard a voice from heaven, as the voice of many waters, and as the voice of a great thunder: and I heard the voice of harpers harping with their harps: and they sung as it were a new song before the throne, and before the four beasts, and the elders: and no man could learn that song but the hundred and forty and four thousand, which were redeemed from the earth. These are they which were not defiled with women; for they are virgins. These are they which follow the Lamb whithersoever he goeth. These were redeemed from among men, being the firstfruits unto God and to the Lamb. And in their mouth was found no guile: for they are without fault before the throne of God.

(Revelation 14:1–5)

In these five verses, we have one of the most remarkable scenes of Revelation. Here is a bright and gladdening vision, the calm after a storm—from the tyranny of the beast to the triumph with the Lamb! This is indeed a welcome transition. Let us now consider these saints, who are no longer exposed to trial but are seated in a position of royalty.

THEIR SAVIOR

Prominence is given to the Lamb on Mount Sion (Zion), around whom this singing multitude gathers. The book of Revelation is essentially a book of the Lamb. Twenty-seven times, our Lord is depicted in this image. And it is as the *slain* Lamb that He is seen. Because of His scars, sovereignty is to be His. In this chapter, we have an anticipative vision of Christ's coming in power. The bleeding lamb is now the Lamb upon His road to ultimate victory. His chosen ones had been as lambs among wolves, and the flock had been harried by the beast. But they overcame through the blood of the Lamb and are now happily at His side.

THEIR STATION

This distinguished multitude is found standing on Mount Sion, the selected seat of the glorious earthly reign for one thousand years of Christ and His saints. Here is the seat of royal power, of God's intervention in grace, of God's sovereignty, all in respect to Israel. *"Sion"* is named only once in Revelation and is an extremely interesting term. To the Jew, Zion is rich in sacred memories. (See Isaiah 2:1–4; Psalm 2:6.) At long last, God's King is on Mount Zion, and surrounding Him are His purchased ones as loyal and loving subjects!

THEIR SUM

A specific number of purchased ones is stated. We have another 144,000 persons, and the question is, Who are these sealed singers? Is this great multitude the same group as the 144,000 in chapter 7? One expositor suggests that this group in chapter 14 represents only a portion of the great harvest of redeemed tribulation saints—a "first installment" marked by high spiritual service. Similarities between these two companies can be noted. In each case, the number, 144,000, is the same. Both groups are on Mount Zion, are sealed on their foreheads, and are happily in deliverance from trouble.

The repetition of the number, however, does not prove that these companies are one and the same. Walter Scott suggested, "The 144,000 here witnessed are of Judah; a similarly numbered company of all Israel (see Revelation 7:4) forms a separate vision.... They are Jews who steadfastly maintained the right of God and of the Lamb; now they are publicly owned of Him....144,000 Jewish saints who occupy the leading place in the earthly millennial kingdom." The number 144,000 indicates governmental number and fullness.

THEIR SEAL

In contrast to the 144,000 in chapter 7, this amazing group in chapter 14 is sealed on their foreheads with the Lamb's name and the name of His Father. A seal, of course, represents a sign of ownership and a guarantee of preservation. William Newell has suggested that it proclaimed their ownership, exhibited their character, and announced their destiny.

It is evident that the seal of these confessors of Christ is in contrast to the mark of the beast on each of his worshippers. "It has occurred to us," said Newell, "that the presence of the heavenly seal in the foreheads of the remnant from chapter 7 onward is so evident to men that Satan is forced to undertake to break its influence by demanding the opposite seal in the foreheads of his devotees. And especially may this be true when we reflect that

God preserves (see Revelation 9:4) those who have His seal from woes to which others are subject."

THEIR SONG

The voices from heaven that John heard were "*as the voice of many waters*" and "*as the voice of a great thunder*" (Revelation 14:2). As is the voice of God, so is the voice of the heavenly choristers, who are in accord with those on Mount Zion. The harp-singing multitude in heaven and the preserved company of Judah form one grand choir. The song and the harp, so beautifully blended, set forth the choral praise of the redeemed and heavenly host.

Their song is called "*a new song*" (Revelation 14:3). The *old* song was related to creation, "*when the morning stars sang together, and all the sons of God shouted for joy*" (Job 38:7). The central theme for this *new* song is one of redemption. That is why it is referred to as the song of Moses and the Lamb. As God and the old song are united, so the Lamb and the new song are conformed.

A. R. Fausset, in commenting on this new song, said, "The song is that of victory after conflict with the dragon, beast, and false prophet; [it was] never sung before, for such a conflict had never been fought before; [it was] therefore new: till now the kingdom of Christ on earth had been usurped. They sing the *new song* in anticipation of His taking possession of His blood-bought kingdom with His saints." The Greek word for "*sing*" indicates continuous singing.

We must not forget that the 144,000 rejoice because they "*were redeemed from among men.*" We have the double phrase "*redeemed from the earth*" (a sinful place) and "*redeemed from among men*" (a sinful race). This high position is the privilege of the 144,000 because they had been redeemed, or *purchased*, not because they were victors over the beast. The angels cannot sing this new song, for they do not know personally what it is to come out of the great tribulation, nor do they have robes that have been washed white through the blood of the Lamb. (See Revelation 7:14.)

THEIR SEPARATION

In Revelation 14:4–5, we are given a wonderful description of the walk and witness of this victorious part of Judah, who had emerged out of the great tribulation and are now standing in triumph with the Lamb on Mount Zion, the seat of royalty and of sovereign grace. A fearful test had been theirs. The grossest corruption, open idolatry, proud boasting, daring blasphemy, and open wickedness had surrounded them, but, like the Jews in Sardis, the 144,000 emerged with garments undefiled.

"They are virgins." We are to understand this in a spiritual sense (see Matthew 25:1), in contrast to the apostate church (see Revelation 14:8), which was spiritually a harlot. (See Revelation 17:1–5.) *"Not defiled with women"* means that they were not led astray from faithfulness to the Lord by the tempters, who jointly constitute the spiritual harlot. William Newell suggests that they are "complete Nazarites unto God as touching their relation to women." But such an interpretation would confine this defined company to men. Does the language not imply that the 144,000 represent those who lived and walked in spiritual purity in a scene abandoned to all that was vile? They had kept themselves unspotted from the world. Virgin love—undivided heart affection for the Lamb—was theirs as the rest of the world followed the beast. They had a separation, thorough and unqualified, from their sinful surroundings. They were virgin souls, clad in stainless purity.

"They...follow the Lamb." Nearness to the Lamb on Mount Zion was the fitting reward for their loyalty to Him while they were on earth. All around them were those who had wandered after the beast and his prophet, but the obedience of the

144,000 was as full and unquestionable as their separation from the world. Following the Lamb in His rejection, they now share His royalty. *"Follow"* is in the present tense, implying an unending obedience.

"They were...the firstfruits." While similar language is used of the church, we are not to confuse the *"firstfruits"* here with the redeemed saints forming the new creation. *"Firstfruits unto God and to the Lamb"* are kingdom words rather than mere salvation words. *"Redeemed from among men,"* these 144,000 form an earnest purchase—a pledge—from among men for the reign of heaven on earth. They form a sample of the full and final harvest.

"In their mouth was found no guile." Several older translations read *"falsehood,"* with the English Revised Version stating, *"In their mouth was found no lie."* Lying wonders and falsehoods characterized the days of the antichrist. The "lie"—that Satan is God and the beast is his Christ, who therefore must be worshipped—was generally believed, but in the mouths of the 144,000, no lie was found. They were truthful in word and way. In spite of fierce persecution, they confessed the true Messiah (see 1 John 2:21–27) and remained true to His Word.

"They are without fault." In outward conduct and ways before men, these saints on earth were without fault. Several versions omit the words *"before the throne of God."* This fitting and condensed epitome of the practical character and life concerned their life on earth. In all their ways, they refused to conform to the edicts of the beast. In respect to the sincerity of their fidelity to the Lamb, they were without fault. They were not absolutely and in themselves *blameless*, but they were regarded as such on the grounds of the Lamb's righteousness. In Him alone they trusted, faithfully served, and followed. What a joy this remnant is to God and to the Lamb!

2. THE FIRST ANGEL AND HIS GOSPEL

And I saw another angel fly in the midst of heaven, having the everlasting gospel to preach unto them that dwell on the earth, and to every nation, and kindred, and tongue, and people, saying with a loud voice, Fear God, and give glory to him; for the hour of his judgment is come: and worship him that made heaven, and earth, and the sea, and the fountains of waters.

(Revelation 14:6–7)

We now come to God's public witness by six angels against the reign of the antichrist and to the fast-coming judgment he deserves. The term *"another angel"* implies a new turn in the unfolding drama, the events of which come with each successive angel. (See Revelation 7:2; 8:3, 13; 10:1). This particular angel-evangelist was seen *"in the midst of heaven,"* implying in the sight and sound of all people on earth. A previous angel *"flying through the midst of heaven"* (Revelation 8:13) announced woe. This angel, however, announces *joy*. This flying angel is a messenger of mercy and shows grace in judgment. He represents the last call for earth-dwellers to repent.

A GLAD ANNOUNCEMENT

We must not forget that this angel does not proclaim an announcement of doom but a *"gospel,"* which means "good news." He announces the good news of the everlasting kingdom of Christ—a kingdom that will begin immediately after the judgment of evil forces, which will be announced as imminent in Revelation 14:7. While the human preachers of the gospel of the kingdom will be converted Jews, angels are commissioned to providentially expedite the declaration of the good news during the last days of the prophetic week.

In unmistakable language, this mighty angel urges people to turn from the beast to God. The hour of divine judgment has come, and men must repent of their gross idolatry if they do not want to endure the wrath of the vials. Here is an urgent call to fear God, the beginning of wisdom (see Psalm 111:10; Proverbs 9:10), and to give glory to Him rather than to the beast and his image. The Creator of all things pleads a final time for man's allegiance. Even as the human race is described under a fourfold designation—nations, tribes, tongues, and peoples—so creation is here stated in four terms: heaven, earth, sea, and fountains.

A GREAT AUDIENCE

The angel flying in heaven preaches his gospel all over the earth, and all classes of people hear his message. Whether there is a general response to the angelic call, we are not told. Our Lord declared that some people are so abandoned to the rejection of God that they would not believe, even if someone rose from the dead and went to them with a message of grace. (See Luke 16:31.) A great preacher like Noah had little success in warning the multitudes of coming judgment. Deaf to his entreaties, they lived on in their corrupt ways until the flood came and took them all away.

3. THE SECOND ANGEL AND BABYLON'S FALL

> *And there followed another angel, saying, Babylon is fallen, is fallen, that great city, because she made all nations drink of the wine of the wrath of her fornication.*   (Revelation 14:8)

The prominence of angels in this chapter indicates that they have a major role in the providential and governmental economy, both prior to and during Christ's millennial kingdom. In

Revelation 14:8, we are given a preface of events to come. It is a preliminary and preparatory announcement of the judgment described in chapters 17 and 18. The destruction of Babylon is being celebrated in heaven, where judgment is treated as something already accomplished.

The intensity of utterance in the repetition *"fallen"* is not a mere Hebraism but speaks of a double judgment. Both as a system and as a city, Babylon is to be destroyed. The word *"is"* in the fallen state of Babylon indicates the anticipation of sure destruction. From heaven's standpoint, Babylon is already fallen, even though its actual doom has not yet occurred.

Babylonianism, as we shall show more fully later, represents a vast system that enslaves professing Christians. It is characterized by worldly pride, idolatry, and spiritual adultery. The reason for Babylon's fall is given in the words *"because she made all nations drink of the wine of the wrath of her fornication."* The wine of the wrath of God is the consequence of her fornication. Because she made the nations drunk with the wine of her fornication, she herself shall be made drunk with the wine of God's wrath. Here, we are given the ultimate fulfillment of Isaiah 21:9: *"And, behold, here cometh a chariot of men, with a couple of horsemen. And he answered and said, Babylon is fallen, is fallen; and all the graven images of her gods he hath broken unto the ground."*

William Newell draws attention to the three distinct subjects in this awesome phrase: "wine, wrath, and fornication."

+ Babylon's wine: *"Babylon hath been a golden cup in the Lord's hand, that made all the earth drunken: the nations have drunken of her wine; therefore the nations are mad"* (Jeremiah 51:7).

+ Babylon's wrath: *"For thus saith the Lord God of Israel unto me; Take the wine cup of this fury at my hand, and cause all the nations, to whom I send thee, to drink it"* (Jeremiah 25:15).

+ Babylon's fornication: *"For all nations have drunk of the wine of the wrath of her fornication, and the kings of the earth have committed fornication with her, and the merchants of the earth are waxed rich through the abundance of her delicacies"* (Revelation 18:3).

The kings of the earth have committed fornication with Babylon. The white heat of God's anger, held back through the ages, is now about to be turned loose upon accumulated corruption.

4. THE THIRD ANGEL AND DOOM

And the third angel followed them, saying with a loud voice, If any man worship the beast and his image, and receive his mark in his forehead, or in his hand, the same shall drink of the wine of the wrath of God, which is poured out without mixture into the cup of his indignation; and he shall be tormented with fire and brimstone in the presence of the holy angels, and in the presence of the Lamb: and the smoke of their torment ascendeth up for ever and ever: and they have no rest day nor night, who worship the beast and his image, and whosoever receiveth the mark of his name. Here is the patience of the saints: here are they that keep the commandments of God, and the faith of Jesus.

(Revelation 14:9–12)

The terrible doom of those who worship the beast, as announced in these verses, is fearful in the extreme. Judgment, unequaled in severity and proportional to the guilt and horrible iniquity that is openly practiced, is now about to fall. With a great voice, this third angel declares the unending torment of all who have followed the beast.

THE WORSHIP OF THE BEAST

Six times in Revelation, the worship of the beast—the devil incarnate—is described as directed to his image. Christ came as *"the brightness of his glory, and the express image of his person"* (Hebrews 1:3). But now, unrelieved torment is to overtake those who have deliberately chosen Satan's false Christ, the antichrist, who commanded all people on earth to worship his image. Retributive justice will be meted out to each and every person who follows the beast and carries his mark.

THE WRATH OF GOD

No alleviating circumstances are permitted. With a loud voice that all can hear, the angel declares that the outpouring of wrath is to be *"without mixture."* A. R. Fausset writes, "Wine was so commonly mixed with water that 'to mix wine' is used in Greek for 'to pour out wine'; [but] this wine of God's wrath is undiluted; there is no drop of water to cool its heat. Nothing of grace or hope is blended with it. This terrible threat may well raise us above the fear of man's threats. This unmixed cup is already mingled and prepared for Satan and the beast's followers."

THE WAIL OF THE DOOMED

"Fire and brimstone" are symbols of unutterable anguish (see Isaiah 30:33; Revelation 20:10), and this eternal doom is to be visited upon the impenitent. "Brimstone," says William Newell, "is [a] most terrible substance...in its action upon human flesh—in torment when it touches the body. Combined with fire, it is absolute agony, unutterable anguish! And it is meant to be so, for it will be the infliction of divine vengeance unlimited."

The eternal doom of the beast-worshippers is described in a dreadful language: *"The smoke of their torment ascendeth up for ever and ever."* Passing from personal pronouns, we have the whole multitude—*"their torment."* Anguish will be unrelieved and unending. The expression *"for ever and ever,"* meaning "ages of ages," is used in Revelation to emphasize...

+ the eternal existence of God. (See Revelation 4:9–10; 5:14; 10:6; 15:7.)

+ the eternal glory of the Lamb. (See Revelation 5:13.)

+ the eternal reign of believers. (See Revelation 22:5.)

+ the eternal doom of the devil. (See Revelation 20:10.)

+ the eternal doom of the lost. (See Revelation 14:11.)

Adding to the remorse of the doomed is the fact that they have *"no rest day nor night."* They will not be able to die or sleep. There will be tormented day and night; no cessation, no alleviation, of anguish can be looked for. Such endless horror and ceaseless agony baffles our comprehension. May grace and power be ours to warn sinners of the inevitable, eternal punishment awaiting all who are not covered by the blood of the Lamb!

Adding to the horror felt by the wicked is the consciousness that the holy angels and the Lamb are onlookers. This will intensify the pungency of the curse. These holy witnesses of doom will not be found gloating over the terrible suffering of the lost. Rather, their presence will indicate the awful and holy approval of a divine sentence. The holy angels, once witnesses of the horrible evils of the beast and his followers, will now witness God's vengeance. Each tormented person will realize that his or her anguish is observed by the angels, as well as by the Lamb, whom the wicked had once openly defied and whose blood they had wantonly rejected. The association of holy angels and the Lamb indicates that both will work together in executing the vengeance of a holy God.

THE WELFARE OF THE SAINTS

In contrast to the self-doomed rebels, we have God's patient elect, who cry for deliverance from the adversary. (See Luke 18:1–8.) The twofold mark of the faithful remnant in a time of unequaled tribulation is the keeping of the commandments of God and the maintenance of faith in Jesus. Now, their faith and patience are fully rewarded.

5. THE FOURTH ANGEL AND A BENEDICTION

And I heard a voice from heaven saying unto me, Write, Blessed are the dead which die in the Lord from henceforth: Yea, saith the Spirit, that they may rest from their labors; and their works do follow them.   (Revelation 14:13)

What a welcome relief this benediction is! It comes as a break between so much judgment and doom. We pause and draw a fresh breath after a revelation of unspeakable torment. But, once we leave this beautiful description of the saint's everlasting rest, we find ourselves again in the terrible atmosphere of wrath and vengeance.

John's meditation was broken by the command to write. The blessedness of the faithful had to be placed on record forever. What the apostle set down must be stored up in the heart. The command to write is repeated twelve times in Revelation, to indicate that all the things it refers to are matters of importance.

While the message John heard has an application to *all* saints, it has a special relation to those who are to be martyred for their faith. In many funeral manuals, this comforting verse is given as one of the Scriptures applicable for recitation at the burial of the Christian dead. But a particular class of martyred saints at a particular junction in human history is intended in this benediction. *"From henceforth"* intimates the imminent end and indicates that the blessing is just about to be entered into. Martyrdom under the beast is the subject. All who die *in* the Lord were willing to die *for* the Lord.

But, after these terrible tortures that only the beast is capable of inflicting upon those who fail to worship him, there comes a rest. Rest will come through dying. For the beast-worshippers, there will be no rest, day or night, but for the faithful unto death, there is eternal life, eternal rest. The rest from toils, weariness, and satanic antagonism will not include rest from activities for those who follow the martyred into heaven. The place of rest is not to be a place of idleness. It will offer the highest form of spiritual service. All believers who are cut short and unwanted in their Christian service here on earth will be amply utilized by the Lord in heaven.

6. THE FIFTH ANGEL AND THE HARVEST

And I looked, and behold a white cloud, and upon the cloud one sat like unto the Son of man, having on his head a golden crown, and in his hand a sharp sickle. And another angel came out of the temple, crying with a loud voice to him that sat on the cloud, Thrust in thy sickle, and reap: for the time is come for thee to reap; for the harvest of the earth is ripe. And he that sat on the cloud thrust in his sickle on the earth; and the earth was reaped. (Revelation 14:14–16)

Armageddon is about to begin, and we are given a comprehensive summary that is amplified in detail in succeeding chapters. Introducing this paragraph, Walter Scott said, "Judicial judgment is about to sweep the guilty earth with the broom of destruction and clear it of evil. The harvest and the vintage are the familiar figures employed to express God's closing dealings. The former is discriminating judgment, the latter unsparing wrath. In the harvest, the wheat is separated from the tares. In the vintage, the tares are alone in the prophetic scene, and form the subjects of the Lord's righteous vengeance."

THE REAPER OF THE HARVEST

The heavenly Reaper whom John saw was, without doubt, the Lord Jesus Christ, referred to as *"the Son of man."* It is under this title that Christ deals with the state of things on the earth and judges the ungodly. (See Matthew 25:31–33; John 5:22–27.) Because of His connection with the human race, Christ exercises all those characteristics entitling Him to universal dominion.

Introducing the vision of the Reaper, John uses another *"behold,"* since subjects of unusual interest are about to be dealt with. The first object attracting the apostle was a white cloud. This cloud was akin to the bright cloud of the transfiguration of Christ. (See Matthew 17:5.) Clouds symbolize divine presence. (See, for example, Ezekiel 10:4; Revelation 10:1.) White constitutes a prominent color in Revelation and, as previously stated, indicates the purity and absolute righteousness of the Reaper in all His actions.

Seated upon a white cloud is the Creator of all clouds. Making this cloud His chariot, He rides to His grim task. Sitting on the cloud suggests calm, deliberative judgment. With no undue haste, the Reaper reaps His harvest.

The golden crown upon His head is a garland of victory, not His diadem as King. Christ's full victory is described in detail later, in Revelation 19:11–21, when many crowns will encircle His brow. His royal dignity and rights are suggested by His golden crowns— *"as it were crowns like gold"* (Revelation 9:7)—but Christ's crown of gold expresses divine righteousness in victorious action and is no imitation crown. It is divinely conferred on its Wearer, who exercises royal authority.

The sharp sickle in the hand of the heavenly Reaper is symbolic of His rights over the harvest. Mosaic law commanded that *"thou shalt not move a sickle unto thy neighbor's standing corn"* (Deuteronomy 23:25). Christ's sickle implies that He will reap the field over which He has authority. The *"sharp sickle"* indicates that the reaping will be quick and thorough. It is significant that the national emblem of the Soviet Union is the hammer and sickle, both of which were used with dreadful effect to gather a harvest for the godless creed of Communism. But God will yet use His hammer—His Word (see Jeremiah 23:29)—to smash the hordes. Then, His sickle will reap a harvest of judgment.

Another angel, distinct from the others already mentioned, comes out of the temple and calls for immediate action on the part of the Reaper. This angel does not command the Son of man but is only a messenger announcing the will of God the Father to the Son. All along, Christ had expected such a message, and now, He hears it. (See Hebrews 10:12–13; Psalm 2:7–9.) God is roused to action, and the angel comes out of the temple; the Sower of the judgment is about to overtake the earth. The temple and the throne, used often in Revelation, represent the presence and authority of God.

THE RIPENESS OF THE HARVEST

The Son of man acts promptly, since *"the harvest of the earth is ripe,"* or "overripe," even "dry." William Newell tells us, "The Greek word used here is the same as is used of the fig tree in Mark 11:20; in Luke 23:31, the adjective form is used: *'If they do these things in a green tree, what shall be done in the dry?'* meaning 'the dreadful state of Israel.'"

"The time is come for thee to reap." This ominous declaration takes us back to the Old Testament prophets, who described a

harvest time for overripe workers of iniquity at the end time period of Gentile dominion. Joel 3:13 says, *"Put ye in the sickle, for the harvest is ripe: come, get you down; for the press is full, the vats overflow; for their wickedness is great."* This can mean only that the ripe are not the saved saints, ripe for glory; they are the wicked, who are overripe for judgment.

THE REAPERS OF THE HARVEST

One brief phrase is sufficient to describe the terrible end of all that proud man has boasted of: *"the earth was reaped."* And what a reaping! It is the awesome second coming of the King of Kings in His great day of wrath.

The Son of man uses the angels as His actual reapers (see Matthew 13:39), and they act swiftly in His harvest work. A separating process is used: discrimination between wheat and tares, good fish and bad, is observed. There is no actual execution of punishment in this harvest, for that is accomplished in the vintage. This harvest is one of discriminating judgment prior to the establishment of the kingdom.

Though described as a single act of reaping, these events cover a considerable time and employ various agencies of God.

7. THE SIXTH ANGEL AND THE VINTAGE

And another angel came out of the temple which is in heaven, he also having a sharp sickle. And another angel came out from the altar, which had power over fire; and cried with a loud cry to him that had the sharp sickle, saying, Thrust in thy sharp sickle, and gather the clusters of the vine of the earth; for her grapes are fully ripe. And the angel thrust in his sickle into

> *the earth, and gathered the vine of the earth, and cast it into the great winepress of the wrath of God. And the winepress was trodden without the city, and blood came out of the winepress, even unto the horse bridles, by the space of a thousand and six hundred furlongs.*   (Revelation 14:17–20)

There are two angels in the vision of the vine of the earth and its judgment. In verse 17, there is the "temple angel" with his *"sharp sickle."* Corresponding with the description given of the Son of man in verse 14, this "angel of vengeance" signifies the association of angels with Christ in His judicial work. Thus, *"another angel came out from the altar."*

The type of altar is not stated. If it represents the brazen altar—the altar of judgment—then, the thought is one of pure, divine judgment upon the vine of the earth. (See Deuteronomy 32:31–35.) But if the altar stands for the altar of incense (see Revelation 8:3–5; 9:13), then, there is a different thought. On this altar were offered the incense-accompanied prayers of all saints, bringing down God's fiery judgment on their foes. The cry of the souls of martyrs under the altar (see Revelation 6:9) is now to be fully answered. The false prophet did great wonders and brought fire down from heaven, but now, the altar angel, having power over fire, moves against all the godless of earth. The tares are now to be cast into the furnace of fire. (See Matthew 13:40–42.)

The subject of judgment is *"the vine of the earth,"* because its grapes are not what the Creator expected, considering its careful culture by Him. The expression *"vine of the earth"* covers the whole religious system in the coming visitation of God's wrath. The grapes of widespread apostasy are "wild grapes" and must be turned into "grapes of wrath." Into the great winepress of the wrath of God must go both apostate Jews and apostate Gentiles. This is the day of vengeance of our God, and mercy will not be shown. (See Isaiah 63:1–3; Jeremiah 25:15–16; Joel 3.) Christ, the true Vine, deals with the grapes of iniquity produced after centuries of cultivation. Such grapes are fully ripe for burning. The phrase "*fully ripe*" means "at their highest point."

"*Without the city*" indicates the sphere where the fullest vengeance of God is to be poured out. Jerusalem is the city, and the valley of Jehoshaphat—where the battle of Armageddon is to be fought—is just outside the city. "*Multitudes, multitudes in the valley of decision: for the day of the LORD is near in the valley of decision*" (Joel 3:14). "*Without the city*" can also imply that the scene of the blood-shedding of Christ and of His people will also be the scene of divine judgment upon all Christ's rejecters.

There is something gruesome about the description John gives us of rivers of human blood reaching up to the bits of the horses for a distance of 200 miles. The phrase "*blood came out of the winepress*" (Revelation 14:20) is symbolic language testifying to the terrible slaughter of the godless when the Lord tramples them in His fury. Manifesting His power, God will trample vast masses into a bloody pulp. The beast and the false prophet, along with all their deluded followers and worshippers, will be exterminated forever.

As we watch the movements of opposing armies in our own day, it seems as if the East will soon become a very important theater of war. On every side of Israel, tremendous forces are poised. Is such a gathering of powers a forerunner of what will happen when the Deliverer of Israel will crush the embattled nations of the earth? Without doubt, the earth is becoming ripe for God's vintage in its strongest form, and, as we see this day approaching, it is imperative for us to warn the ungodly to flee from the wrath to come. Today is still the day of grace, and, as it lingers, we must beseech the wicked around us to be reconciled to God.

14

THE SEVEN VIALS

REVELATION 15:1–16:21

We now approach two chapters of exceptional awe. Having considered the instigators of earth's horrible iniquity, we now come to the terrible judgment of the vials. Severe and final chastisements are about to be inflicted in sharp and rapid succession. As the sin of man reaches its climax in the Man of Sin, so now, the judgments of God are to fall upon a guilty earth. Within the chapters before us, we have the details regarding God's judgments preceding His great day of wrath. As we shall see, the pouring out of the seventh vial completes the wrath of God. Then follows the wrath of the Lamb.

Of this double wrath, William Newell wrote, "Remember constantly that Christ must come Himself, at the last, and tread the winepress alone in His anger. (See Isaiah 63:3–5.) The wrath of God is general, worldwide, and in view of man's iniquity and idolatry. The wrath of the Lamb is particular against antichrist and his king and [against the] armies gathered for the double purpose of cutting off Israel from being a nation (see Psalm 83:4) and of making war against the Lamb (see Revelation 19:19; Zechariah 12:10)...to prevent His rescue of beleaguered Israel."

These two chapters should be studied together, because they provide details for what is stated in general terms in the opening words of Revelation 11:18: *"And the nations were angry, and thy wrath is come, and the time of the dead, that they should be judged."* In chapter 15, we are given the reparation for the vials; in chapter 16, we witness the performance of the vials.

> *And I saw another sign in heaven, great and marvelous, seven angels having the seven last plagues; for in them is filled up the wrath of God.*   (Revelation 15:1)

The sign, or wonder, of chapter 15 extends to the end of chapter 16. In fact, Revelation 15:1 is a summary of all that follows. The angels do not actually receive the vials until Revelation 15:7, but, here in the opening verse, they are seen by anticipation as already having them. In this great and marvelous sign that John saw, we have the completion of a trio of signs. The "great sign" of the woman—Israel—is presented in Revelation 12:1. Another sign—that of the dragon, the antagonist of Christ and His counsels—is presented in Revelation 12:3. And here, we have *"another sign in heaven, great and marvelous."* All three signs are seen in heaven, God's immediate dwelling place. This third sign—more solemn than the first, because of its association with God's wrath upon the beast—is great in that something of outstanding importance is to be revealed. *"Marvelous"* indicates that divine patience is exhausted and that terrible visitations of divine judgment are about to overtake earth's apostates.

It would seem as if the contents of chapter 15 revolve around three weighty phrases: *"the wrath of God"* (Revelation 15:1, 7), *"the harps of God"* (verse 2), and *"the glory of God"* (verse 8).

> *And I saw another sign in heaven, great and marvelous, seven angels having the seven last plagues; for in them is filled up the wrath of God. And I saw as it were a sea of glass mingled with fire: and them that had gotten the victory over the beast, and over his image, and over his mark, and over the number*

of his name, stand on the sea of glass, having the harps of God. And they sing the song of Moses the servant of God, and the song of the Lamb, saying, Great and marvelous are thy works, Lord God Almighty; just and true are thy ways, thou King of saints. Who shall not fear thee, O Lord, and glorify thy name? for thou only art holy: for all nations shall come and worship before thee; for thy judgments are made manifest. And after that I looked, and, behold, the temple of the tabernacle of the testimony in heaven was opened: and the seven angels came out of the temple, having the seven plagues, clothed in pure and white linen, and having their breasts girded with golden girdles. And one of the four beasts gave unto the seven angels seven golden vials full of the wrath of God, who liveth for ever and ever. And the temple was filled with smoke from the glory of God, and from his power; and no man was able to enter into the temple, till the seven plagues of the seven angels were fulfilled. (Revelation 15:1–8)

THE WRATH OF GOD

Seven angels and seven plagues form the media of expression of God's wrath. Occurring five times, the expression *"the wrath of God"* is indeed a fearful one, and one that should strike terror into the hearts of all unsaved people now on earth. (See Revelation 14:10, 19; 15:1, 7; 16:1.)

The *"seven angels"*—distinct from the seven highly honored angels connected with trumpets—come out of the temple (see Revelation 15:6), the immediate residence of God and the angels. Out of the temple of old, priests came as ministers of grace. But now, angels emerge as ministers of judgment.

The *"temple of the tabernacle of the testimony"* is a suggestive phrase. With Israel, the temple, or tabernacle, was a pledge of

God's presence with, and His provision for, His people. But now, the holiness of God demands punishment of the wicked, and, therefore, we have the testimony of judgment, according to the nature of God against the beast and all the enemies of His people. David Brown writes, "The tabernacle of the testimony, appropriately here, comes to view, where God's faithfulness is avenging His people with judgments on their foes about to be set forth. We need to get a glimpse within the Holy Place to understand the secret spring and the end of God's righteous dealing."

These seven angels are clothed in a way befitting the righteous character of their mission, and also in a way resembling the Lord. (See Revelation 1:13.) By comparison with Revelation 19:8, we find that the *"pure and white linen"* indicates righteousness, while *"their breasts girded with golden girdles"* suggest the work of judgment compatible with God's holy nature.

"The seven plagues" suggests finality and completion; thus, the appearance of *"seven"* is especially appropriate. We have come to the final cycle of judgmental visitation. Of course, the vials do not bring the end of divine wrath, since further strokes of vengeance are to fall when Christ comes in person. (See Revelation 19:11–21.) What we have at this point is the conclusion of God's providential judgments. These vials are *"full of the wrath of God."* "Full" means "finished," or "consummated." To God, the future is as certain as though it were the past, so sure of accomplishment is His Word.

THE HARPS OF GOD

This preface to the last of the devastating judgments of God includes a beautiful description of the victorious martyrs who are with the Lord. The paragraph from Revelation 15:2–4 is taken up with victory, praise, and worship. Heavenly choral praises are represented by the harp, which, with its combination of solemn, grand notes and soft, tender strains, indicates the praise and worship of God. (See 1 Chronicles 25:6.) The harps of God—indicating that the instruments, musicians, and themes are His—were part of the instruments of heaven, used solely for the divine praise. It would seem as if the two heavenly groups of harp singers mentioned in Revelation 14:2 and Revelation 15:2 represent the same victorious host.

The stage upon which the harpists stand is likened to *"a sea of glass mingled with fire,"* suggesting a fixed state of holiness, of inward and outward purity. The sea suggests vastness, while glass suggests a solid calm or a settled, unruffled peace. Pictured as standing upon the sea of glass, the martyred company has come to their rest, as well as to this new position as conqueror-worshippers.

The *"sea of glass mingled with fire"* introduces another element. These saints have emerged victorious from their fiery trial. We have three foes to face—the world, the flesh, and the devil—but the singers had a fourth foe to defy: the beast. Victory was gained over the beast, over his image, over his mark, and over *"the number of his name,"* and now, they triumph because of a victory that is thorough and complete.

The song accompanying the harps has the ring of great poetry about it. It is a song of victory like that of Moses after crossing the Red Sea. Two songs are combined: *"the song of Moses the servant of God"* and *"the song of the Lamb."* The song of Moses is the triumph over evil by God's judgments. It is a song celebrating the overthrow of Pharaoh and his hosts at the Red Sea. (See Exodus 15.) This Mosaic song must not be confused with the prophetic one in Deuteronomy 32, which, magnificent as it is, celebrated an *earthly* redemption only. The grace and glory in the song that was sung on the eastern bank of the Red Sea were associated with power over Israel's foes in Egypt, by God's judgments.

The song of the Lamb, however, is of a different nature. This song, led by the Lamb as the Captain of our salvation, implies the exaltation of the rejected-Messiah, the suffering One. Sung by the faithful slain remnant amidst unfaithful and apostate Israel, this song celebrates God and the Lamb by victorious sufferers in heaven.

Coming to the subjects of this double song, we find God magnified in several ways. First, His works are praised. The phrase *"great and marvelous"* is repeated in Revelation 15, verses 1 and 3, implying the vindication of the justice of God, so that He may be glorified at the grand end of God's dealings. In the combined divine title *"Lord God Almighty,"* we have a vast reservoir of strength—consoling to the saint but foreboding to the enemy of God.

The ways of God are extolled as being *"just and true."* In the chastisement of His enemies, God will act in harmony with His own character. This equitable judgment will be meted out by the *"King of the ages"* (RV)—not *"King of saints,"* as in the King James Version. The point at issue in the Lord's controversy with the earth is whether He or Satan's man, the beast, is king of the nations. At this eve of the vials descending on the kingdom of the beast, the victorious singers hail the Lord as the true *"King of the ages."* The worship of God also contributes to this remarkable song. The three repetitions of *"for"* supply the reasons why the Lord should be glorified.

*"**For** thou only art holy."* The singers on the glassy sea celebrate the holiness of God. They fear and glorify Him as the only One entitled to be called "holy." The beast set himself up as God, but the victorious choir chooses holiness in the face of a world gone over to sin. Now, they are where all true holiness reigns.

*"**For** all nations shall come and worship before thee."* God's judgments will strike fear into His foes. Anticipating the universal domination of the Lord, the saints celebrate the worldwide recognition of His supremacy. Here, we see the fulfillment of such prophecies as Psalm 148, Isaiah 2:2–4; 56:6–7, and Zechariah 14:16–17.

"For thy judgments are made manifest." He should be glorified. These are indeed the most beautiful words that come from those who passed through the horrors of the torment of the beast.

Commenting on this unique scene, F. B. Meyer said,

Those who were brought up under the dispensation of Moses, and the followers of the Lamb in the present dispensation, together with all holy souls who have overcome, shall constitute one vast choir. But search the song of Moses as you will, you will fail to find one note that equals this in sublimity. Here are the saints of God, trained in distinguishing the niceties of righteous and holy government and behavior, enabled from their vantage ground in eternity to survey the entire history of the divine dealings, adoring Him as King of the ages, and acknowledging that all His ways had been righteous and true. What confession! What an acknowledgment!

THE GLORY OF GOD

The last section of this remarkable chapter is introduced by another *"behold"* (omitted by some versions). This paragraph opens with the dwelling of God and closes with the glory of God. Because everything in this section is connected with the glory of God, let us examine these verses with that thought in mind.

William Newell argues for a literal temple of God in heaven, but we feel that the word *"temple"* is used because of what it represents symbolically—namely, the dwelling place of God, where He is approached and worshipped. Out of the temple come the seven angels with the seven plagues, which represent God's final visitation of judgment upon the nations.

The presentation of the vials to the angels by one of the living creatures indicates that these living creatures are the executors of the judicial government of God. These dignified beings are deep in the understanding of the purposes of God and therefore present to the angels previews of dreadful events. It has been pointed out that there are three steps in God's work of judgment:

1. The angels are commissioned and equipped in the sanctuary. (See Revelation 15:6.)

2. The angels receive the golden vials full of God's fury from one of the living creatures. (See Revelation 15:7.)

3. The angels cannot take a step in the act of judgment until God authoritatively gives the command. (See Revelation 16:1.)

All of this suggests that the works and ways of God, even in judgment, are calm and measured. And this is what we would expect of the One *"who liveth for ever and ever."* It is the eternal God who is about to plague the guilty earth with His fury. We must never forget that He is glorified in judgment as well as in grace.

Before we leave this preparatory chapter, we are introduced to God's smokescreen, which covers everything within the sanctuary. Smoke, as we've said, is symbolic of God's presence. (See Exodus 19:18; Isaiah 6:4.) No man was able to enter the temple because of God's presence in His manifested glory and power during the execution of the vial judgments. Smoke from the glory and power of God filled the temple. Moses was unable to enter the tent of testimony—just as the priests were unable to enter the temple—because of the glory of the Lord. (See Exodus 40:34–35; 1 Kings 8:10–11.) What we have here is not glory itself but *smoke* from the glory of God. It is not incense filling the temple but smoke, which is the glory of God manifested in judgment. During this entire scene, the finality of it should fill our hearts with utmost awe! God is about to deal with all earth-rebels.

*And I heard a great voice out of the temple saying to the seven
angels, Go your ways, and pour out the vials of the wrath of
God upon the earth.*   (Revelation 16:1)

The opening verse of Revelation 16 is rich with significance. First,
there is the *"great voice out of the temple,"* which has been variously
interpreted. Possibly God's voice is the one meant, since we are now
brought to the vials of God's wrath. Christ is not mentioned until
after God has personally executed judgment. As we have already
hinted, Revelation is a book of the "voice," and wherever the voice is
found, it implies an intelligent understanding of the subject in question. We read of a strong and loud voice. Such adjectives describe the
character of the voice and also the nature the announcement.

Here, the great voice comes out of the temple, out of the Holy
of Holies. Because God's holiness demands judgment upon an
apostate world, God's wrath burns fiercely: *"Go…and pour out the
vials of the wrath of God upon the earth."* A different command came
for Christ as He was about to leave His own: *"Go ye into all the
world, and preach the gospel to every creature"* (Mark 16:15). Now,
grace is withdrawn. It is no longer the cup of salvation but the cup
of the wrath of God.

Pentecost witnessed the pouring out of the Spirit with such
an effusion that there was the manifestation of blessing. But now,
we have come to another outpouring: unmixed fury is about to
descend upon the earth. The fullness of divine wrath is emptied
into every bowl, which, in turn, is poured out without reserve
upon a guilty world. The prayer of the suffering Jewish remnant is
answered in the seven terrible plagues about to fall: *"Render unto
our neighbors sevenfold into their bosom their reproach, wherewith they
have reproached thee, O Lord"* (Psalm 79:12).

In the golden vials, we have a further glimpse into the fury
of God. The Greek word for *"vials"* means "bowls" or "cups" and
represents the broad-rimmed vessels used in the sanctuary, where

they were filled with fragrant incense. Now, the vessels, hallowed by temple use and service, are filled with God's righteous wrath and are devoted to judgment.

THE FIRST VIAL—UPON THE EARTH

And the first went, and poured out his vial upon the earth; and there fell a noisome and grievous sore upon the men which had the mark of the beast, and upon them which worshipped his image. (Revelation 16:2)

There is something expressive about the execution of these seven plagues. The vials as a whole imply swift action. Sudden destruction will overtake the beast and his worshippers, and they shall not escape.

The trumpet judgments are limited, more or less, to the Roman world, but the vial judgments are to cover the earth and constitute God's total war upon the world. The vials are God's answer to Satan, and they will blast his empire. In the trumpets, Satan's power is released to further his objectives. In the vials, God unleashes all His power to finish His grim work. Direct control over all the forces of nature is committed to the angels, who, in turn, execute the judgment that is written.

In the first vial, or bowl, of wrath, we see a plague akin to the sixth Egyptian plague (see Exodus 9:8–12), the first of the plagues to afflict the bodies of the Egyptians. David Brown remarks, "The reason why the sixth Egyptian plague is the *first* here is because it was directed against the Egyptian magicians, Jannes and Jambres, so that they could not stand before Moses; and so, here, the plague is sent upon those who, in the beast-worship, had practiced sorcery. As they submitted to the mark of the beast, so they must bear the mark of the avenging God."

In this connection, we wonder whether the *"noisome and griev-ous sore"* will not afflict the very part of the body bearing the mark of the beast—namely, the forehead and the palm of the hand. Walter Scott wrote, "Physical suffering, no doubt, will also add to the anguish endured by men, but the chief and predominating fea-tures will be judicial, dealing with the soul and conscience—a suf-fering far exceeding any bodily affliction." But surely, we cannot get away from literal sores—bad, malignant, and suppurated wounds!

The Greek word translated as "sore" means "an ulcer...pro-ducing a discharge of pus." In Exodus 9:8, Aaron and Moses took ashes from the furnace and tossed them into the air in the sight of Pharaoh. It became *"small dust in all the land of Egypt, and [was] a boil breaking forth with blains upon man, and upon beast, throughout all the land of Egypt"* (verse 9). Both those plagues and these must be taken literally, as is proven by the fact that the fearful sores of the first vial are still upon the men by the time the fifth vial of darkness is revealed, where we read, *"because of the boils"* (Exodus 9:11). Hopelessness, as well as hideousness, is implied by these unhealed sores. These wounds are to be endured as a foretaste of the anguish of hell.

THE SECOND VIAL—UPON THE SEA

> *And the second angel poured out his vial upon the sea; and it became as the blood of a dead man; and every living soul died in the sea.* (Revelation 16:3)

In this second bowl of wrath, we are given a picture of a mur-dered man weltering in his own blood. The sea, and all that is within it, became *"as the blood of a dead man."* Under the third trumpet, only a third part of the sea became blood (see Revelation 8:8); here, however, the destruction is not partial but complete.

Once the judgments are over, there will be only a few people left to enter the millennium.

Because the sea covers the greater portion of the earth, this plague will be widespread in its death-dealing power. Blood, the vivid and terrible mark of death, was shed most plentifully by the beast. But the blood of the martyrs is now avenged. The beast is beginning to reap what he has sown.

It is blood for blood! Words fail to describe the terrible condition of things as millions of expired sea creatures cover the surface of the oceans. The stench from these horrible, rotting carcasses will be overwhelming. With every living thing in the sea dead, what pollution and disease such a blood-soaked sea will hold!

THE THIRD VIAL—UPON THE RIVERS

And the third angel poured out his vial upon the rivers and fountains of waters; and they became blood. And I heard the angel of the waters say, Thou art righteous, O Lord, which art, and wast, and shalt be, because thou hast judged thus. For they have shed the blood of saints and prophets, and thou hast given them blood to drink; for they are worthy. And I heard another out of the altar say, Even so, Lord God Almighty, true and righteous are thy judgments. (Revelation 16:4–7)

The third angel, presiding over the waters, empties his vial upon *"the rivers and fountains of waters"*—that is, the sources of the sea. All sources of progress and national well-being come under judgment, because commerce and life as a whole are so dependent on rivers, canals, and streams. We reject the wholly symbolic application of *"rivers"* as "the ordinary life of a nation characterized by known and accepted principles of government," and of *"fountains of water"* as "the sources of prosperity and well-being turned to blood—morally poisoned." We hold that the guardian angel controlling the actual waters instantly pollutes them.

Two angels combine in this declaration of God's righteous, reciprocal, and retributive judgments. First, the angel of the waters uses the peculiar idiom for God's eternity—*"which art, and wast, and shalt be."* As the Righteous One, God does not overstep the just measure of strict righteousness in the least degree. Apostates had shed the blood of saints and prophets, and now retributive justice operates as the murderers of God's people are made to drink water as blood. A terrible doom is earned. They are worthy of a fearful death, which comes now as a preview of the second death in the lake of fire.

The second angel is referred to as the angel *"out of the altar."* More correctly, it is the altar itself that speaks; *"another out of"* is omitted in the best manuscripts. We can translate the phrase, *"I heard...the altar* [personified] *say...."* On this altar, the prayers of the saints are presented before God, and beneath it are the souls of the martyrs crying for vengeance on their foes and the foes of God. Thus, the angel and the altar, representing the whole of heaven, concede that God's judgments are just and true. Everyone within the heavenly temple is on God's side, as He acts as the great avenger of His own.

The cries of altars from the time of Abel onward are now forever vindicated. (See Matthew 23:35.)

THE FOURTH VIAL–UPON THE SUN

And the fourth angel poured out his vial upon the sun; and power was given unto him to scorch men with fire. And men were scorched with great heat, and blasphemed the name of God, which hath power over these plagues: and they repented not to give him glory. (Revelation 16:8–9)

Under the fourth trumpet, the sun was darkened by a third (see Revelation 8:12), but here, the sun's scorching power is intensified. *"Power was given unto him"*—that is, unto *it*, the sun—to scorch mankind with great heat. This is to be the release of God's nuclear weapon. We do not interpret the sun symbolically in this passage but as the actual sun, from which is *"nothing hid from the heat thereof"* (Psalm 19:6). Having complete control over His created works, God intensifies the heat of the sun and thereby causes a terrible death roll. Describing the great and terrible day of the Lord, the prophet Joel declared, *"The earth shall quake before them; the heavens shall tremble: the sun and the moon shall be dark, and the stars shall withdraw their shining"* (Joel 2:10).

Under the first trumpet, the trees and grass were burned up, but now, God applies His scorched-earth policy to the bodies of men. Can we imagine the terrible anguish that multitudes will experience as they are scorched with this great heat? The Greek translation has an emphasis that we miss in the King James Version. It literally reads, "The men were scorched with great heat"—that is, the same men who, in verse 2, were described as having the mark of the beast. As with the plagues of Egypt, so here, in these judgment plagues, God's people are immune. As the three Hebrew youths were preserved as they remained in the fiery furnace (see Daniel 3:27), so the remnant will be protected by God.

And as Pharaoh's heart was hardened in spite of the display of God's absolute power over His creation, so here, the extreme physical suffering fails to produce any change of heart: *"They repented not to give him glory."* Instead of being crushed by the judgment of God and crying out for mercy, these men only blasphemed the name of God. Deserved punishment coarsens the lips and hardens the heart; the fires of judgment fail to purify. Because it is the goodness of God that leads to repentance (see Romans 2:4), men who are not won by grace will never be won at all.

We can only speculate about what might have happened if there had been godly repentance on the part of these men with their burning flesh. Would God, with authority over the plagues, have halted the storm of His wrath and, once again, blessed the repentant with His favor? The tragedy will be the absolute lack of man's humility and sorrow over sin. Such a double judgment, as scorching heat and absence of water to drink, will fail to produce any change of heart. Because these people are thoroughly reprobate, God gives them up.

THE FIFTH VIAL—
UPON THE BEAST'S THRONE

> *And the fifth angel poured out his vial upon the seat of the beast; and his kingdom was full of darkness; and they gnawed their tongues for pain, and blasphemed the God of heaven because of their pains and their sores, and repented not of their deeds.* (Revelation 16:10–11)

In this fifth bowl of wrath, judgment is poured out upon the throne of the beast that was given to him by the dragon and set up in arrogant mimicry of God's throne. (See Revelation 13:2.) Satan's masterpiece is now smitten in the center and seat of his power. The beast, as a real person, stands condemned as the tool of Satan. And it is clear that the subjects of this "mock kingdom," as well as the executive of it, feel the stroke of divine vengeance. William Newell suggests that the beast's throne will be the rebuilt Babylon on the Euphrates River—Satan's ancient capital city in the land of Shinar, where wickedness is to be *"set there upon her own base"* (Zechariah 5:11) in the end time.

At last, the impious and insolent challenge *"Who is like unto the beast? who is able to make war with him?"* (Revelation 13:4) is answered forever. Under the beast, Satan builds up a vast empire, but God will not be outdone: He smites the kingdom of the beast with darkness.

Because they loved darkness rather than light, physical darkness as black as that of the Egyptian plague (see Exodus 10:21–23) falls upon the followers of the beast. It is a darkness that causes men to gnaw their tongues in anguish. This horrible darkness suggests the blackness and darkness they are to endure forever. This judgment seems to run concurrently with the effects of previous plagues. Pains and sores out of the first vial are rendered more appalling by the darkness. William Ramsay reminds us that the expression *"gnawed their tongues"* is the only one of its kind in the Bible, and it indicates the most intense and excruciating agony. Such an action suggests rage over the baffling of their hopes and the overthrow of their ruler and kingdom. They meditate revenge but are unable to effect it, hence their fury. Suffering from mental and physical anguish, they bite their lips and tongues.

It is interesting to notice that the part of the body that these rebels sinned with is the very part now afflicted with anguish. They blasphemed the God of heaven, the One controlling light and darkness. Terrible oaths went forth from their lips against the name of God and against God Himself. Now, these blasphemers gnaw their tongues!

Even the accumulation of plagues, rather than a mere succession, fails to produce a change of heart, for, again, we read that they *"repented not of their deeds."* Their will is unbroken. No tears of penitence flow. To those abandoned to their evil deeds, even heavier strokes must descend from God to break their stubborn wills.

It should be pointed out that this vial of darkness must not be confused with the darkening of the heavenly bodies just before Christ's appearing. (See Revelation 19:11–16.) What we see in this fifth vial is one of the signs our Lord gave us in His description of the tribulation period. (See Luke 21:8–38.) For the remnant on earth, there will be plenty of light, just as Israel had light in their dwellings during the Egyptian plagues.

THE SIXTH VIAL—
UPON THE RIVER EUPHRATES

> *And the sixth angel poured out his vial upon the great river Euphrates; and the water thereof was dried up, that the way of the kings of the east might be prepared. And I saw three unclean spirits like frogs come out of the mouth of the dragon, and out of the mouth of the beast, and out of the mouth of the false prophet. For they are the spirits of devils, working miracles, which go forth unto the kings of the earth and of the whole world, to gather them to the battle of that great day of God Almighty. Behold, I come as a thief. Blessed is he that watcheth, and keepeth his garments, lest he walk naked, and they see his shame. And he gathered them together into a place called in the Hebrew tongue Armageddon.*
>
> (Revelation 16:12–16)

Scholars differ over the interpretation of this passage. One commentator suggests that the drying up of the Euphrates is figurative of Babylon itself, which is situated on it. But nothing will suit the context except the literal Euphrates River, whose broad barrier is difficult to cross by individuals or armies. The drying up of this ancient river will allow the Asiatic armies—as described in Revelation 19—to march without hindrance to the Promised Land, of which the Euphrates is the eastern boundary.

The important point to remember is that both the Nile River (see Isaiah 11:15) and the Euphrates River are to be literally dried up. Thus, the western and eastern boundaries of Israel will be open to invaders. With the drying up of the Euphrates, the eastern armies under their respective kings will then achieve their objective.

These kings will march without hindrance to the Promised Land. Is it not dreadful to realize that countless millions of Asians are to cross the dry bed of the Euphrates and join forces with the beast against Israel? Such a united rush of the nations before the great day of wrath is fearful in the extreme. Blindly, they rush toward wholesale slaughter, when blood will come up to the bridles of the horses.

Note the frequent use of *"great"* in this chapter. Through the miraculous ministry of the beast, the multitudes will become accustomed to great things. Sensationalism will be the order of the day. Great events, with their deceptive influences, will be daily occurrences. But God Himself will give the people a few *"great"* things, not for pleasure but for discipline:

- Great voice (Revelation 16:1)
- Great heat (Revelation 16:9)
- Great river (Revelation 16:12)
- Great day (Revelation 16:14)
- Great voice (Revelation 16:17)
- Great earthquake (Revelation 16:18)
- Great city (Revelation 16:19)
- Great Babylon (Revelation 16:19)
- Great hail (Revelation 16:21)
- Great plague (Revelation 16:21)

In Revelation 16:13–16, which some writers treat as a parenthesis, we have the satanic trinity directing the most gigantic combination of opposing forces ever witnessed on earth. Personally superintended by Satan, mighty world powers gather for their doom.

Within this sixth vial of wrath, we have a trinity of evil—the dragon, the beast, and the false prophet—marshaling all the kings of the earth for their battle, not only for Israel but also for the overthrow of God Himself.

> *The kings of the earth set themselves, and the rulers take counsel together, against the LORD, and against his anointed, saying, Let us break their bands asunder, and cast away their cords from us.* (Psalm 2:2–3)

THE THREE FROGS

The evil trinity of the mystery of iniquity is likened to three unclean spirits like frogs. (See Revelation 16:13.) Although three frogs were the original coat of arms of France, a country that has been a center of infidelity, socialism, and spiritualism, we do not believe in the exclusively historical interpretation of this part of Revelation 4 through 22. Because prophecy is frequently progressive or cumulative, there is a modified view of the principle of interpretation which seeks to combine the historical and futurist systems. Thus, there can be partial fulfillments of some sections of Revelation without exhausting their significance. They point onward to complete fulfillment in the future. Interpreters of this double view see in Nazism, Fascism, and Communism the three frogs that John saw.

Here, we have the antitype to the plague of frogs send on Egypt, a miracle that the pharaoh's magicians were able to duplicate. (See Exodus 8:7.) A conspicuous feature of the ministry of the best will be the great signs and wonders performed by satanic means. The dragon, the beast, and the false prophet are appropriately likened to loathsome frogs. As frogs croak by night in marshes and quag-mires, so these unclean spirits in the darkness of error teach lies in the mire of filthy lusts. Alford speaks of "the uncleanliness and the pertinacious noise of the frog." Frogs were regarded by Greek writers and poets as the proper inhabitants of the Stygian lake, or the river of hell. These spirits issue out of the mouths of the unholy three who form hell's trinity—the mouth being the chief seat of influence. From various Scriptures, we gather that the mouth is the *source* and *means* of destruction. (See Isaiah 11:4; Revelation 1:16; 2:16; 9:17; 19:15.) The dragon is to be consumed with the breath of the Lord's mouth. (See 2 Thessalonians 2:8.)

The unclean spirit out of the dragon's mouth symbolizes the proud infidelity opposing the Lord and His Anointed One, Christ. The unclean spirit out of the beast's mouth represents the spirit of the world in the politics of men, whether lawless democracy or despotism, in which man is set above God. The unclean spirit out of the false prophet's mouth depicts the lying spiritualism and reli-gious delusion rampant in the days of satanic deception.

In this satanic trinity, with its miracle-working ministry, we have a combination of direct hellish power, brute apostate force, and terrible malignant influence for the dread purpose of gather-ing the millions of earth for war. The final effort of hell to over-throw heaven is at hand, and it results in Christ taking over the kingship of the world. (See Revelation 19:17–21.) At His return, He will deal effectively with these three unclean spirits, just as He did with those who antagonized Him while He was here on earth.

Because the gathering of world kings with the beast is a signal for Christ's coming to destroy His foes, the saints are exhorted to watch for His return. A word of cheer and of warning is sent to the faithful remnant: *"Behold, I come as a thief. Blessed is he that watcheth, and keepeth his garments, lest he walk naked, and they see his shame"* (Revelation 16:15). Here, we have a parenthesis of great spiritual importance. It must be understood clearly that this is not a message for the church, even though the underlying principle of blessedness being associated with watching—and shame with careless living—is applicable to saints of all times.

"Behold" and the *"blessed"* are definitely related to tribulation saints. Around them will be multitudes asleep and in moral and spiritual darkness. Living in a state of false security, they congratulate themselves on a condition of "peace" and "safety." But suddenly, and unexpectedly, the Lord, as a thief in the night, will surprise and destroy the peoples gathered by satanic agency against the Lord and His anointed. Those who believe that the church is to go through the great tribulation make much of this verse, but Christ is not coming for His church as a "thief." He returns for the church as *"the bridegroom"* (see, for example, Joel 2:16; Matthew 9:15; 25:1, 5), since the church is His bride. With the coming of a thief, there is dread and fear, since he is coming to rob us of our possessions and destroy our goods. (See 1 Thessalonians 5:2, 4; Matthew 24:43; 2 Peter 3:10). *"We are not of the night, nor of darkness"* (1 Thessalonians 5:5); therefore, we have no fear of our Lord's return.

Of course, in connection with our walk, we must endeavor to have garments without stain and a life without shame and moral nakedness. The danger faced by saints who live at the time when the unclean spirits are operating is that of neglecting the advent hope and thereby exposing themselves to the gaze of angels and a godless world, publicly lacking divine direction and protection.

Bishop Lightfoot suggests that there may be an allusion in this exhortation to watchfulness to a Jewish custom in the service of the temple. By Jewish tradition, each night, twenty-four wards, or companies, were appointed to guard the various entrances to the sacred courts. One individual was appointed as captain, or marshal, over the others, and he was called "the man of the mountain of the house of God." His duty was to patrol during the night to see that his subordinates were faithful to their charge. Preceded as he was by men bearing torches, it was expected that each wakeful sentinel should hail his appearance with the password, "Thou man of the mountain of the house, peace be unto thee!" If, through unwatchfulness and slumber, this were neglected, the offender was beaten with the staff of office, his garments were burned, and he was branded with shame.

THE BATTLE OF ARMAGEDDON

How we tremble as we try to visualize what will happen to the nations combined in undying hatred to God and to His Christ as they are gathered by the unclean spirits to the battle of that day of God Almighty! What universal slaughter! History proves that there are times when nations are seized with a passion for war that historians cannot fully explain. It will be this way with the war against God.

How blindly will the hordes of earth be led against the One who created them! (See Psalm 2; Revelation 17:14; 19:19.) The phrase *"he gathered them together"* (Revelation 16:16) can be translated as "they [the unclean spirits of verses 13 and 14] gathered them together." If the *"he"* is retained, it can stand for God, who gives them over to the unclean spirits. No one can read Revelation as a whole without realizing that God is behind the scenes and the actors in the judicial judgment of the book. In righteous retribution, He permits the apostate chiefs of the earth to gather the multitudes together to the mountain of Megiddo.

Because Armageddon will witness the bloodiest battle in history, we should briefly consider the historical and prophetical significance of earth's most terrible battlefield. Armageddon is situated at the foot of Mount Carmel, the scene of much past slaughter. *Armageddon* means "mountain of destruction" or "slaughter" and is well named. The name is from *Har*, meaning "mountain," and *Mageddon*, or *Megiddo*, from a root word meaning "to cut off" or "to slaughter." The limited area of Megiddo would forbid the presence of vast numbers of men, but the name can also stand for the larger vicinity of Israel, where, by satanic agency, the nations of the earth will be crushed.

Megiddo was the scene of the overthrow of the Canaanite kings by God's miraculous interposition under Deborah and Barak. (See Judges 5:19–20.) As an ally of Babylon, Josiah was defeated and slain at Megiddo. (See 2 Chronicles 35:22–25.) The mourning of the Jews at the time just before God shall interfere for them against all the nations ranged against them is compared to the mourning of Josiah at Megiddo. (See Zechariah 12:11.)

But the question can be asked: Why is Armageddon chosen as the gathering place? Well, the nations assemble there to crush and exterminate Israel!

> *They have taken crafty counsel against thy people, and consulted against thy hidden ones. They have said, Come, and let us cut them off from being a nation; that the name of Israel may be no more in remembrance. For they have consulted together with one consent: they are confederate against thee.* (Psalm 83:3–5)

God, however, overrules and intervenes. Though the nations fling themselves with combined might against the Lord and His people, divine fury is unleashed, and destruction overtakes the arrogant hordes. Israel is delivered, and her cruel foes are slain. And in the complete overthrow of the nations, the sovereignty of the earth is decided, as well as Israel's right to her own land.

THE SEVENTH VIAL—INTO THE AIR

And the seventh angel poured out his vial into the air; and there came a great voice out of the temple of heaven, from the throne, saying, It is done. And there were voices, and thunders, and lightnings; and there was a great earthquake, such as was not since men were upon the earth, so mighty an earthquake, and so great. And the great city was divided into three parts, and the cities of the nations fell: and great Babylon came in remembrance before God, to give unto her the cup of the wine of the fierceness of his wrath. And every island fled away, and the mountains were not found. And there fell upon men a great hail out of heaven, every stone about the weight of a talent: and men blasphemed God because of the plague of the hail; for the plague thereof was exceeding great. (Revelation 16:17–21)

All that we have under the previous vial is preparatory to the final outpouring of God's wrath, the great day of wrath of Revelation 19:11–16. Then, and not until then, will the rebels be crushed and removed from the earth. (See Matthew 13:40–43.) In the sixth vial, we have the gathering of the nations of the earth to Israel for actual warfare against God and the remnant of His people. (See Isaiah 11:15–16.) Now comes a destruction exceeding in magnitude anything ever witnessed since man began his sorrowful history outside the garden of Eden.

The seventh angel *"poured out his vial into the air."* Because all men breathe air, which is essential to life, we have divine judgment visiting the life-breath of the people. And, because Satan is spoken of as *"the prince of the power of the air"* (Ephesians 2:2), we also have in this vial the consummation of judgment upon all the pernicious influences of the devil. Thus, Satan's realm suffers under this awful plague. The *"great voice"* is the voice of God, as in Revelation 16:1, except that, here, the temple and the throne unite. In the temple, God *resides*, while on the throne, He *reigns*. The divine voice cries, *"It is done,"* meaning that the whole series of plagues is now complete. It is done! It is come to pass. Compare God's voice in this final consummation with Christ's voice on the cross when the work of expiation was completed: *"It is finished"* (John 19:30).

The Savior's *"It is finished"* was totally rejected, so, here comes the Judge's *"It is done"* of the terrible divine retribution.

The end of God's wrath has come. Later will come the fearful exhibition of the Lamb's wrath. Under this seventh vial, God is giving to Babylon *"the cup of the wine of the fierceness of his wrath."* This phrase suggests boiling rage and settled anger, both of which are referred to in Jeremiah 30:23–24. Here, the fact of Babylon's overthrow is stated. In Revelation 17 and 18, we will read a detached account of the brief resume given under this vial. God is the Creator; He produces convulsions of nature such as threw the earth into chaos before the creation of man.

THREE TOKENS OF WRATH

In the *"voices, and thunders, and lightnings"*—always expressive of almighty power in judgment—we have a formula of divine visitation calculated to strike terror in the hearts of men. These signs and tokens of retributive anger are visited upon the earth in the form of the greatest earthquake the earth has ever experienced. Until this moment, the severity of all earthquakes in history will fade into insignificance alongside this unparalleled upheaval. (See Hebrews 12:25–26.)

THREE PARTS OF THE CITY

So destructive is this vast earthquake that Jerusalem is *"divided into three parts."* Rome and all the great cities of the earth are reduced to ruins. All the sovereignty over the kings of the earth that Rome and Babylon represented is forever destroyed. *"Great*

Babylon" is singled out as being ripe for "*a great earthquake*," for "*the plague thereof was exceeding great*." The place and its pride are doomed to eternal destruction (see Jeremiah 51:62–64), which doom is celebrated in heaven in Revelation 19:1–4.

Adding to the terror of the hour is the banishment of islands and mountains. Under the sixth seal, these "*were moved out of their places*" (Revelation 6:14). Here, they "*fled away, and...were not found*." What a massive catastrophe!

The crowning act of judgment is the descent of enormous hailstones over the earth. Hail, as we have shown, is a symbol of divine wrath. (See, for example, Isaiah 28:2; Ezekiel 38:22.) No one can fully imagine what the sudden, disastrous effects of this last hailstorm will be like. The crushing, overwhelming nature of this judgment becomes clear when we remember that the hailstones are each "*about the weight of a talent*." A talent is somewhere between 100 and 180 pounds. Thus, the severity of judgment reserved against the day of battle and war in Jehovah's "*great hail out of heaven*" is frightful in the extreme. (See Job 38:22–23; Psalm 105:32.)

But these judgments call forth blasphemy instead of repentance! Hardening of conscience is the effect of sin. The tragedy is that man does not become broken and repentant but remains unchanged. With the display of God's judgmental power, men should turn and glorify Him, but instead they perish, cursing God. What a different effect the display of God's power has upon His own people: they give glory to the God of heaven. (See Revelation 11:13.)

15

THE SEVEN DOOMS

REVELATION 17:1–20:15

In the highly dramatic chapters we are now to consider, Christ as the Conqueror moves swiftly in the subjugation of all His foes. What fast-moving action we have in this section! How majestic is the scene of our omnipotent Lord taking to Himself His power and reigning supreme! Once He rises to deal with all antagonistic forces, none will be able to withstand His might. With a rod of iron He will break the strongest enemy. Proud, arrogant rulers, both hellish and human, are to be dashed in pieces as a potter's vessel. Whether systems, cities, or citizens, everything and everyone contrary to His will and rule is to fall before His withering look and judgments. Although He is the gentle Lamb, Christ now reveals His lionlike power.

> Tyrant thrones and idol shrines,
> Let them from their place be hurled;
> Enter on Thy better reign,
> Wear the crown of this poor world![11]

What a memorable occasion that was when Jesus went into the synagogue at Nazareth, took the Old Testament scroll from the minister, and read from Isaiah the passage He related to His own ministry:

---

11. John Page Hopps, "Father, Let Thy Kingdom Come," 1911.

*The Spirit of the Lord is upon me, because he hath anointed me...
to preach the acceptable year of the Lord.* (Luke 4:18–19)

Then, He closed the book without finishing the quotation from Isaiah, namely, *"...and the day of vengeance of our God"* (Isaiah 61:2).

"The acceptable year" covers our Lord coming as the Savior, as well as the dispensation of grace during the church age—Revelation 1–3. *"The day of vengeance of our God"* belongs to what follows the day of salvation, the day of judgment during the great tribulation—Revelation 4–20. With flaming fire, the righteous God takes vengeance on the ungodly. (See 2 Thessalonians 1:8.) This is a reason why *love* is mentioned in this judgment section of Revelation. Because the love of the Lamb is rejected, the day of His wrath comes upon all who love and make a lie.

Zephaniah was one of the prophets who, by the Spirit, testified beforehand of events far removed from his own time. Describing *"the great day of the LORD"* (Zephaniah 1:14), Zephaniah said that it would be...

- *a day of trouble and distress* (verse 15),
- *a day of wasteness and desolation* (verse 15),
- *a day of darkness and gloominess* (verse 15),
- *a day of clouds and thick darkness* (verse 15),
- *a day of the trumpet and alarm* (verse 16)...
- *the day of the LORD's wrath* (verse 18)

1. THE DOOM OF BABYLON

An introductory word on the close relationship between chapters 17 and 18 is necessary, since both chapters deal with Babylon, albeit from different angles. Brief notices of Babylon's destruction are given in Revelation 14:8 and Revelation 16:19, but chapters

17 through 19 fill in all the details of God's judgment on a guilty religious system. It is essential to take all these passages together and read them as one.

In Revelation 17, we have...

+ *mystical* Babylon,
+ a corrupt system,
+ an apostate Christendom,
+ the whore and the beast,
+ religious pretension, and
+ the delight of the kings of the earth over the drunken harlot, "Mystery Babylon."

In Revelation 18, we have...

+ *material* Babylon,
+ a doomed city,
+ godless commercialism,
+ God and Babylon,
+ worldly pride, and
+ the rulers and merchants of the earth wailing and lamenting over the destruction of commercial Babylon.

It is fitting that one of the seven angels responsible for pouring out the seven bowls of wrath should explain to John the judgment already pronounced upon Babylon. Two significant phrases seem to divide this seventeenth chapter:

+ *"I will show unto thee the judgment"* (Revelation 17:1).
+ *"I will tell thee the mystery"* (Revelation 17:7).

The twofold development of the chapter is clearly evident:

+ The great whore dominates the beast. (See Revelation 17:1–7.)
+ The beast destroys the great whore. (See Revelation 17:8–18.)

THE GREAT WHORE DOMINATES THE BEAST

And there came one of the seven angels which had the seven vials, and talked with me, saying unto me, Come hither; I will show unto thee the judgment of the great whore that sitteth upon many waters: with whom the kings of the earth have committed fornication, and the inhabitants of the earth have been made drunk with the wine of her fornication. So he carried me away in the spirit into the wilderness: and I saw a woman sit upon a scarlet colored beast, full of names of blasphemy, having seven heads and ten horns. And the woman was arrayed in purple and scarlet color, and decked with gold and precious stones and pearls, having a golden cup in her hand full of abominations and filthiness of her fornication: and upon her forehead was a name written, MYSTERY, BABYLON THE GREAT, THE MOTHER OF HARLOTS AND ABOMINATIONS OF THE EARTH. And I saw the woman drunken with the blood of the saints, and with the blood of the martyrs of Jesus: and when I saw her, I wondered with great admiration. And the angel said unto me, Wherefore didst thou marvel? I will tell thee the mystery of the woman, and of the beast that carrieth her, which hath the seven heads and ten horns.

(Revelation 17:1–7)

In Scripture, a woman and a city are both used as symbols of the church. (See 2 Corinthians 11:2; Revelation 21:2, 9–10.) Both figures are also used in this description of apostate Christendom. By Revelation 7:18, the woman is identified as the city: "*And the woman which thou sawest is that great city, which reigneth over the kings of the earth.*" The scarlet woman, one of the profound marvels of Scripture, is Satan's masterpiece of counterfeiting. What a travesty the mother of harlots is of the true church!

+ The true church is a chaste virgin; the apostate church is a whore.

+ The true church is espoused to one husband; the apostate church engages in promiscuous intercourse with the kings of the earth.

+ The true church is the mystery of godliness; the apostate church is the "*MYSTERY, BABYLON.*"

+ The true church is the "*pillar and ground of the truth*" (1 Timothy 3:15); the apostate church is called Babylon, "*the city of confusion*" (Isaiah 24:10).

+ The true church offers the cup of salvation; the apostate church holds the golden cup full of abominations.

+ The true church is purchased by the blood of Christ; the apostate church is drunk with the blood of martyrs.

The woman is pictured as sitting—she "*sitteth upon many waters*" (Revelation 17:1), as well as on "*seven mountains*" (verse 9). Sitting "*upon many waters*" receives the following exposition by John in Revelation 7:15: "*And he saith unto me, The waters which thou sawest, where the whore sitteth, are peoples, and multitudes, and nations, and tongues.*"

The "*many waters*" typify the vast multitudes of the human race over whom the woman has cast her spell. Ancient Babylon got its wealth by means of the Euphrates River and its numerous canals for irrigation. The apostate church fattens on the nations she governs.

"*O thou that dwellest upon many waters*" (Jeremiah 51:13) indicates that the great whore rules and dominates the nations religiously, just as the beast upon which she rides rules politically. Representing a vast religious system, the woman has a following that is universal in scope. The great whore and the beast are companions in wickedness and apostasy. Combined, they represent ecclesiastical and governmental power.

Sitting *"upon the beast"* (Revelation 17:3) means that the harlot sits astride the beast. She not only exercises religious dominion over the multitudes, but she also is able to manage and guide the beast. All vassal kings and human rulers, especially within the revived Roman Empire, are under her sway. Civil and political powers are subservient to her rule and supremacy. And such thorough and complete subjugation over the vast imperial and apostate power headed up in the beast is already in the making.

Two contrasting ideas are represented by the woman and the beast. We can express them this way:

+ The woman personifies corruption of truth; the beast personifies open defiance of God.

+ The woman embodies all that is licentious; the beast embodies all that is cruel and ruthless.

Thus, corruption and violence, which brought about the flood (see Genesis 6:11), are to reach their climax in the woman and the beast. This position astride the beast is a prophecy that the apostate church will be carried and supported by the nations and will rule and reign with temporal power.

The seven mountains on which the woman sits (see Revelation 17:9) depict seven kings, or successive forms of political government. Of seven Roman emperors, five "fell" (by natural death or by violent means) before John's day. The five are usually listed as Julius Caesar, Tiberius, Caligula, Claudius, and Nero. The sixth, who resigned as John wrote Revelation, was the blasphemous Domitian, who was assassinated. The other emperor, who had not yet come in John's day, might have been the seventh head. And it is the woman who dominates this last sovereign expression of every anti-Christian movement and sect then in existence, consolidated and controlled by Satan. The following contrasts might prove helpful.

The True Church:	The Mother of Harlots:
Chaste, virgin	Great whore
Subject to Christ	Subject to none
Out of heaven	Out of the earth
God-adorned	Satanically adorned
Preserved by Christ	Destroyed by the beast
Eternal glory ahead	Eternal ruin
True bride	Counterfeit church
Has a heavenly calling	Covets earthly possessions
Christ's masterpiece	Satan's masterpiece
Indwelt by the Holy Spirit	Possessed by evil spirit
Mystery hidden from ages	Mystery of iniquity
Caught up into the air	Cast down to perdition
Exercises spiritual power	Seeks secular power
Exhibits the glory of Christ	Glories in sensuous things

The beast is to be the head of a federated empire. Executive power, commencing with Nimrod, will conclude with the beast, both of whom stand related to Babylon. God is to permit executive power in the prophetic earth, the nations clustered around the Mediterranean Sea with allies from the empire of the caesars. These will form the federation of the beast. All of these nations are earthly-minded. The beast's dominion is both *external* (extending to all nations) and *internal* (conforming to the world).

The historic Babylonian system of paganism was a double mixture of the union of religious and civil government and of outward forms and meanings. Secret initiation rites were used, and worshippers were consecrated by rituals of cleansing, even when they were guilty of practicing evil. The *"woman,"* the mystery of iniquity, is the symbol of a pagan religion with a priestcraft dominant over all civil power. Her machinations are secret and internal, while those of the beast are manifest to all. In the conflict for supreme authority and control, the beast is victorious.

The removal of the harlot will mean the lifting of spiritual, mental, political, and financial burdens from the nations. Although they are to rejoice over her destruction, yet they commit fornication with her and give her reverence.

The word *"mystery"* implies a spiritual fact hitherto hidden and incapable of discovery by mere reason, but now revealed. The union between Christ and His church is a mystery. In contrast to the mystery of godliness will be the mystery of iniquity. This part of the mystic name stamped indelibly upon the woman's forehead fittingly describes the terrible system she represents—a travesty of the true church. Christ's place of supremacy over the nations is usurped. Instead of being the depository of all that is true and holy, the woman is shown as the embodiment of error and iniquity.

"BABYLON THE GREAT" is called great because of its terrible reputation and its embodiment of widespread confusion. This description of the woman suggests a widespread system of spiritual evil, representing the culmination of all evils operating against the true church while it was on the earth.

The "Babylonianism" of Revelation 17 is the ecclesiastical system of the apostate church. It is the state religion of the beast. Such a system is called "BABYLON THE GREAT" to distinguish it from the Babylon of Nebuchadnezzar, known as "Great Babylon." The word *Babylon* means "confusion" and is associated with Babel and its unfinished tower. As used of the woman, the name Babylon represents apostate Christendom from the divine standpoint.

From God's view, such Babylonianism is the mystery of abomination. Professing Christianity minus a regenerate membership, and wholly without God, is to expand into the full outline of the scarlet-clad Babylonian woman. It is a religious Babylonianism that the rulers of earth will find to be a heavy burden and that will ultimately cause these leaders to join the beast in an attempt to free themselves from a system that has enslaved them.

What is the meaning of "THE MOTHER OF HARLOTS AND ABOMINATIONS OF THE EARTH"? In ancient Rome, harlots wore a label on their brow bearing their name. Forehead names are worth tracing and contrasting. In Revelation 19:16, Christ has a name on His garments and thigh. The redeemed have the name of God in their foreheads. The harlot's name on her forehead is another example of Satan's mimicry. All the names borne by the woman are in sharp contrast to the miter of the high priest, with its wording: "Holiness unto the Lord." The offspring of this mother of harlots will be numerous. Apostate Christendom will be the parent of all kinds of religions, idolatries, and arts used by Satan to turn men from God. Under the figure of the mother of harlots, we have religion at its worst and the source of all that is morally loathsome.

Apostate Christendom will be an abomination on the earth and in the eyes of the Lord because of the amalgamation it will offer. The parable of the woman mixing leaven until all the meal was penetrated aptly describes the poison of an evil system about to permeate the religious world. (See Matthew 13:33.) *Babylon*, as we have already seen, means "confusion" or "mixture." *Babel*, meaning "the gate to God," was the rendezvous for lawless sinners. God intervened, however, with the mixture or confusion of languages, and scattered the people abroad. (See Genesis 11:5–8.) Abraham was called out from such an apostate civilization to begin a new race. Thus, ancient Babylon, chief of idolatrous cities, is a fitting emblem of the monstrous guilt and extensive influence of latter-day apostate Christendom. But the destruction of this evil system will come when the beast challenges the woman's claim of supreme authority and control.

Two phrases describe the abominable nature of the great whore: *"the wine of her fornication"* (Revelation 17:2) and the *"filthiness of her fornication"* (verse 4). Fornication is illicit intercourse, and spiritual fornication is tantamount to idolatry. *"With their idols have they committed adultery"* (Ezekiel 23:37). The solemn indictment against the inhabitants of the earth is that they have allowed themselves to succumb to the seductive glitter and gaudy display of the harlot. Kings and people are depicted as being ensnared by the corrupt and licentious charms of the scarlet-clad woman, but all who drink of her cup, even though it is golden, must perish with her.

John portrays the woman as sitting upon a scarlet-colored beast with a golden cup in her hand, full of abominations and filthiness of her fornication. (See Revelation 17:4.) It was the same with Babylon of old. While still in all its glory, it had its doom proclaimed by Jeremiah: *"Babylon hath been a golden cup in the LORD's hand, that made all the earth drunken: the nations have drunken of her wine; therefore the nations are mad"* (Jeremiah 51:7).

As the scarlet beast is full of names of blasphemy (see Revelation 17:3), so the golden cup is *"full of abominations and filthiness of her fornication"* (verse 4). The twin coils of idolatry and corruption are to characterize the last phrase of apostate religion, and the worldwide influence of this monstrous harlot can be gathered from the fact that she makes others drunk with the wine of her fornication.

It is said of the scarlet-colored beast that he was *"full of names of blasphemy, having seven heads and ten horns"* (Revelation 17:3). Here we have the final king, the federated head of nations, a king of kings and lord of lords. Being "*full of names of blasphemy*" implies that the beast's entire domain is wholly corrupt, characterized by open, blatant blasphemy. (See Revelation 13:1–10.) In the various names, we have the varied form of rebellion and self-will. Thus, both the beast and his empire are blasphemous and impious.

"*Full of names*" can also mean all over—not only on their heads, but on every part of their bodies. In the "*seven heads*," we have completeness of administrative power, covered by successive forms or systems of government. (See Revelation 13:1.) The "*ten horns*" represent royal personages who reign in royal authority with the beast. This scarlet-colored beast is identified with the fourth beast of Daniel's vision. (See Daniel 7:23–24.)

In order to see the woman astride the beast, John tells us that the angel carried him away into the wilderness—that is, into a place of loneliness and utter desolation. What did John mean by the wilderness? One explanation is that the splendor of the woman and the beast captivates the heart and intoxicates the senses of all people, except for the faithful remnant, to whom this gaudy show is as a wilderness, for God is not in it.

THE BEAST DESTROYS THE GREAT WHORE

And the angel said unto me, Wherefore didst thou marvel? I will tell thee the mystery of the woman, and of the beast that carrieth her, which hath the seven heads and ten horns. The beast that thou sawest was, and is not; and shall ascend out of the bottomless pit, and go into perdition: and they that dwell on the earth shall wonder, whose names were not written in the book of life from the foundation of the world, when they behold the beast that was, and is not, and yet is. And here is the mind which hath wisdom. The seven heads are seven mountains, on which the woman sitteth. And there are seven kings: five are fallen, and one is, and the other is not yet come; and when he cometh, he must continue a short space. And the beast that was, and is not, even he is the eighth, and is of the seven, and goeth into perdition. And the ten horns which thou sawest are ten kings, which have received no kingdom as yet; but receive power as kings one hour with the beast. These have one mind, and shall give their power and strength unto the beast. These shall make war with the Lamb, and the Lamb shall overcome them: for he is Lord of lords, and King of kings: and they that are with him are called, and chosen, and faithful. (Revelation 17:7–14)

Here, the *"I will show unto thee"* of Revelation 17:1 changes to *"I will tell thee."* John is given the divine interpretation of the mystery of the woman and of the beast carrying her. The apostle had wondered with the amazement of a horrible surprise; now, the earth is to wonder at and admire God's outpoured judgment upon the woman and the beast. A double mystery is revealed:

+ The mystery of the beast (Revelation 17:7–14)
+ The mystery of the whore (verses 15–18)

The woman and the beast are treated separately, since they are distinct—even though they are companions in wickedness and apostasy. The woman depicts ecclesiastical power, and the beast personifies civil power. The four phases of the beast's history are explained to John. In four brief, crisp words and phrases from Revelation 17:8, John learns of the course and consummation of the greatest empire of the world:

+ *"...was..."*
+ *"...is not..."*
+ *"...out of the bottomless pit..."*
+ *"...go into perdition..."*

"The beast which thou sawest was..." signifies the *past.* Here, we have the ancient Roman Empire as it existed in imperial form up

to John's day and until its destruction in A.D. 476. Under a long succession of imperial rulers, the beast existed as one vast, consolidated empire. Even though the beast is an actual person, he is also used as a figurehead of an apostate system, just as the woman is. Thus, the beast—and the empire he personifies—is an integral part of biblical prophecy.

"*The beast that thou sawest...is not*" signifies the *present*. Even though the countries incorporated within the past empire of worldwide fame still remain, the consolidated empire, as such, is nonexistent. Fragments of the old Roman life and law characterize many of the nations that were once part of this mighty empire.

"*The beast which thou sawest...shall ascend out of the bottomless pit, and go into perdition*" signifies the *future*. In lifting the veil, God enables John to look down the corridor of centuries and behold the satanic revival of the Roman Empire. Out of heaven comes the bride of the Lamb, but out of the abyss comes the empire of the beast.

In this marvelous survey of the beast's future, we are given a glimpse into the final phase of apostate Gentile civil power. The hour of vengeance is at hand. The beast and his Babylon are about to be destroyed. Emphasis is given to their everlasting doom in the repeated phrase "*into perdition*" (Revelation 17:8, 11). In verse 11, the "*he*" is emphatic in the Greek. Peculiarly and preeminently, "*he*" is marked out for destruction. This "*little horn*" (Daniel 8:9), with eyes like a man and a mouth speaking great things, is to be cast alive into the lake of fire—alive and with his companions in crime. (See Revelation 19:20.) "*Perdition*" is used of another individual in Scripture: Judas. (See John 17:12.) This leads some writers to affirm that the beast is a reincarnation of Judas. The empire itself is destroyed by Christ at His coming, when He will lay hold of the kings of the world and fashion them into His world empire.

Twice we are told of a guilty, deluded world, wondering over the appearance of the beast. (See Revelation 13:3; 17:8.) But such a

The Seven Dooms 271

marvelous phenomenon does not amaze the elect, who understand the exact character of the beast. It is only those *"whose names were not written in the book of life from the foundation of the world"* who behold and wonder at Satan's handiwork. The elect have the mind of wisdom and therefore understand the prophetic significance of what is written.

Among the prominent features of the beast are its political history and war with the Lamb. We have already written of the seven heads. The ten horns, we are told, represent the ten kings, or their kingdoms. The seven heads express successive forms of government, whereas the ten kings are contemporaneous, being viewed as covering actual territory at the time of the beast. The ten kings coexist with the beast and indicate the appearance of his empire in a ten-kingdom form.

The respective heads of these kingdoms receive power as kings, which means that they reserve their kingly rights. They have the title of kings, but they do not have undivided kingly power. Bowing implicitly to the will of the beast, these ten kings give their power and strength to the beast. With one sentiment, they carry out his will and become his dependent allies.

These ten kings reign *"one hour with the beast."* The duration of the kings is measured by the reign of the beast. *"One hour"* indicates a definite time of short duration. The beast, though setting himself up as a king of kings, is quickly deposed by the true King at His coming. The victory of the Lamb over the beast and his coalition of kings is swift and complete.

In Revelation 17:14, the full and final victory of Christ—fully described in Revelation 19:19–21—is anticipated by the angel. This war and wrath of the Lamb is specific: against the antichrist and his kings, who have gathered for the double purpose of cutting off Israel from being a nation (see Psalm 83:4) and making war against the Lamb as an expression of their hatred for Him.

Note that the Lamb is seen as the Lord of Lords and King of Kings. The word for *"Lamb"* is the diminutive *arnion*, meaning "the little lamb." In contrast to the arrogance and wickedness of the beast, we have the meekness and innocence of the Lamb. But, as the all-powerful Lamb, He overcomes the beast. The titles used of our Lord combine His meekness and might, His tenderness and power.

The entire book of Revelation revolves around Christ as the Lamb:

+ Chapter 1: The vision of the Lamb

+ Chapters 2–3:The message of the Lamb

+ Chapters 4–5: The adoration of the Lamb

+ Chapters 6–19: The wrath of the Lamb

+ Chapter 19, verses 7–10: The marriage of the Lamb

+ Chapter 19, verses 11–22: The reign of the Lamb.

"Lamb" occurs twenty-seven times in Revelation and provides an extremely profitable study.

+ The slain Lamb (Revelation 5:6; 7:14)

+ The worshipped Lamb (Revelation 5:8; 21:22)

+ The worthy Lamb (Revelation 5:12)

+ The eternal Lamb (Revelation 5:13–14)

+ The revealing Lamb (Revelation 6:1)

+ The wrathful Lamb (Revelation 6:16–17; 14:10)

+ The reigning Lamb (Revelation 7:10)

+ The sustaining Lamb (Revelation 7:17)

+ The recording Lamb (Revelation 13:8; 21:27)

+ The coming Lamb (Revelation 14:1)

+ The attractive Lamb (Revelation 14:4)

+ The conquering Lamb (Revelation 12:11; 14:10; 17:14)

+ The married Lamb (Revelation 19:7–9; 21:9)

+ The illuminating Lamb (Revelation 21:23–25)

+ The refreshing Lamb (Revelation 22:1)

+ The adored Lamb (Revelation 22:3–4)

How true is the hymn that reads "The Lamb is all the glory in Immanuel's land"![12]

This seventeenth chapter of Revelation is one of *wonder*, and another outline can be worked out with the references to this word.

+ The wonder of heaven (Revelation 12:1)

+ The wonder of Satan's personality (Revelation 12:3; 13:3)

+ The wonder of the beast's power (Revelation 13:13)

+ The wonder of the harlot church (Revelation 17:6)

+ The wonder of a godless world (Revelation 17:8)

The three features of those who share in the victory of the Lamb apply to His saints, *"they that are with him"* (Revelation 17:14). As the beast marshals all his hosts, so Christ has His militant hosts to assist Him. The heavenly armies, consisting of the entire body of redeemed saints, accompany Christ as He descends to the earth. What a scene! The beast and his armies are on one side, and the Lamb and His armies on the other side, and, of the outcome, there is no doubt. Christ will be exalted among the nations. He will be exalted in the earth.

> *And he saith unto me, The waters which thou sawest, where the whore sitteth, are peoples, and multitudes, and nations, and tongues. And the ten horns which thou sawest upon the beast, these shall hate the whore, and shall make her desolate and naked, and shall eat her flesh, and burn her with fire. For*

12. Anne R. Cousin, "The Sands of Time Are Sinking," 1857.

> *God hath put in their hearts to fulfill his will, and to agree,*
> *and give their kingdom unto the beast, until the words of God*
> *shall be fulfilled. And the woman which thou sawest is that*
> *great city, which reigneth over the kings of the earth.*
>
> (Revelation 17:15–18)

The waters that John saw are explained as representing *"peoples, and multitudes, and nations, and tongues."* Here, we have the immense moral influence of apostate Christendom over vast masses of mankind.

"These shall hate the whore" (Revelation 17:16.) What abject desolation awaits the apostate church! Determined to rid himself and his empire of the subtle and impoverishing influences of the harlot, the beast now turns and removes the harlot from her exalted seat. The rulers of the federated empire strip the harlot of all her seductive, gaudy ornaments. The combined nations, with their masterful head, combine in hatred of the whore. The downfall of the great whore comes because of a sudden change in the enslaved peoples. Not only is there loathing for the harlot and plunder of all her wealth and finery, but her flesh is eaten. *"Flesh"* is plural and signifies masses of flesh—earthly possessions, the fullness of carnality. But the beast and the ten kings, once the harlot's admirers and slaves, are now her bitter foes, and they gorge themselves on the gathered possessions of the harlot.

Then, the harlot is burned with fire. In this step of graduated punishment, there may be a reference to the legal punishment of abominable fornication. In ancient times, harlots sometimes were burned. God's permissive will comes into focus in the perfect agreement between the ten kings and the beast. At the back of the alliance of nations and their union with the beast—and the final overthrow of the harlot—is the will of God. He has decreed the destruction of Gentile dominion and apostate Christendom, and God will triumph. God can even use evil men to accomplish His purposes. (See, for example, Genesis 50:20.) The wrath of man can be made to praise Him.

Walter Scott wrote:

God works unseen, but not the less truly, in all the political changes of the day. The astute statesman, the clever diplomatist, is simply an agent in the Lord's hands. He knows it not. Self-will and motives of policy may influence to action, but God is steadily working toward an end—to exhibit the heavenly and earthly glories of His Son. Thus, instead of kings and statesmen thwarting God's purpose, they unconsciously forward it. God is not indifferent, but is behind the scenes of human action. The doings of the future ten kings in relation to Babylon and the Beast—the ecclesiastical and secular powers—are not only under the direct control of God, but all is done in fulfillment of His words.

At a critical time like this, we must keep our eyes open for evidences of God's overruling hand among the nations.

Next, we turn to the doom of material Babylon. History, both biblical and secular, provides us with an adequate description of the ancient City of Babylon, which reached its greatest glory and magnificence during the reign of Nebuchadnezzar (604–562 B.C.). With its high walls, towers, avenues, gardens, and palaces, Babylon of old must have had a fascination that was compelling and unsurpassed. That its fortunes have been both wonderful and woeful is a fact emphasized by prophets and historians alike. At present, there is no Babylon, leading some expositors to affirm that all Old Testament prophecies of its destruction have been fulfilled and that, therefore, it cannot be rebuilt. Today, the territory covered by the biblical Babylon is a region in Iraq known as Hillah.

Babylon, where Alexander the Great drank himself to death, was the third world kingdom to oppress Israel in the times of

Gentile supremacy. Derived from *Bab-el*, meaning "the gate of God," it also became *Babel*, meaning "confusion." Thus, the gate of God became the gathering place for lawless sinners, and, to check spreading apostasy, God intervened with the confusion of tongues.

The history and prophecy of Babylon can be summarized briefly.

1. Nimrod was its founder. (See Genesis 10:8–11.) Its first queen—and symbol of a wicked system and a city—was Semiramis I (811–824 B.C.). Being the first of all idolatrous cities, Babylon is the most suitable emblem to declare the enormous guilt and the extensive and withering influences of apostate Christendom.

2. As a kingdom, Babylon was an inferior one when, under Assyria, it helped her against Israel and Judah. (See 2 Kings 17:24–31; 2 Chronicles 33:11.)

3. It is prophesied as being Judah's captor. (See 2 Kings 20; Jeremiah 25:9–14.)

4. It was chosen by God to chasten Judah. (See 1 Chronicles 9; Jeremiah 25:9.)

5. It was to be severely punished for its sins. (See Jeremiah 25:9–14; Daniel 5.)

6. It was the oppressor of Israel under *"the head of gold"* (Daniel 2:38) and *"a lion...[with] eagle's wings"* (Daniel 7:4).

7. It will be prominent again as a symbol under the antichrist. (See Revelation 17:5, 18.)

After the destruction of Nineveh, the great metropolis of the world was Babylon, which, according to the great historian Herodotus, had one hundred gates of solid brass, with walls thirty-five feet high, and was so thick that six chariots could race abreast on top of them. Prophets foretold Babylon's destruction.

(See Isaiah 13:1–22; Jeremiah 50:9–46.) Alexander the Great tried to restore Babylon, but God had declared, *"I will sweep it with the besom of destruction"* (Isaiah 14:23), and it has remained a ruin ever since.

The Babylon of the book of Revelation occupies the same relation to the Babylon of the Old Testament prophets as does the New Jerusalem to the Jerusalem of the prophets. In Revelation, both cities are used in a *mystical* sense; in the case of the prophets, the cities are to be understood in their *literal* meaning. Because we have no record of a Christian church amid the ruins of that ancient city, the Babylon from which Peter sent his first epistle must have been Rome. (See 1 Peter 5:13.)

The revival of Babylon as an actual city is a disputed question. There are many biblical scholars who affirm that all references in Revelation to Babylon are strictly symbolical. According to *The Scofield Reference Bible*, the notion that a literal Babylon is to be rebuilt on the site of ancient Babylon is in conflict with Isaiah 13:17–22:

> Verses 17–22 have a near and far view. They predict the destruction of the literal Babylon then existing; with the further statement that, once destroyed, Babylon should never be rebuilt. (See Jeremiah 51:61–62.) All this has been literally fulfilled.

Without doubt, the antichrist is before us as the "king of Babylon," which a restored Israel is to triumph over.

Returning to the prophecies, we likewise discover Jeremiah presenting the double prophecy of Babylon. We have the overthrow of the city by the Medes and Persians, and then, there is the prophecy of a future enemy. (See Jeremiah 50:1–7.) The reference here to the regathering of Israel and Judah is definitely intended for the future. In Jeremiah 50:8–16, the plagues are similar to those of

Revelation 18. The past and future of Babylon are before us again in Jeremiah 50:21–46. In Jeremiah 51:5–10, we have language nearly identical to that used in Revelation 14:16; 16:17–21; and 18:1–24.

Ancient Babylon, with all its mysticism and paganism, will be destroyed suddenly with the seventh vial. (See Revelation 14:8; 18:1–24; Isaiah 21:9.)

Zechariah is another Old Testament prophet who predicted the return of Babylonianism. The figurative significance of the language used in Zechariah 5:5–11 can be expressed in this way:

1. The *"ephah,"* a three-peck measure, speaks of commerce going forth throughout the earth.

2. The *"talent of lead,"* a 158-pound weight, symbolizes the heaviness of the traffic and the richness of the business.

3. The *"woman"* is interpreted as the wickedness in the measure. The Hebrew word *rasha* indicates the restless, fallen nature of man as manifested in all lawlessness and unrestraint. (See Job 3:17; Isaiah 57:21.)

4. The *"wings of a stork"*—considered an unclean bird—and the *"wind...in their wings"* represent the speedy accomplishment of material Babylon as the great business hub of the world.

In Revelation 18:1–3, John is given a complete and detailed revelation of the destruction of an actual city. Old Testament prophecies of Babylon provide a mixture of past and future destinies, but John presents a wholly prophetic declaration of doom. The phrase *"And after these things"* (Revelation 18:1) implies a fresh beginning and introduces us to a distinctive revelation. Chapter 17 gives us the description of the power and perdition of mystical Babylon. Chapter 18 records the continuation of the seventh vial (see Revelation 16:17–21), which is interrupted by the parenthetical chapter on mystical Babylon. The opening phrase, therefore, serves to emphasize the distinctive unity of the themes revealed. Thus, while the subject of Babylon is carried over from Revelation 17, chapter 18 offers a distinct and subsequent revelation. After the perdition of mystical Babylon comes the destruction of commercial or material Babylon.

> *And after these things I saw another angel come down from heaven, having great power; and the earth was lightened with his glory. And he cried mightily with a strong voice, saying, Babylon the great is fallen, is fallen, and is become the habitation of devils, and the hold of every foul spirit, and a cage of every unclean and hateful bird. For all nations have drunk of the wine of the wrath of her fornication, and the kings of the earth have committed fornication with her, and the merchants of the earth are waxed rich through the abundance of her delicacies. And I heard another voice from heaven, saying, Come out of her, my people, that ye be not partakers of her sins, and that ye receive not of her plagues. For her sins have reached unto heaven, and God hath remembered her iniquities. Reward her even as she rewarded you, and double unto her double according to her works: in the cup which she hath filled fill to her double. How much she hath glorified herself, and lived deliciously, so much torment and sorrow give her: for she saith in her heart, I sit a queen, and am no widow, and shall see no sorrow. Therefore shall her plagues come in one day, death, and mourning, and famine; and she shall be utterly burned with fire: for strong is the Lord God who judgeth her.*
>
> (Revelation 18:1–8)

Evidently, the authoritative angel announcing Babylon's doom is not John's guide from Revelation 17. (See verses 1, 7, 15.) Various features of this important angelic announcer should be noted. First, he descends *"down from heaven,"* suggesting the heavenly character of Babylon's judgment and the interest that heaven shows in the affairs of the earth. Whoever the human agents may be in the overthrow of Babylon, it is heaven that ultimately judges her.

The *"great power"* of the angel of doom suggests that there are orders and degrees among the angelic hosts. Some angels are more distinguished than others, and some receive authority to act for God in unusual circumstances. That the angel here is no ordinary being is clearly evident from the fact that *"the earth was lightened with his glory."* So recently has this angel come from the presence of God that, in passing, he flings a broad belt of light across the dark earth. But is there the thought here of inherent glory, as well as that of gathered glory? Walter Scott suggests that this angel may be none other than Christ Himself, as in Revelation 8:3 and 10:1. Combining these passages, we have...

+ Christ, the Angel-Priest, on behalf of His suffering remnant (see Revelation 8:3.);

+ Christ, the Angel-Redeemer, taking possession of His inheritance (see Revelation 10:1);

+ and Christ, the Angel-Avenger of His people, taking vengeance on Babylon (see Revelation 18:1–19:5).

Because angels *"excel in strength"* (Psalm 103:20), the strong cry of this angel announcing the judgment of Babylon is not prospective but retrospective. From His point of view, the mighty iniquitous system is already destroyed. (See Revelation 18:2.) The repetition is like the solemn dirge of the damned: *"...is fallen, is fallen."*

+ A degenerate state becomes beast-like.

+ An apostate church becomes harlot-like.

+ An apostate Christendom, incapable of change, must be destroyed.

In Revelation 17, a corrupt religious system is stripped of possessions and wealth, which, in turn, are transferred to the treasuries of empire rulers. But apostate civil authorities triumphing over the great whore face more terrible days than they imposed upon the woman, through yielding themselves and their kingdoms to the bestial and brutal will of the antichrist.

The language used in this opening section of Revelation 18 provides us with the reason for Babylon's doom. The illicit intercourse with nations and kings under the guise of religion in Revelation 17 passes into illicit intercourse in the realm of commerce in chapter 18. It is almost beyond belief that we can conceive of a city becoming a habitation of demons, whose proper home is in the abyss of the underground world. Babylon is also the center of unparalleled wickedness and degradation, as well as being the capital of demonism. By unclean spirits—and unclean and hated birds—we can understand the varied agents of Satan of a highly pernicious nature, all helping to turn Babylon into a sink of iniquity and an abomination in the sight of a holy God.

Also included within this grave indictment against Babylon is judgment upon those nations—covering a wide geographical area—who fell easy prey to the seductive charms of a godless metropolis. *"The kings of the earth"* are not to be confused with the personal heads of the ten kingdoms. Offering a tempting bait to all those willing to associate with Babylon for mere worldly gain, the merchants of the earth traffic with its luxury, the abundance of which was taken from the great whore by civil and apostate powers coveting it. But such advancement of temporal interests is short-lived, for these very merchants weep and wail over the vanishing of their source of enrichment.

Of all plagues smiting the earth, those of Babylon are to be the worst, because, in their intensity, they are to overtake the city *"in one day."* The plagues of Egypt came by installments, but here, death, mourning, famine, and fire are permitted by the strong Judge to come together, and suddenly.

The heavenly voice calling God's people to come out of the city is different from that of the angelic voice of Revelation 18:1. Possibly, it is God Himself inviting His own people to leave the sins and plagues of Babylon. (See Jeremiah 50:4–9; 51:5–8, 45.) Such a call for separation is applicable at all times wherever the Babylonian spirit and principle are found. (See 2 Corinthians 6:17.) *"Be not partakers of her sins"* means "Have no fellowship with Babylon, and you will not receive its plagues." This earnest call also suggests that God has His own people, even in an apostate city, but that their only safety is in separation from it.

By *"her sins,"* we are to understand the utter and terrible corruption of the morals of Babylon, a condition requiring God's stern judgment: *"For her sins have reached unto heaven."* The first Babel confederacy was one *without* God; piled stones tried to reach heaven. (See Genesis 11:4.) But here, piled sins *are* able to reach heaven. What a monument of shame! Here, we have a Babel tower not of *stones* but of *sins*—sins so bold and impious that they call for heaven's stern and unsparing judgment.

The executioners of God's wrath were commanded to mete out a full compensation to Babylon: *"double unto her double."* The cup of destruction is to be filled *"double."* The cup of luxury and prominence must give way to the cup of torment and humiliation; death must take the place of life; mourning must dethrone exaltation; famine must substitute delicacies; fire must consume all of Babylon's boasted works. *"Double unto her double"* speaks of a full acquittal, a double recompense according to Levitical law. Vengeance here goes beyond "eye for an eye." In God's retributive justice, measure is doubled. But such terrible judgment will not be mere spiteful vindictiveness. Like all divine judgments, this one will be deserved and just.

A unique description of the confident boast of security is before us in the words *"she hath glorified herself, and lived deliciously."* Presumption is added to Babylon's many crimes. The city is judged not only for *conduct* but also for *character*. Haughtiness within is indicated by a boastful, queenly state. But whatever hope was entertained of retrieving former grandeur, Babylon's doom is sealed: *"she shall be utterly burned with fire."* The mighty God is to be Babylon's Judge. The doom of Babylon is certain because of the justice and power of God.

And the kings of the earth, who have committed fornication and lived deliciously with her, shall bewail her, and lament for her, when they shall see the smoke of her burning, standing afar off for the fear of her torment, saying, Alas, alas that great city Babylon, that mighty city! for in one hour is thy judgment come. And the merchants of the earth shall weep and mourn over her; for no man buyeth their merchandise any more: the merchandise of gold, and silver, and precious stones, and of pearls, and fine linen, and purple, and silk, and scarlet, and all thyine wood, and all manner vessels of ivory, and all manner vessels of most precious wood, and of brass, and iron, and marble, and cinnamon, and odors, and ointments, and frankincense, and wine, and oil, and fine flour, and wheat, and beasts, and sheep, and horses, and chariots, and slaves, and souls of men. And the fruits that thy soul lusted after are departed from thee, and all things which were dainty and goodly are departed from thee, and thou shalt find them no more at all. The merchants of these things, which were made rich by her, shall stand afar off for the fear of her torment, weeping and wailing, and saying, Alas, alas, that great city, that was clothed in fine linen, and purple, and scarlet, and decked with gold, and precious stones, and pearls! For in one hour so great riches is come to nought. And every shipmaster, and all the company in ships, and sailors, and as many as trade by sea, stood afar off, and cried when they saw the smoke of her burning, saying, What city is like unto this great city! And they cast dust on their heads, and cried, weeping and wailing, saying, Alas, alas, that great city, wherein were made rich all that had ships in the sea by reason of her costliness! for in one hour is she made desolate. (Revelation 18:9–19)

One cannot read this passage without realizing the luxurious centralization of the great city of Babylon. The wealth of nations increases, and universal influence is exercised from such a capital. Potentates, merchant princes, and all who go down to the sea in ships share in Babylon's prosperity. All alike are caught by surprise in the holocaust of destruction. Let us separate the three classes affected by Babylon's ruin.

Kings lead in the general mourning, since they profited most by Babylon's worldwide commercial influence. And by these *"kings of the earth,"* we can understand chiefs and rulers generally—not only the ten kings associated with the beast in Revelation 17. All rulers associated with the licentiousness and luxury of material Babylon up to the hour of its overthrow are found wailing over its burning. Under the impact of the great earthquake (see Revelation 16:17–21), these corrupt rulers will flee from the doomed city in a frenzied state, crying, *"Alas, alas that great city Babylon, that mighty city! for in one hour is thy judgment come."* Thus, God's judgments inspire fear, even in the most worldly.

Because commerce plays a large part in the greatness of the city, the merchants are also among the chief mourners. The varied items of merchandise in these verses indicate what a great commercial metropolis Babylon had become in the approximately three years since the harlot has been abolished. In the days of the antichrist, markets will be controlled from this great trading post of the nations. At this crossroads of the world, all business is to be centralized. The wording here suggests luxury in the extreme. Everything a person could possibly lust after is provided in this universal emporium. Expensive jewelry, costly furniture, unusual perfumes, delicious banquets, crowded markets, rich fabrics—all are here. Buying and selling, unbridled passion and pleasure, and musical resorts will reproduce the days of Noah and Lot.

Altogether, some twenty-nine items are singled out, proving that a great world market will be seriously affected by the ruin of Babylon. The sevenfold classification of all the articles traded in this world's storehouse can be categorized this way:

1. Valuables: *"gold, silver, precious ornaments stones, and pearls."*

2. Costly array: *"fine linen, and purple, and silk, and scarlet."*

3. Sumptuous furniture: *"vessels of ivory, and all manner vessels of most precious wood, and of brass, and iron, and marble."*

4. Rich odors: *"cinnamon, and odors, and ointments, and frankincense."*

5. Abundant living: *"wine, and oil, and fine flour, and wheat."*

6. Livestock and triumphant pageants: *"beasts, and sheep, and horses, and chariots."*

7. Infamous traffic: *"slaves, and souls of men."*

Slave merchants are sometimes called "body merchants," and Babylon has its human slave market. Besides slaves for mere labor, women sell their bodies, and men their souls, to satisfy lusts. Undoubtedly, there will be slaves, dazzled by the splendor and seductive influence of Babylon. Yet, in one hour, such great riches will be destroyed. No wonder the millionaire merchants of the earth, whose affluence came from silver, stones, sheep, slaves, and souls, will weep and wail over the destruction of all the sources of their wealth. Merchandise will be completely ruined. Everything catering to pride and prosperity will perish in the unexpected and sudden blow from the divine hand.

As a world center of finance and commerce, Babylon will engage in an extensive sea trade. Ships loaded with all kinds of merchandise will travel to and from its ports. The pathetic cries of shipmasters and sailors are occasioned by the fact that the desolation of Babylon means the end of all seagoing traffic and, consequently, the end of their livelihood. (See Revelation 18:17–19.) No wonder all who were made rich by ships in the sea weep and wail and cast dust on their heads! Their testimony is, *"What city is like unto this great city!"* To all the seafarers, nothing is equal to Babylon. It is the epitome of great worldly prestige and power. By policies, diplomacy, and unholy ends, its worldwide influence has been gained. By sword and money, its domain has been spread far and wide. But all such unholy greatness is swiftly banished by Him who is able to cast the mighty from their seats of power.

Gathering together the lamentations of the monarchs, merchants, mariners, and musicians, we have an insight into the terror of Babylon's judgment.

The double *"alas"* of the monarchs ends with *"in one hour is thy judgment come"* (Revelation 18:10). Here we have the swiftness of divine action. The stroke of vengeance from the hand of God is sudden and unexpected.

The double *"alas"* of the merchants gives their viewpoint of Babylon's ruin: *"In one hour so great riches is come to nought"* (Revelation 18:17), indicating the complete banishment of prideful material prosperity.

The double *"alas"* of the mariners gives us another phase of the anguish experienced over the city's downfall: *"In one hour is she made desolate"* (Revelation 18:19). Loaded with riches one moment, in the next she is stripped bare of all her costliness.

Rejoice over her, thou heaven, and ye holy apostles and prophets; for God hath avenged you on her. And a mighty angel took up a stone like a great millstone, and cast it into the sea, saying, Thus with violence shall that great city Babylon be thrown down, and shall be found no more at all. And the voice of harpers, and musicians, and of pipers, and trumpeters, shall be heard no more at all in thee; and no craftsman, of whatsoever craft he be, shall be found any more in thee; and the sound of a millstone shall be heard no more at all in thee; and the light of a candle shall shine no more at all in thee; and the voice of the bridegroom and of the bride shall be heard no more at all in thee: for thy merchants were the great men of the earth; for by thy sorceries were all nations deceived. And in her was found the blood of prophets, and of saints, and of all that were slain upon the earth.   (Revelation 18:20–24)

In the utter doom of the Babylon of Revelation 18, the violence of destruction caused by the mighty angel is expressed by the words *"Thus with violence shall that great city Babylon be thrown down, and shall be found no more at all"* (Revelation 18:21), a phrase occurring six times in Revelation. The obliteration of the city fulfills all prophetic statements as to its destruction. Two chapters, Jeremiah 51 and Revelation 18, should be studied and compared carefully. By fire and earthquake, the city will be destroyed from center to circumference, and that without warning.

By a direct visitation of God, Babylon's destruction is complete. The world's best singers and players are silent, for nothing but cries of anguish are heard. Craftsmen who prostituted their art to further the sensuous worship of apostate Christendom cannot repair the damage. All illumination will fail, for not even the light of a candle can be found.

In this remarkable section of Revelation, we have a striking illustration of Scripture interpreting Scripture. We read of a mighty angel taking up a stone like a great millstone and casting it into the sea crying.

In Jeremiah, we have the prophet instructed by God to bind a stone to the book and cast it into the midst of the Euphrates River, and to then say, "*Thus shall Babylon sink, and shall not rise from the evil that I will bring upon her*" (Jeremiah 51:64). Turning to Daniel's prophecy of the final world empire, we find him predicting the time when a "*stone…cut out of the mountain without hands*" (Daniel 2:45) will completely destroy the image representing the great Gentile age.

"*The sea*" is a symbol of the restless, turbulent Gentile nations, and "*that great city Babylon*" is the final expression of Gentile monarchy and dominion. Thus, it is not difficult to see in Christ the "*stone*," made out of the mountain of God, destroying a godless civilization.

By comparing Scripture with Scripture, we can summarize the various causes of Babylon's absolute ruin:

1. Pride of heart and position (Isaiah 13:19; 14:4; Jeremiah 50:29–34; Revelation 18:7–8)

2. Oppression and suppression of Israel (Isaiah 14:2–22; Jeremiah 51:24–25)

3. Worldly lusts and luxuries (Isaiah 47:8–11; Revelation 14:8; 18:3–9)

4. Sorceries and demonism (Isaiah 47:12–13; Revelation 18:2, 23)

5. Idolatry (Jeremiah 50:2; 51:47; Revelation 18:6–24)

6. Persecution of the saints (Revelation 18:6–24)

Babylon is distinguished in Scripture as being subject to the Lord's vengeance, since she is prominent as the enemy and enslaver of His people. The martyrdom of the righteous, commencing with the death of Abel and gaining intensity throughout the ages, reaches its final concentration of martyrdoms in the reign of terror in Revelation 17–18. But the destruction of both Babylons avenges the blood of the saints and culminates the wrath of God.

The divine command to destroy Babylon is followed by a divine call to the saints to delight over her total destruction. (See Revelation 18:20–19:6.) *"Rejoice over her"* is used in the opposite sense to the rejoicing company of Revelation 11:10, where we had the joy of the godless over the death of the two witnesses. At last, God has approved the case of heaven. Rejoicing over such terrible ruin may not appear to be very heavenly, but the execution of righteous justice always elicits the approval of God's own people. Heaven rejoices over just vengeance upon the great whore and the beast. It is here that we can understand many of the imprecatory psalms, full of the sighs of the righteous for judgment to overtake the wicked.

> *And after these things I heard a great voice of much people in heaven, saying, Alleluia; Salvation, and glory, and honor, and power, unto the Lord our God: for true and righteous are his judgments: for he hath judged the great whore, which did corrupt the earth with her fornication, and hath avenged the blood of his servants at her hand. And again they said, Alleluia. And her smoke rose up for ever and ever. And the four and twenty elders and the four beasts fell down and worshipped God that sat on the throne, saying, Amen; Alleluia. And a voice came out of the throne, saying, Praise our God, all ye his servants, and ye that fear him, both small and great. And I heard as it were the voice of a great multitude, and as the voice of many waters, and as the voice of mighty thunderings, saying, Alleluia: for the Lord God omnipotent reigneth.*   (Revelation 19:1–6)

In Revelation 18:24, we have *"the blood of prophets, and of saints, and of all that were slain upon the earth."* When it falls, all of the persecuted are avenged. This "Hallelujah Chorus" between

290 Revelation: Drama of the Ages

the second and third dooms is an extension of Revelation 18:20. What the notables of earth mourn over, heaven rejoices over. It is significant that the first *"Alleluia"* (Revelation 19:1) in the New Testament is raised over the judgment of the great harlot. The four alleluias uttered by the great multitude, the four beasts, and the twenty-four elders constitute a cry of victory in which praise is ascribed to God. At last, the eternal desolation of Babylon, as prophesied in the Old Testament, is an accomplished fact. (See Isaiah 13:1–22; Jeremiah 50:13, 23, 29–40; 51:26, 37, 62.)

The eternal, ascending smoke testifies to the doom of Babylon as being an everlasting witness to the righteous judgment of God poured out upon all fornication and upon the martyrdom of His people. The Greek word translated as *"rose up"* in reference to the ascending smoke of verse 3 means "kept going up" and is somewhat different from the ascending incense of Revelation 8:4. Some writers affirm that this may be one passage indicating that the eternal lake of fire will be visible to earth-dwellers in the new earth after the millennium.

The opening phrase of Revelation 19, *"And after these things,"* describes a turn of events and is the climax of the previous chapters. Vengeance is, at last, enacted. The doom of Babylon indicated in Revelation 14:8 is now fully accomplished.

Briefly reviewing this "Alleluia" section that celebrates the utter and eternal ruin of Babylon, we note that the same destruction is viewed differently in heaven and on earth. On earth, a dirge of sorrow is heard, but in heaven, a paean of praise arises. That beautiful word *"Alleluia,"* meaning "Praise Jehovah," rolls through the vault of heaven. Note the three divine possessions:

+ Salvation—divine deliverance from judgment

+ Glory—divine moral glory in judgment

♦ Honor—divine might displayed in judgment

The grounds of the triumph of the redeemed and heavenly hosts is that of divine truth and righteousness: *"true and righteous are his judgments."* A fundamental principle is that all of God's dealings with His creatures, whether in grace or in judgment, are essential attributes that are conspicuously displayed in these judgment chapters.

The second *"Alleluia"* is related to the finality and perpetuity of a divinely executed judgment. Two further exclamations of this word swell the volume of praise. God is the Judge of Babylon, as Christ is the Judge of the beast. At last, an angelic voice summons all the servants of God to join in antiphonal praise to God, and their united voices are like the roar of a mighty waterfall. From God's throne, the very center and source of judicial action, the call goes forth to praise Him, *"for the Lord God omnipotent reigneth."*

Let us now look at this title given to God, *"the Lord God."* He is the Lord of creation, of compassion, and of completion. Some versions read *"The Lord our God."* When the apostle John wrote these words, there were hundreds of false gods in Rome, but this is "our God." This is the final song in the Bible, and it is fitting that it should be a song of the total triumph of God over all His enemies. It corresponds to the first song in the Bible, especially at Exodus 15:11: *"Who is like unto thee, O Lord...?"* There is a challenge in these songs. In Psalms, unbelief asks, *"Where is thy God?"* (Psalm 42:3, 10). This is the question many people are asking today. But in that day, the tables will be turned when all people finally recognize that God is upon His everlasting throne.

Our God is all-powerful; He has no limitations. This is one of His supreme attributes. The devil cannot claim this, nor can any dictator, nor will the antichrist. Omnipotence belongs to God alone. In Ephesians 1:19–20, the apostle Paul wrote of *"the exceeding greatness of his power...which he wrought in Christ, when he raised him from the dead."* Paul then proceeded to exalt Christ *"far above all principality"* (verse 21).

God's love is both omnipotent and everlasting. (See Jeremiah 31:3.) His purpose is also omnipotent; it cannot be thwarted, no matter how the nations of men or the invisible forces of evil may seek to foil it. God's will is also omnipotent. God's will is the mightiest thing in the universe. After Nebuchadnezzar had been in the fields with oxen for seven years, he declared, "[God] *doeth according to his will in the army of heaven, and among the inhabitants of the earth: and none can stay his hand, or say unto him, What doest thou?"* (Daniel 4:35). In these days of tragic suffering upon the earth, we can only exclaim, *"Alleluia: for the Lord God omnipotent reigneth."*

Our God also has kingship over the universe. Not merely does He live, but He *lives and reigns.* When this supreme fact grips us, nothing else matters. Our God's throne is intact. Amid all that is bringing desolation and death on this earth, let us keep the eye of faith on that throne, which can never be shaken.

Revelation 19 is an interlude in which John turns aside to describe all he heard and saw as to the reaction of heaven to the manifestation of divine vengeance. In some respects, it is one of the most impressive chapters in the entire book of Revelation, since it begins with an opened heaven as Christ descends as the Warrior-Judge to commence His task of final judgment. At Christ's baptism, there was an opened heaven (see Matthew 3:16), and Ezekiel commenced his ministry in a similar manner. (See Ezekiel 1:1.)

Three sections of this parenthesis are clearly marked:

1. The four exclamations of *"Alleluia"* (Revelation 19:1–6)

2. The marriage supper of the Lamb (Revelation 19:7–10)

3. The return of the Redeemer in glory (Revelation 19:11–21)

As to the four instances of *"Alleluia,"* it is interesting to note that this is the only place in the King James Version where this word is actually used. The repeated Old Testament phrase "Praise ye the Lord" is from the Hebrew word allelujah, a term much loved by ancient Jews. The first *"Alleluia,"* or "Praise ye the Lord," is uttered over God's punishment of the wicked, and the four alleluias are the response of the host of heaven and the godly saints of earth to the divine destruction of Babylon.

The first two are an extension of the previous section, in which heaven rejoices over the doom of Babylon, and these alleluias come from a mighty host in heaven who praises God for His true and righteous judgments. The third *"Alleluia"* is echoed by the twenty-four elders and the four living creatures, who add a loud *"Amen"* to their tribute of praise. (See Revelation 19:4.) The fourth comes from the multitudes of earth, and from creation as they bless God for his omnipotence.

"The marriage supper of the Lamb" (Revelation 19:9) is a precious revelation to the hearts of all God's people. What a moment this will be when the *"church of the firstborn"* (Hebrews 12:23) is forever united to Him who bought her with His own blood! This is to be the marriage supper of the Lamb. Our presence there will be due to all of His grace, and only those washed through the blood of the Lamb will be present at this nuptial celebration.

This supper will be one of delight, but *"the supper of the great God"* (Revelation 19:17) will be one of *destruction*. At this supper, the fowls of the air will eat the flesh of kings, while, at the marriage supper of the Lamb, the saints will feast with Christ as the King of Kings. Our beautiful wedding garments represent the righteousness that the Lamb imputes and imparts to all His saints.

As to the "return of the Redeemer in glory," there is no doubt as to the identity of the Rider of the white horse. His names correspond to all that He is in Himself, as well as to the nature of His judgments. He is called…

+ *"Faithful and True"* (Revelation 19:11),
+ *"The Word of God"* (Revelation 19:13),
+ *"King of Kings"* (Revelation 19:16), and
+ *"Lord of Lords."* (Revelation 19:16).

The diadems encircling His brow are royal ones and are therefore different in character from the mock ones on the head of the beast. As for the striking phrase *"a vesture dipped in blood"* (Revelation 19:13), we understand this to refer to the blood of Christ's enemies, who are not sprinkled with the blood of Calvary. One of Christ's names, *"The Word of God,"* offers one of the strongest arguments for His incarnation. (See John 1:1, 14; 1 John 1:1–3.) Jesus Himself is the final and perfect revelation of God. (See Hebrews 1:1–4.)

2. THE DOOM OF KINGS AND ARMIES

And I saw an angel standing in the sun; and he cried with a loud voice, saying to all the fowls that fly in the midst of heaven, Come and gather yourselves together unto the supper of the great God; that ye may eat the flesh of kings, and the flesh of captains, and the flesh of mighty men, and the flesh of horses, and of them that sit on them, and the flesh of all men, both free and bond, both small and great. And I saw the beast, and the kings of the earth, and their armies, gathered together to make war against him that sat on the horse, and against his army. And the beast was taken, and with him the false prophet that wrought miracles before him, with which he deceived them that had received the mark of the beast, and them that worshipped his image. These both were cast alive into a lake of fire burning with brimstone. And the remnant were slain with the sword of him that sat upon the horse, which sword proceeded out of his mouth: and all the fowls were filled with their flesh. (Revelation 19:17–21)

The promise and prophecy given to Christ by His Father was that, when He came to reign, He would dash His enemies to pieces. (See Psalm 2:9.) Here, in the battle of Armageddon, with its terrible carnage, is the fulfillment of that fearful prophecy concerning the catastrophe overtaking Gentile world powers. Before us is the terrible day of the Lord predicted by the prophets. (See Joel 2:11; Micah 1:6.)

In the gathering for *"the supper of the great God,"* John gives us a bold and powerful picture of the battlefield after the victory of Christ: a sacrificial feast spread on God's table for all the vultures of the sky. In this grim conflict, there are some interesting contrasts to observe.

Fowls eat up the flesh of the mighty men of earth. Opposing the armies of the beast and the kings of the earth are the armies of the Rider on His white horse, and there is never any doubt about the outcome. (See Revelation 19:14, 19.) Even the escaping few are captured by the sword of the One sitting on His horse. In connection with Satan's effort to destroy the Jewish remnant, God graciously protected *"the remnant of her seed"* (Revelation 12:17), but these people fleeing from the armies of kings cannot escape the vengeance of the King of Kings.

3. THE DOOM OF THE BEAST

At last, this desolator (see Daniel 9:27) and *"abomination of desolation"* (Matthew 24:15) and *"man of sin"* (2 Thessalonians 2:3) reaps the harvest of his diabolical hatred of God and his saints. As earth's last and most terrible tyrant, he suffers a well-deserved punishment. We read that *"the beast was taken"* (Revelation 19:20), and this particular Greek word for *"taken"* is different from other Greek terms. It means "to take hold of forcefully," "to apprehend"—as a policeman lays hold of a criminal and compels him to go to jail. Who is it that seizes the beast, along with his companion in crime, the false prophet? None other than the strong Son of God, with eyes as a flame of fire, flashing with righteous anger!

> *These both were cast alive into a lake of fire burning with brimstone.*   (Revelation 19:20)

They were not allowed to die, nor were they slain—as their dupes were—but they were *"cast alive"* into everlasting punishment. The three Hebrew youths in the book of Daniel also were cast alive into the fiery furnace, but God withheld the action of the fire and graciously preserved the courageous young men. But the beast and the false prophet are cast alive into a fire from which there is no deliverance.

As for *"a lake of fire,"* we do not claim to know all that is implied by such eternal suffering. Granted that the language may be symbolical, the reality must be far more terrible than the terms used. Jesus was a "hellfire" Preacher. To Him, eternal punishment was a terrible reality, and He had no pleasure in the eternal misery of sinners. He died upon the cross that men *"should not perish, but have everlasting life"* (John 3:16). It is our urgent task to warn the lost to flee from the wrath to come.

4. THE DOOM OF THE FALSE PROPHET

> *And the devil that deceived them was cast into the lake of fire and brimstone, where the beast and the false prophet are, and shall be tormented day and night for ever and ever.*
>   (Revelation 20:10)

Once united in their defiance of God, these two powerful and noxious beings are now united in their doom. Although the false prophet will have been the murderer of multitudes who would not worship the image of the beast, he himself will not be permitted to die. Even his professed miraculous power cannot now save him from being *"cast alive into a lake of fire."* No doubt, the everlasting punishment of the false prophet will be all the worse because of his religious pretensions. The doom of the beast and the false prophet represents the end of a false statecraft and a false priest-craft. Both these personages suffer together because they fought together against the Lamb.

5. THE DOOM OF THE DEVIL

And I saw an angel come down from heaven, having the key of the bottomless pit and a great chain in his hand. And he laid hold on the dragon, that old serpent, which is the Devil, and Satan, and bound him a thousand years, and cast him into the bottomless pit, and shut him up, and set a seal upon him, that he should deceive the nations no more, till the thousand years should be fulfilled: and after that he must be loosed a little season. (Revelation 20:1–3)

At long last, the head of the serpent is forever bruised. (See Genesis 3:15.) The victory secured over the devil at Calvary is now completely operative. Cast out of heaven in ancient times because of his rebellion, and then cast out of the air to the earth (see Revelation 12:9), the devil is now cast into the bottomless pit for a thousand years. His liberty to walk about devouring souls (see 1 Peter 5:8) is now abolished as an angel from heaven binds Satan, confining him in the abyss, and seals his prison for a thousand years. John wrote that the dragon is imprisoned so that *"he should deceive the nations no more, till the thousand years should be fulfilled."*

Satan's thousand years in the abyss will produce no change in his evil character. Once released, he will prove himself to be the same old devil. But while he is confined, the earth will breathe a purer air, and Christ's millennial reign will cause peace and righteousness to cover the earth as the waters cover the sea. Six times, the phrase *"thousand years"* is mentioned, and this period is the glorious kingdom age predicted by the prophets, as well as by Christ and His apostles.

After his final, postmillennial work of deception, the devil is forced to join his deluded devotees, who had already endured the flames for a thousand years. With them, he *"shall be tormented day and night for ever and ever"* (Revelation 20:10). At last, the "trinity of evil" imitating the Trinity of heaven reap their unrelieved doom. The devil, along with the beast and the false prophet, are, together, forever in the lake of fire. No wonder the devil strives to keep people from reading this final book of the Bible! It is heavy with his deserved doom, and he does not want those he deceives to know of his terrible future.

6. THE DOOM OF GOG AND MAGOG

And when the thousand years are expired, Satan shall be loosed out of his prison, and shall go out to deceive the nations which are in the four quarters of the earth, Gog and Magog, to gather them together to battle: the number of whom is as the sand of the sea. And they went up on the breadth of the earth, and compassed the camp of the saints about, and the beloved city: and fire came down from God out of heaven, and devoured them. (Revelation 20:7–9)

The mention of Gog, the prince, and Magog, the land, takes us back to Ezekiel 38, where Gog represented all the nations forming the great northern confederacy. In Revelation, we have come to the final revolt of the nations and to their destruction. Some people ask why the Lord would release Satan from the bottomless pit after Christ's prosperous thousand-year reign. Why set Satan free, even for a little while, to head up a massive revolt? The only answer is that the Lord wants to prove the utter depravity of man.

One would think that, after a thousand years of Christ's blessed and beneficial reign, no one on earth would want to revolt. But, even as Adam sinned in the most perfect environment of the garden of Eden, so large numbers of these millennial dwellers will rebel against Christ, in spite of the peace and provision accompanying His reign. Of course, He rules them with a rod of iron, and they *must* bow before Him. But their instant response to Satan's call reveals that their obedience to Christ is only feigned; they recognize His power only because they have to.

Judgment, however, is as swift as the rebellion of the nations of the four corners of the earth; fire comes down from God out of heaven and devours the multitudes. *Fire*, as we know, is related to all of God's judgments—even the judgment of the saints at the judgment seat of Christ, where our works are to be tried by fire. (See 1 Corinthians 3:13.) In this final conflict, there is no battle, no fighting. The almighty God, who is Himself *"a consuming fire"* (Hebrews 12:29), immediately destroys all the deceived and brutalized nations. Man's last attack against God, and against *"the camp of the saints about, and the beloved city,"* ends in complete failure, as hell enlarges its mouth to receive the hordes of earth whom the devil had deceived and led in rebellion. No wonder we go on to read of a new earth—one forever without a devil!

7. THE DOOM OF THE LOST

Law courts have witnessed some tense and terrible scenes, but the most famous and fearful of these pale into insignificance alongside the staggering scene of the final judgment we are now to consider. Before we study what is involved in this somber scene, let us familiarize ourselves with the language used in the narrative.

> *And the devil that deceived them was cast into the lake of fire and brimstone, where the beast and the false prophet are, and shall be tormented day and night for ever and ever. And I saw a great white throne, and him that sat on it, from whose face the earth and the heaven fled away; and there was found no place for them. And I saw the dead, small and great, stand before God; and the books were opened: and another book was opened, which is the book of life: and the dead were judged out of those things which were written in the books, according to their works. And the sea gave up the dead which were in it; and death and hell delivered up the dead which were in them: and they were judged every man according to their works. And death and hell were cast into the lake of fire. This is the second death. And whosoever was not found written in the book of life was cast into the lake of fire.*
>
> (Revelation 20:10–15)

This judgment, which occurs after the millennium and the final disposition of Satan and the present heavens and earth, will be the most solemn and awful ever witnessed. The eternal Judge is to settle all accounts. Having dealt with Satan, the god of the world, Christ now prepares to deal with the sinners of the world. At last, the end of the world is reached, for creation flees from the face of the One sitting upon the throne. There are those who refer to this as a general judgment, but Revelation knows no "general" judgment. Any judgment in this book is particular and specific. All men of all ages of earth's history, whether good or bad, are not to gather at this great scene. It is only for *"the dead,"* just as the judgment seat of Christ is only for believers.

John's vision is in two parts, indicated by the repeated phrase "*I saw*":

- The Judge: "*And I saw a great white throne, and him that sat on it*" (Revelation 20:11).
- The judged: "*And I saw the dead, small and great, stand before God*" (verse 12).

THE JUDGMENT THRONE

Revelation is a book of thrones and judgments. In Revelation 19:11–21, we have Christ's judgment against living persons. Here, in Revelation 20:10–15, it is the judgment of the dead. Matthew 25:31 speaks of "*the throne of his glory*," which is related to Christ's judgment of the living nations. But among the thrones of Scripture, the one identified as "*a great white throne*" is the most dreadful of all.

What kind of throne is this one set up not on earth or in the heavens? It is not the throne of a Sovereign about to reign and rule but is that of a Judge about to pronounce doom upon the guilty. It is a throne set up for a specific purpose; it is not a permanent throne, for it ceases to be as soon as its judgments have been meted out to the condemned. At this throne, the position in Pilate's day will be reversed. Then, the Creator was judged by the creature, but now, the creature appears before the Creator for the pronouncement of his sentence. In Pilate's hall, God stood speechless before man, but here, man is speechless before God. He who stood condemned before the earthly tribunal will now decide the destinies of the human race and will reveal the principles of divine government.

Having rejected the great salvation offered by Christ, sinners are now made to stand before God's great white throne. It will be great for several reasons:

- Because of the dignity of the Judge Himself

+ Because of the greatness and unparalleled solemnity of the occasion

+ Because of the vastness of the scene

+ Because of the eternal consequences involved

+ Because of the great destinies it will decide

The *white* throne corresponds to the character of its Occupant: "*He hath prepared his throne for judgment. And he shall judge the world in righteousness, he shall minister judgment to the people in uprightness*" (Psalm 9:7–8). The Infinite One, before whom the finite must stand, is holy and righteous in "*the day of wrath and revelation of the righteous judgment of God*" (Romans 2:5). There will be no unfair, unjust treatment, such as He Himself received at Pilate's hands. Being white, the throne symbolizes the purity and righteousness of the judgments of the Judge. It is white because of its immaculate purity. Here we have the undimmed blaze of divine holiness, purity, and justice. How terrible it will be for sinners to face the unapproachable light of the Lord's presence!

THE JUDGE

The Judge is the Lord God, even the Savior, who Himself declared that His Father had "*given him authority to execute judgment*" (John 5:27). Since salvation was planned by God, achieved by Christ, and applied by the Holy Spirit, it may be that all three Persons of the Godhead will be at the judgment of those who despise such a salvation. Christ, however, is left to pronounce the solemn judgment of the lost. (See John 5:22; Acts 10:42; 17:31; 2 Timothy 4:1.)

With eyes as a flame of fire, Christ will search for and scorch those before Him. (See Revelation 1:14; 19:12.) Everyone and everything will wither up as those eyes gleam with righteous judgment. On that day, they will not sparkle with mercy, for, with majesty unlimited, the Owner of those piercing eyes has earned the right to dispose of the destiny of His willful creatures. Because the Judge is "the righteous One," His judgment will correspond to His nature. *"Shall not the Judge of all the earth do right?"* (Genesis 18:25). Of course He will, as He always does. *"In righteousness he doth judge"* (Revelation 19:11); *"true and righteous are thy judgments"* (Revelation 16:7).

Mention of the *"face"* (Revelation 20:11) of the Judge is noteworthy. In Revelation 12:13–16, Israel was forced to flee *"from the face of the serpent"* (verse 14), but, here, *"earth and the heaven"* (Revelation 20:11) flee from the face of the Savior, who is now the Judge. Once that face was spat upon, buffeted, and marred beyond human recognition, but now it is adorned with fearful majesty. And in this countenance, sinners will read their doom.

How different will be the church's sight of that face! *"They shall see his face; and his name shall be in their foreheads"* (Revelation 22:4). And Christ's saints are to be honored by participation in this judgment. *"To execute upon them the judgment written: this honor have all his saints"* (Psalm 149:9).

THE JUDGMENT

The courts of democratic countries attempt to offer criminals a fair trial. This court in heaven, however, is not set up to discuss the pros and cons of any sinner's case but to carry out a sentence already declared. Unsaved people, here and now, are condemned already. (See John 3:18.) In that future day, the dead will be raised and made to stand before the Judge, not to be judged as to their guilt or innocence but to receive the ratification of a condemnation already pronounced.

> He that believeth on him is not condemned: but he that believeth not is condemned already, because he hath not believed in the name of the only begotten Son of God.
>
> (John 3:18)

He that believeth on the Son hath everlasting life: and he that believeth not the Son shall not see life; but the wrath of God abideth on him. (John 3:36)

This judgment is called *"eternal"* (Hebrews 6:2) because its consequences are eternal. It also acts as a guarantee that sin will never be allowed to invade God's new creation. The child of God is happy to know that he will never face such condemnation: *"There is therefore now no condemnation to them which are in Christ Jesus"* (Romans 8:1). By our acceptance of Christ, who bore our condemnation, we are saved from sin and its just and eternal punishment.

THE JUDGED

Several objects of judgment are enumerated in the awesome account of the great white throne, and it is important to note these respective judgments.

"The earth and the heaven" (Revelation 20:11). There will be a quick disappearance of the old creation, because the One sitting on the throne was its Creator, and, therefore, it immediately obeys His command. Why will the earth vanish? Because it was the scene of sin and rebellion, and it bore the stain of the Judge's blood. Man held on to it for many centuries, but now earth flees away. Why does the heaven also vanish? The aerial heavens cannot remain, because they were polluted by Satan, the prince of the power of the air. How can the heavens continue if they are not clean in God's sight? Among the new creations are *"a new heaven and a new earth"* (Revelation 21:1).

"Angels which kept not their first estate" (Jude 6). Because the chief rebel has been dealt with, Christ now proceeds to deal with all those whom Satan influenced. While we have no direct proof in the narrative that Satan's host of evil spirits are to appear at this throne,

we feel that they will be judged at this time. *"And the angels which kept not their first estate, but left their own habitation, he hath reserved in everlasting chains under darkness unto the judgment of the great day"* (Jude 6). If, as Paul affirms, we are to judge angels—that is, fallen ones—then it would seem as if the saints will be at this tribunal in a judicial capacity. It is not hard to understand why Satan hates the book of Revelation and attempts to keep people from reading and studying it! He does not want them to know of his terrible doom, as well as the stern punishment awaiting his angelic and human dupes.

"The dead, small and great" (Revelation 20:12). By this group we are to understand all the dead in sin, whether dead spiritually or physically. The godless on earth at the time this throne is set up are immediately transferred to it, while the dead in hell are raised and made to appear with them. Here they stand, like condemned prisoners at the bar, awaiting their sentence of doom.

The dead in Christ were raised at His return for the church. (See 1 Thessalonians 4:16–17.) This is the final resurrection of all the wicked dead for their final disposition. All the wicked dead *before* Christ came to earth will have the book of the law to judge them. (See Romans 2:12; 3:19.) All the wicked dead *since* Christ will be judged by the gospel of grace. (See Romans 2:16; John 3:18–19; 12:48.) All the wicked dead *after* Christ's second coming will be judged by the everlasting gospel. Infants and those who are mentally deficient will not be there. Because they never had any conscious accountability, the blood of Christ, which covers Adamic sin, guarantees their presence in heaven.

All ranks and degrees of sinners are to appear at this awesome throne, as indicated by the phrase *"small and great,"* a phrase occurring five times over in the book of Revelation. Now we have various classes and distinctions, social and racial. But all distinctions are to be swept away as the Judge takes His seat, for *"God is no respecter of persons*" (Acts 10:34). The proud and mighty, as well as the insignificant, are to enter the lake of fire.

The fearful. These are people who were full of fear while on earth. They were always afraid to confess Christ, to identify themselves with the gospel, and to live for the Lord. Their hearts failed them for fear. Though courageous enough in other realms, they were cowards when it came to receiving Christ as their Savior.

The unbelievers. Here, we have the most numerous class, found in all ranks. Jesus Himself declared that travelers on the broad road are many. (See Matthew 7:13.) It is sad to realize that the vast majority of men and women are unbelievers. So many of our centers of secular learning produce polished pagans. Too often, the natural mind refuses to receive and believe the message of the crucified and risen Savior.

The abominable. By this group, we are to understand all who are morally and physically filthy. The corruption of Noah's days is here again. Wars bring with them the liberation of detestable forms of sin.

The murderers. Statistics inform us that murder is on the rise. Jesus called Satan a murderer (see John 8:44), and he is the parent of all who destroy the lives of others. What a day of reckoning awaits those butchers and hangmen in the world who wantonly kill innocent men, women, and children!

The fornicators. Scripture uses the word *fornication* to imply sexual immorality of every kind. Adultery, incest, and idolatry are cited as fornication. (See Matthew 5:32; 1 Corinthians 5:1; 2 Chronicles 21:11). Unscriptural doctrine is likewise likened to *spiritual* fornication. (See Revelation 19:2.)

The sorcerers. We have already drawn attention to the fact that this word is connected with our English word *pharmacy*. Long ago, drugs played an important part in witchcraft, and, once again, we have a drunken, drugged, and doped society! In this category, we can place all those who are identified with spiritism and demonism.

The idolaters. The general interpretation of this class is that they represent the heathen who worship idols of wood and stone. But all the idolaters are not in Africa or India; there are countless numbers of idolaters around us in so-called Christian countries. People worship themselves, their money, their businesses, and their sports. What is an idol? An idol is anyone or anything that takes the place of God in our lives.

The liars. Every kind of liar must stand before God's throne. Satan, the father of lies and the master liar, is already in the lake of fire, and now his children are about to follow him. All who are contrary to God and His Word are liars.

None of the foregoing people will be able to appeal their judgment. They will be only too conscious of their guilt. While the punishments will be proportional in *intensity* to the sins committed, the *duration* of punishment will be eternal in every case.

"The sea" (Revelation 20:13). In his description of the new creation, John declares that the sea exists no more. This meant much to John, who in his Patmos prison knew that the Aegean Sea separated him from those to whom he loved to minister. But what is the full implication of this phrase about the sea giving up *"the dead which were in it"* (Revelation 20:13)? Is *"sea"* to be treated as symbolic of the unsettled condition of mankind and, therefore, descriptive of the surrender of the seething masses to judgment? Or, are we to accept the usual interpretation: that all those drowned at sea are to emerge from their watery grave? To our mind, it seems that the next phrase, *"death...delivered up the dead which were in* [it]," covers all whose who died and were buried in the earth or sea.

George Pember, in his stirring book *Earth's Earliest Ages*, suggested that the sea is the prison of vast numbers of demons who followed Satan in his expulsion from heaven and who, when the sea was formed, were confined within it. This may be the prison of darkness referred to in Jude 6. With the passing of earth and heaven, the sea will also vanish, and, therefore, all beings within this liquid tomb must appear before Him who made the sea.

"Death and hell" (Revelation 20:13). Death, or the grave, held the bodies of the lost, while Hades held their spirits. Now, bodies and spirits are united, and, in their eternal bodies of shame and in their eternal spirits, the condemned go out to the death of death. But, at last, this monster is destroyed: *"The last enemy that shall be destroyed is death"* (1 Corinthians 15:26). Hades, or hell, is the present abode of the lost. But this temporary abode gives way to the more fearful, eternal judgment of the lake of fire. Such a resurrection is spoken of as one of shame (see Daniel 12:2), of the unjust (see Acts 24:15), and of damnation (see John 5:29). How different will be the resurrection of the saved at the return of Christ! (See 1 Thessalonians 4:16–17; Philippians 3:21; 1 Corinthians 15.)

Death and hell quickly follow their occupants into the lake of fire. (See Revelation 20:14.) Brought into existence because of Satan's work, they now follow him into eternal perdition. Because the keys of hell and death dangle at Christ's waistband, He is able to act as He likes with such abodes. *"I am he that liveth, and was dead; and, behold, I am alive for evermore...and have the keys of hell and of death"* (Revelation 1:18). Thus, the lake of fire becomes the final depository of all that was contrary to God and to Jesus Christ. The terrible term *"the lake of fire"* occurs five times in Revelation, and we should consider the significance of this final abode of Satan, the beast, the false prophet, the dead, death, and hell. Surely, such striking language suggests the finality and eternity of unspeakable, unrelieved doom!

There are those who argue that the language is only figurative, and that actual flames are not meant. If this is so, then the reality symbolized must be even more terrible than the figure. "Remember," says Broadus, "that language may be highly figurative without being fictitious. Only ascertain what the figures of Scripture were designed to mean, and that meaning is as certainly true as if stated in plain words. Thus, the fire that cannot be quenched may be called a figure, if you choose; yet it assuredly means that in hell there will be something as bad as fire, as torturing as fire is to the earthly body—nay, the reality of hell, as well as of heaven, does no doubt greatly transcend the most impressive imagery that earthly things can afford." To this, we may add the fact that Christ never made idle threats, and that, when He spoke of eternal fire, He was warning against a real punishment so vividly described by figures of the most extreme suffering.

This judgment of fire was prepared for the devil and his angels: "*Then shall he say also unto them on the left hand, Depart from me, ye cursed, into everlasting fire, prepared for the devil and his angels*" (Matthew 25:41). They are the first to endure the torment of flames.

Truly, the language used of the eternal caverns of the lost is sufficient to stroke terror into the heart of every sinner. The teaching of our Lord makes it plain that the torment is to be eternal. (See Luke 16:24–26.) In the lake of fire, there will be full consciousness, which will make anguish more intense. There is no purgatory, no probation, and no ultimate escape. "*And beside all this, between us and you there is a great gulf fixed: so that they which would pass from hence to you cannot; neither can they pass to us, that would come from thence*" (Luke 16:26). All the condemned "*shall be tormented day and night for ever and ever*" (Revelation 20:10).

The repeated phrase "*the second death*" is easily explained. The first death was physical—separation of the spirit from the body. The second death is eternal—separation of the spirit from God. Over the saved, this second death has no power. (See Revelation 20:6.) Donald G. Barnhouse, in *God's Last Word*, remarked, "As though to give one final word of comfort to those whose names are written in the Lamb's book of life, and one final word of warning to those who know Him not, the distinction is once more clearly drawn. Whoever was not found written in the book of life was cast into the lake of fire."

THE JUDGMENT BOOKS

We now come to the somewhat difficult question of the various records that John mentions as being before the Judge as He deals with the condemned persons standing at the throne. *"Books," "another book," "the book of life,"* and *"the Lamb's book of life"* are terms to be distinguished and interpreted.

"The books" (Revelation 20:12) implies that there is more than one set of records in heaven. By these books, we can understand the record of the works of the people about to be judged. *"The dead were judged out of those things which were written in the books, according to their works"* (Revelation 20:12). The Lord is keeping a faithful record of the thoughts, deeds, and words of sinners. Nothing is too trivial to set down.

This is not a general judgment; the merits of each person will be considered, *"every man according to his deeds"* (Romans 2:6). The rich man of Luke 16 died, went to Hades, and cried out, *"I am tormented in this flame"* (verse 24). But Abraham replied, *"Son, remember..."* (verse 25). And the rich man remembered past, and lost, opportunities. He remembered what Moses and the prophets had said. He remembered the message of God's Word. He remembered, but now it was too late!

While a person may have a good record, evidently it is Christ's insertion of his name into *"the book of life"* (Revelation 20:12) that counts. "*Notwithstanding in this rejoice not, that the spirits are subject unto you; but rather rejoice, because your names are written in heaven*" (Luke 10:20). It is not the absence of *works* but of a *name* that condemns.

> *Many will say to me in that day, Lord, Lord, have we not prophesied in thy name? and in thy name have cast out devils? and in thy name done many wonderful works? And then will I profess unto them, I never knew you: depart from me, ye that work iniquity.* (Matthew 7:22–23)

Christ has control of this register, as indicated in Revelation 3:5. (See also Revelation 13:8; 17:8; 21:27.) "*The Lamb's book of life*" (Revelation 21:27) is the golden record of those belonging to the Lord. Names in this book were written long before the events of the great white throne.

Donald G. Barnhouse notes the following points on the various books in heaven.

"Books" is a plural form. There is more than one set of books kept in heaven. There are at least two records in heaven concerning the believers in the Lord Jesus Christ. There is one that is the roll of the elect chosen in Christ before the foundation of the world, and this is called "the Lamb's book of life" (Revelation 21:27), or simply "the book of life" (Philippians 4:3; Revelation 13:8; etc.). It was of this that the Lord spoke to His disciples when He told them that they were to rejoice that their names were written in heaven. (See Luke 10:20.) There is another book concerning the believers that is the record of all their thoughts and meditations concerning their Lord. We read of this in the beautiful passage in Malachi: "Then they that feared the LORD spake often one to another: and the LORD hearkened, and heard it, and a book of remembrance was written before him for them that feared the LORD, and that thought upon his name" (Malachi 3:16). It is very possible that this book contains the difference between those who are saved plus the reward of having a crown, and those who are saved so as by fire with all their works burned away. (See 1 Corinthians 3:14–15.)

In our passage it is also evident that there are books that concern the unsaved....The easiest to describe is the book of the records of the life and works of the unsaved. Here, we read, in no uncertain terms, that the deeds of the unbelievers are recorded in heaven. How this is done, we do not claim to know or venture to guess. It is hidden in God, but there should be no difficulty in believing this when man himself is able to record great symphonies and speeches in wax, and reduce whole libraries to microfilms. The fact is there. God states it. The unbeliever may scoff at it, but he will be judged by it. Then, there is another book that definitely concerns the unbeliever, and which is called also "the book of life," though it is evidently very different from the Lamb's book of life! The names of the unbelievers are in this book, but are blotted out. This is evident from a study of certain passages of the Scriptures.

It would seem that there is a book, something like a census record, in which the names of every individual to whom physical life is given are recorded, and that these names are blotted out of the book, leaving at the end a checklist that would be identical with the list in the book of the elect, chosen in Christ before the foundation of the world. We have already seen that one of the promises made to the born-again ones—"Who is he that overcometh the world, but he that believeth that Jesus is the Son of God?" (1 John 5:5)—is that their names shall never be blotted out of the book of life. This would indicate that some names are blotted out, and since the names of the elect cannot be blotted out, it must be the names of the lost are in that particular book, along with the names of the saved, and that the names of the lost are blotted out. This would be further indicated by the statement in the last paragraph of the Bible—Revelation 22:19—that the names of those who subtract anything from the whole of God's revelation in the Scriptures shall be subtracted from the book of life.

16

THE SEVEN NEW THINGS

REVELATION 21:2–22:1

With Satan, sin, and sinners forever removed, with death and hell vanquished, and with Christ recognized and revered as Lord of all, a perfect age begins in which God becomes all in all. At last, the eternal state appears. Gloom has been banished, and glory begins. An everlasting sunrise ushers in a new creation, for the world's last dark day has gone. Man's history has been consummated, and God's new order is now introduced.

These last chapters of Revelation comprise a fitting close to God's eternal purpose and marvelous provision for His own people. (See Ephesians 2:7.) Here, we are at the goal of all revelation! Satan's will and purpose throughout the ages were to separate God from man, but God is ultimately victorious. At long last, every divine purpose for man's eternal well-being is realized, and every divine promise is fulfilled.

In sublimity of language, the description of the transportation of the glorified to the pinnacle of eternal peace that John gives stands unsurpassed. The moral competence of the apostle to behold and grasp the glories of eternity was not in himself but in the Holy Spirit. Under His absolute control, John lived and moved in another realm of existence, and he was thus prepared to receive the vision of the realities of heaven.

Somehow, we feel that the chapters before us call for contemplation more than interpretation, for reverence rather than research. We find ourselves wishing that more had been recorded of our eternal abode. One reason for the scarcity of facts regarding the eternal state is the limitation of language to express what John saw and felt. The best of words are only words, at best—a poor medium of expression when it comes to eternal glories. Once we are in heaven, amid its splendor, ours will be the exclamation of the Queen of Sheba: *"The half was not told me"* (1 Kings 10:7).

The key phrase of the closing section of Revelation is found in chapter 21, verse 5: *"Behold, I make all things new."* Some writers suggest that, now, the millennial age and the eternal age blend into one perfect portrayal of unending glory. Chronologically, verses 9 through 27 of Revelation 21 may actually precede verses 1 through 8. Verses 7 and 8 point to a time before the dawning of the eternal age. The scene presented is indeed magnificent. At last, Christ is the Victor of the ages, and He is about to hand over the kingdom to His Father. What a thrill this act of surrender will be for both Father and Son! How we need to live more in the future than we do! Like the apostle Paul, let us learn how to balance the gloomy *now* with the glorious *then.*

1. A NEW HEAVEN

And I saw a new heaven...: for the first heaven...passed away. (Revelation 21:1)

Comparing this entire verse with Revelation 20:11, we find the order reversed. At the great white throne, *"the earth and the heaven fled away."* Now, it is *"heaven"* then *"earth."* And this reversal is significant. In the old creation, which terminates at Revelation 20:11, God was intimately related with earth, on which He had a temple for His people. But now, with His people *as* a temple (see Revelation 21:3), everything is of a heavenly nature.

"Heaven" does not mean God's immediate presence but rather the *aerial* heavens—that is, all that is between the earth and God Himself. The old heaven was where Satan operated, and it was therefore not clean in God's sight. The *"new heaven"* is to be constituted so differently that the sun, moon, stars, and atmospheric properties will no longer be necessary. At last, there will be a sunrise without a sunset.

There are three heavens referred to in Scripture:

1. *The third heaven* is the place to which Paul was caught up in the immediate presence of God. It is the region of divine glory and also the dwelling place of angels and saints. (See 2 Corinthians 12:1–5).

2. *The second heaven*, or astronomical heaven, is the setting of the sun, moon, and starry host. (See Job 38:31–33.)

3. *The first heaven*, or atmospheric heaven, is the air around and above us. Satan is referred to as the prince of this region. (See Ephesians 2:2.)

Because the first heaven—God's abode—is eternal, it is, not subject to any change. *"The new heaven"* implies the transformation of the aerial and astronomical heavens. With our heavenly bodies, we shall be able to roam around the new heaven and the new earth.

A new "midheaven" is necessary, because the present heavens are polluted by Satan's presence as the prince of the power of the air. It is for this reason that the stars are not pure in God's sight. (See Job 25:5.) The space between us and God's abode is also cluttered with missiles, rockets, satellites, and miscellaneous orbital debris, placed there by twentieth-century man.

2. A NEW EARTH

And I saw...a new earth: for...the first earth...passed away.
(Revelation 21:1)

Truly, it will pass with little regret. The old earth must disappear, because it has witnessed the sin and violence of man. It has also been soaked with the blood of millions of martyrs and has been stained with the blood of the Redeemer. It has been drenched with oceans of the tears of godly men and women. The new earth will never experience sin, sorrow, or slaughter. Some scholars suggest that the new heaven is to be the abode of the redeemed saints in glory, while the new earth is to be the abode of the redeemed ones saved in the tribulation who passed into the millennium.

One conspicuous omission from God's new creation is that of oceans: *"There was no more sea"* (Revelation 21:1). How John's heart must have been comforted by such a revelation! On the Island of Patmos, the apostle was experiencing the separation that the sea can cause. In heaven, however, nothing will ever cut us off from our dear ones. All who are the Lord's will be together forever.

There is a difference of opinion among biblical scholars as to whether the new creation—which will not appear before the old one disappears—is to be totally new or simply a remaking of the old. Some argue that fire does not symbolize *annihilation* but *purging*, and that God will merely purify the old creation, making it a fit habitation for His glorified saints. Other writers say that the language used in the New Testament is definite and emphatic, and that there is to be a total disappearance of the old creation. It is to *"pass away with a great noise, and…be burned up"* (2 Peter 3:10), implying, it is contended, not a mere transformation but an obliteration. The old creation is to be laid aside as an outworn garment, folded up and utterly discarded.

And yet, do not old rags have a way of reappearing as new clothes? When God said, *"Behold, I make all things new"* (Revelation 21:5), the Greek word translated as *"new"* is not the one meaning new in time or of recent appearance, but new as to form or quality, of a different nature from the old. Thus, *"the new man"* of Ephesians 4:24 implies a different man altogether from the first man, Adam. Paul described a new character of manhood that is spiritual and moral, after the pattern of Christ. And it is so with the new heaven and the new earth, which will differ completely in form and quality from the original heaven and earth.

No matter which view we hold, the time from the first creation to the new creation spans the Bible. The first creation is the sphere and scene of first things. Sin, commencing in heaven by Lucifer, has wrecked the first creation. The new creation is altogether different, as can be seen by a study of John's "no mores." When it came to describing the glories of the new creation in Revelation 21, John could only use a series of negatives:

+ No more sickness

+ No more pain

+ No more hunger

+ No more thirst

+ No more sorrow

+ No more tears

+ No more sea

+ No more death

+ No more sin

+ No more night

With Satan forever banished, temptation will be forever absent. With the vista of the ages of the ages, we reach a world without tragedy, tribulation, or evil practices—*"a new earth, wherein dwelleth righteousness"* (2 Peter 3:13). With such a glorious prospect awaiting us, should we not strive to live with eternity's values in view? Present trials and disappointments are not to be compared with the glory to be revealed in that eternal day.

3. THE NEW JERUSALEM

*And I John saw the holy city, new Jerusalem, coming down
from God out of heaven, prepared as a bride adorned for her
husband.*   (Revelation 21:2)

In the perfect description of perfect unity, John gives us an
insight into the church's governmental relationship to everything
else. Here again, we should note John's verbs of experience: *"I saw"*
and *"I heard."* The new Jerusalem is contrasted with the old one.
The present earthly Jerusalem, the so-called "Holy City," is most
unholy, but the new Jerusalem is perfect, holy, and *"out of heaven."*
As a bride dressed in beautiful bridal robes, the church descends
in all her glory. Formed by the wooing of the Spirit in the wilderness below, she was caught up at the return of the Bridegroom and,
after her marriage to Him, is now adorned with eternal loveliness.

Some writers believe that Revelation 21:1 is an elaboration of
the marriage supper of the Lamb. (See Revelation 19:7.) The first
bride of the Bible (see Genesis 2:18–24) can be used as a picture
of the church's origin and relationship to Christ. The false bride,
the harlot (see Revelation 17:5), shone in the glory of man, but the
Lamb's bride shines in the reflected beauty and glory of God. Even
in the eternal state, she lacks any inherent glory, *"having the glory
of God"* (Revelation 21:11).

John likens the church to a city. William Newell's exposition
of the society of the redeemed as a city is extremely helpful. Here
is an adapted summary of some of his points.

It is a literal city. Everything suggests literalness—gold, streets,
dimensions, stones. This city comes down, for it is impossible to
build a holy city here. In this new home of the church, all the materials are provided by God.

It is a heavenly city. It comes down out of heaven, for it is for heavenly people. Without a heavenly nature, which the Holy Spirit makes possible in regeneration, one cannot respond to his eternal environment. *"But now they desire a better country, that is, an heavenly: wherefore God is not ashamed to be called their God: for he hath prepared for them a city"* (Hebrews 11:16).

It is a home city. The city John so fully describes is to be the eternal home of Christ and His own, whose glorified bodies will correspond to Christ's. Others, of course, will also share this glory (see Revelation 21:24–26), but the church will be as a wife at home. What a prospect—at home with the Lord forever!

It is a vast city. The figures used of this city stagger the imagination.

> *And the city lieth foursquare, and the length is as large as the breadth: and he measured the city with the reed, twelve thousand furlongs. The length and the breadth and the height of it are equal. And he measured the wall thereof, an hundred and forty and four cubits, according to the measure of a man, that is, of the angel.* (Revelation 21:16–17)

The length and width and height of this cube-like city are equal: twelve thousand furlongs, or about 1,500 miles. Governmental perfection is suggested by the constant repetition of the number 12. *"And [it] had a wall great and high, and had twelve gates, and at the gates twelve angels, and names written thereon, which are the names of the twelve tribes of the children of Israel"* (Revelation 21:12). The twelve gates are identified with Israel (see Matthew 19:28), and the twelve foundations, with the church (see Ephesians 2:20).

It is a glorious city. The glory of God is to be its light: *"Having the glory of God: and her light was like unto a stone most precious, even like a jasper stone, clear as crystal"* (Revelation 21:11). The Lamb is to be the lamp—that is, the source of all necessary illumination.

There will be no need for natural lights. The mention of *"a golden reed to measure the city"* (Revelation 21:15) implies that when God measures something, He intends to use what belongs to Him. And everything will measure up to *His* requirements, for the glorified—His church—will be adorned with eternal loveliness.

It is a capital city. God's eternal home is to be in this capital city of the new creation, more resplendent than any renowned capital in the world today. This is the center of divine presence and government in the universe of God and the Lamb. With each view of the city, the Lamb is named, and the sevenfold reference to Him (see Revelation 21:9, 14, 22–23, 27; 22:1, 3) indicates that even though Christ delivers the kingdom to the Father, nevertheless, He shares it with the redeemed.

4. THE NEW FELLOWSHIP

At last, the broken fellowship of the first garden (see Genesis 3) is fully, completely, and eternally restored. Never again will Satan or man be able to rupture such fellowship. What is heaven? Is it not a society of perfectly restored souls in ecstatic, unrestrained fellowship with God? Here, then, is a heaven coming down out of heaven:

> *And I heard a great voice out of heaven saying, Behold, the tabernacle of God is with men, and he will dwell with them, and they shall be his people, and God himself shall be with them, and be their God.* (Revelation 21:3)

But God will not come down to dwell with men until the old creation passes away. This present earth is too corrupt to be God's abode. God's delight is to dwell with the sons of men. (See Proverbs 8:31.) The result of this precious fellowship is a world without tears, for only God is able to dry our tears: *"And God shall wipe away all tears from their eyes; and there shall be no more death, neither sorrow, nor crying, neither shall there be any more pain: for the former things are passed away"* (Revelation 21:4). What a day!

5. THE NEW TEMPLE

> *And I saw no temple therein: for the Lord God Almighty and the Lamb are the temple of it.* (Revelation 21:22)

At long last, the shadows give way to the substance. (See Hebrews 9:23–24.) Everything associated with the tabernacle and the temple merely typified the Lord God and the Lamb. Ezekiel's millennial temple was the center of worship for an earthly city, but now, everything centers around the throne, to which all have access. In ancient times, God had a temple for His people, and, in this church age, He has a redeemed people as His temple. But John describes the eternal age, when God will provide Himself as a temple for His own.

When John speaks of the temple of God being opened in heaven, he uses the Greek word for *"temple"* meaning "the holiest of all," "the shrine of shrines," into which the high priest alone entered, and only once a year. God makes good His unchanging grace to His people, and His throne and presence in their midst will gloriously supersede the ark in the tabernacle and the temple of old. This reference, along with the previous one about measuring the temple (see Revelation 11:1–2), implies that the secret abode of the safeguarded children of God is now revealed.

Amid the crash of empires and the passing of the old world, John assures us that all the saints are under the shadow of the Almighty and that there is immediate access to God without the mediation of a priest or other mediator. *"No temple"* thus signifies full and free access to all true worshippers. As Walter Scott so fittingly expressed,

What need of a temple? God, in the greatness of His Being, and as the One who has acted and ruled of old, is now revealed in glory by the Lamb. The divine Presence is equally diffused. God and the Lamb make themselves known throughout every part of the vast city of gold.

God had regarded His people as His temple, but now He is their true and living Temple, as well as their true Ark and their everlasting hidden Manna. The habitation of God is always an open sanctuary to faith but a clouded and lightning-crowned Sinai to all who reject God. (See Hebrews 12:18–24.)

> Lo! what a glorious sight appears
> To our believing eyes!
> The earth and sea are passed away,
> And the old rolling skies
> The God of glory down to men
> Removes His blest abode;
> Men, the dear objects of His grace,
> And He, the loving God.[13]

6. THE NEW LIGHT

And the city had no need of the sun, neither of the moon, to shine in it: for the glory of God did lighten it, and the Lamb is the light thereof. And the nations of them which are saved shall walk in the light of it: and the kings of the earth do bring their glory and honor into it. And the gates of it shall not be shut at all by day: for there shall be no night there.

(Revelation 21:23–25)

---

13. Isaac Watts, "Lo! What a Glorious Sight Appears," 1707.

And there shall be no night there; and they need no candle,
neither light of the sun; for the Lord God giveth them light:
and they shall reign for ever and ever.   (Revelation 22:5)

The eternal Holy City is to have a remarkable, supernatural lighting system. Now, we have natural illumination provided by the sun, moon, and stars. The sun is the source of life and light for all on earth, and the moon and stars are only reflectors. But these heavenly bodies that were called into being from ancient times to perform certain functions now pass away with the old heavens. At present, we have artificial illumination, for technology has succeeded very well in lightening our darkness at night. But, in the new city, God and the Lamb provide all necessary light. Christ referred to Himself as the Light of the world, and He will be the Light of the eternal world. Along with God, He will be the Light of the new world as well as the old. Together, they are to provide all necessary illumination. There will be *"no night there"* in that eternal day.

The gates of the new city will never be closed. Police will be unnecessary to guard the city dwellers, and there will be no more theft. Nations can come and go. All that goes with sinful darkness disappears. Everything natural and artificial has vanished. Truly, the prospect of such perfect provision overwhelms us!

Amid the darkness of this present world, we are to shine as lights (see Philippians 2:15), and, in the new world, we shall still shine as we reflect Christ's eternal glory.

7. THE NEW PARADISE

There are several important features to bear in mind in the study of this chapter as a whole.

1. A book is valuable only in proportion to the truth it reveals. *"These sayings are faithful and true"* (Revelation 22:6). Here, we

have a solemn affirmation as to the veracity of Scripture. An angel from heaven authenticates the prophecies of Revelation. All the prophets of old were under the control of the Spirit of truth.

2. A book is closely associated with its writer. Five times, the name *John* appears as the writer of Revelation. (See Revelation 1:1, 4, 9; 21:2; 22:8.) *"What thou seest, write in a book"* (Revelation 1:11). Indeed, this entire dramatic book was written by John, who was familiar with writing. (See 2 John 12; 3 John 13.) Higher criticism may reject John as the writer of Revelation and name some "other John" who was not the apostle, but, as Hilgenfield aptly remarks, "An unknown John whose name has disappeared from history, leaving hardly any trace behind, can scarcely have given commandments in the name of Christ and the Spirit to the seven churches." The fivefold use of John's name demonstrates that the John who wrote the fourth gospel and the three epistles bearing his name also penned Revelation, as he was divinely instructed to do.

3. A book not sealed is open for perusal and profit. What was sealed in Daniel's day (see Daniel 12:4) is now exposed. Let us not forget that *Revelation* means "an unveiling," and this is what the whole of the book is. The nearer we approach the events recorded in it, the clearer the prophecies become. (See Revelation 22:10.)

And he showed me a pure river of water of life, clear as crystal, proceeding out of the throne of God and of the Lamb. In the midst of the street of it, and on either side of the river, was there the tree of life, which bare twelve manner of fruits, and yielded her fruit every month: and the leaves of the tree were for the healing of the nations. And there shall be no more curse: but the throne of God and of the Lamb shall be in it; and his servants shall serve him: and they shall see his face;

*and his name shall be in their foreheads. And there shall be no
night there; and they need no candle, neither light of the sun;
for the Lord God giveth them light: and they shall reign for
ever and ever.* (Revelation 22:1–5)

The climax of redemption, which is now reached, is the wonder
of a garden from which the serpent and sin are forever excluded.
Let us briefly note one or two features of the glorious future of
the people of God. In the old creation, all the rivers ran into the
sea, but here we have a river without a sea—a river responsible for
fertilization and vegetation in the new creation. Rivers open the
Bible (see Genesis 2:10–14) and close it (see Revelation 22:1). This
river flows from the throne, which is its source. The water of this
divine river is clear as crystal—that is, totally pure, requiring no
treatment to purify it. All thrones give place to the throne of God
and of the Lamb. (See 1 Corinthians 15:24–28.)

The Bible also opens with a tree of life and finishes with
another one *"in the midst of the street"* (Revelation 22:2), signifying no seclusion or exclusion. All are to have access to this healing tree. The leaves of this tree yield wholeness and health. The
fruit is for the saints, and the leaves are for the nations. (See
Ezekiel 47:12.) Because all sickness and death have passed away
(see Revelation 21:4), the *"healing"* provided by the tree is not associated with the body. Because healing implies sickness, the translation "for the health of the nations" is more accurate.

In Genesis 2:8–15, God created a material home for man
within a garden. But that original garden witnessed Satan's rebellion and man's transgression. (See Genesis 3:1–7.) Now, we have
a garden surpassing the first one in every way. Nothing will ever
wither or die within it. The curse pronounced by God in earth's
first garden is forever removed. The calamity of Eden will not
happen again. With sin forever banished, there will be no more
curse. The last word of the Old Testament is *"curse"*: *"And he shall*

turn the heart of the fathers to the children, and the heart of the children to their fathers, lest I come and smite the earth with a curse" (Malachi 4:6). The New Testament opens with Jesus Christ, the One who came to bear the curse. (See Galatians 3:13). With the grand finale of the Bible, instead of a curse, we have a benediction.

The ultimate triumph of Christ can be presented this way:

In Genesis: "In the beginning God created the heaven and the earth" (Genesis 1:1).

In Revelation: "I saw a new heaven and a new earth" (Revelation 21:1).

In Genesis: "The darkness he called Night" (Genesis 1:5).

In Revelation: "There shall be no night there" (Revelation 22:5).

In Genesis: "Thou shalt surely die" (Genesis 2:17).

In Revelation: "There shall be no more death" (Revelation 21:4).

In Genesis: "I will greatly multiply thy sorrow" (Genesis 3:16).

In Revelation: "Neither shall there be any more pain" (Revelation 21:4)

In Genesis: "Cursed is the ground for thy sake" (Genesis 3:17).

In Revelation: "There shall be no more curse" (Revelation 22:3).

In Genesis: banishment from the tree of life.

In Revelation: the tree of life appears.

In Genesis: Satan appears.

In Revelation: Satan disappears.

John goes on to declare that in the new creation, God's servants are to be ceaselessly active. We are to reign through the ages of ages: "They shall reign for ever and ever" (Revelation 22:5). This means that the saints are not going to sit around playing harps all the time. With perfect, glorified minds and bodies, it will be our joy to serve the Lord as we cannot do now because of the hindering influence of sin. Privileges undreamed of are to be ours in the land that is fairer than day: we will see His face. Whose face? That of the Lamb! (See Revelation 22:3–4.) Are we living in anticipation of the thrill when, for the first time, our eyes will behold the King in all His beauty?

> Face to face with Christ, my Savior
> Face to face—what will it be,
> When with rapture I behold Him,
> Jesus Christ, Who died for me?[14]

Speechless wonder will be ours as we look upon that face before which heaven and earth fled away. The greatest wonder will be our transformation into His likeness. *"His name,"* says John, *"shall be in their foreheads"* (Revelation 22:4). By the name, we are to understand the character or nature of God. The seal, of course, is the sign of ownership and security. But why the reference to the forehead? The implication is that the seal will be in a place easily seen by others. We are publicly and perfectly to reflect the character of God. How expressive are these lines:

> I want to be marked for Thine own,
> Thy seal on my forehead to wear;
> And have that new name on the mystic white stone,
> Which none but Thyself can declare.[15]

Before closing his marvelous description of "the bright inheritance of saints, Jerusalem above," John has another word regarding its radiance of glory and light beyond compare: *"And there shall be no night there; and they need no candle, neither light of the sun; for the Lord God giveth them light"* (Revelation 22:5). No night, no candle, no sun—just a glorious city of light that stands in contrast

14. Carrie E. Breck, "Face to Face with Christ, My Savior," 1898.
15. Charlotte Elliott, "I Want That Adorning Divine," 1868.

to the present world of darkness. Now, only half the world can have light at one time, but when the Lord God gives light, it will be diffused everywhere at the same time. Such eternal light is outside the scope of scientific investigation; it transcends our finite human comprehension. What a city! No night, with its darkness and fear; no candlelight services; no sunrises or sunsets!

> There is a land of pure delight,
> Where saints immortal reign,
> Infinite day excludes the night,
> And pleasures banish pain.[16]

The revelation of Jesus Christ is accomplished. The great unveiling of Him as the all-powerful Lamb is both ratified and enforced. After the wonderful panorama of His glory, grace, and government, Revelation closes with the simplest, sweetest, and shortest of benedictions: *"The grace of our Lord Jesus Christ be with you all"* (Revelation 22:21). In both the prologue and epilogue of Revelation, the second coming of our Lord is declared. (See Revelation 1:7; 22:20.) In the epilogue (see Revelation 22:6–21), we have short, concise sentences that provide a striking conclusion to this remarkable book. As we examine the words closely, we find that they contain a condensation of main themes presented throughout—namely, the certainty of the fulfillment of prophecy and the imminence of this fulfillment.

The angel who appears speaks of himself in the third person and adds a beatitude to the promise of Christ's return. (See Revelation 22:6–7.) John is so overwhelmed with emotion as he contemplates the astonishing vision and climactic scene of the Holy City that he falls in worship at the feet of the angelic herald. But John is reminded that all adoration, praise, and reverence belong to God alone.

---

16. Isaac Watts, "There Is a Land of Pure Delight," 1707.

Then, John is instructed to regard Christ's second coming as being near. The visions that John received were not to be kept secret, as if the day were far off. They belong to the present, for Christ is about to appear. There is a solemn declaration of the fixed, unalterable fate of a deliberate human choice, with human character continuing to produce its inevitable development and fruit; the doom of the godless is sealed. (See Revelation 22:10–11.)

In the repeated designation "*I am Alpha and Omega*" (Revelation 1:8, 11; 22:13), we have a striking evidence of Christ's deity. As for "*dogs*," they symbolize the offensive, uncontrolled uncleanness of all who rejected the cleansing blood of the Lamb and were shut outside the Holy City. (See Revelation 22:15.)

The bright and morning star shines most brightly just before the dawn of day and is a fitting symbol of the return of Christ, who will bring the dawn of an age of radiant light. (See Revelation 22:16.) Even as a blessing is attached to the proper use of this book, there is also a solemn warning against the abuse of the book:

> *For I testify unto every man that heareth the words of the prophecy of this book, If any man shall add unto these things, God shall add unto him the plagues that are written in this book: and if any man shall take away from the words of the book of this prophecy, God shall take away his part out of the book of life, and out of the holy city, and from the things which are written in this book.* (Revelation 22:18–19)

A woe is pronounced upon all who tamper with any of its teachings. This warning refers to the willful perversion and distortion of its great truths. All who love the book must guard its integrity and declare the whole counsel of God.

17

THE SEVEN LAST THINGS

REVELATION 22:8–21

Genesis is a book of firsts, and Revelation is a book of lasts. It is useful to compare and contrast commencements with completions. In this last section of the last book of the Bible, there are seven last things to observe.

1. THE LAST WITNESS TO THE REALITY OF THE VISION

And I John saw these things, and heard them. And when I had heard and seen, I fell down to worship before the feet of the angel which showed me these things.
(Revelation 22:8)

Verbs of experience are prominent in this verse: "*I...saw*" and "*I...heard.*" There may be a reference here to the crowning vision that John had of the new heaven (see Revelation 22:1–7), the consummation of the Revelation of Jesus Christ. But these verbs of experience also confirm the authenticity of Revelation as a whole.

2. THE LAST APOSTOLIC BEATITUDE

Blessed are they that do his commandments, that they may have right to the tree of life, and may enter in through the gates into the city.   (Revelation 22:14)

Previously, we described all the beatitudes of Revelation. Here, we are reminded that obedience to all that God has revealed brings a rich reward. (See John 13:17.) As believers, we walk on two feet: trust and obedience.

3. THE LAST DIVINE TESTIMONY

I Jesus have sent mine angel to testify unto you these things in the churches. I am the root and the offspring of David, and the bright and morning star.   (Revelation 22:16)

For I testify unto every man that heareth the words of the prophecy of this book, If any man shall add unto these things, God shall add unto him the plagues that are written in this book.   (Revelation 22:18)

He which testifieth these things saith, Surely I come quickly. Amen. Even so, come, Lord Jesus.   (Revelation 22:20)

Alive forevermore, Christ confirms all the prophecies of the book of Revelation, which are divinely designed to reveal Him in all His glory and majesty. Three times, we have the word *"testify"* or *"testifieth."* The phrase *"I Jesus"* declares Him to be the Jesus of all history. What a calm yet emphatic assertion of dignity this is—*"I Jesus"*! The personal pronoun is emphatic. Revelation is the book of His unveiling, and He is the medium of its communication. A *"root"* is of the earth and symbolizes

His humanity, but the *"star"* is from above and speaks of His deity. If the words of Jesus mean what they say, then to tamper with any part of this sublime book is tragic. To mutilate any part of it—or any other part of the Bible, for that matter— merits divine judgment.

4. THE LAST HEAVENLY INVITATION

And the Spirit and the bride say, Come. And let him that heareth say, Come. And let him that is athirst come. And whosoever will, let him take the water of life freely.
(Revelation 22:17)

To rightly understand the trinity of uses of the word *"come"* by John, we must examine them in the light of the context. The first two actually mean "Come Thou!" The first *"come"* is a double invitation. *"The Spirit and the bride say, Come."* Whom are they addressing? The One who, three times over in the chapter, says, *"I come quickly"* (Revelation 22:7, 12, 20). The Holy Spirit speaks through His bride, the church, and adjoins with her in response to the voice of Him who is coming as the *"bright and morning star"* (Revelation 22:16). Then, the individual saint—as well as the saints collectively—says, "Come Thou!" Do we have a strong personal desire to welcome the returning Lord? The third *"come"* is related to the sinner, who, as a thirsty one, is bidden to take of the living waters before it is forever too late.

5. THE LAST ADVENT PROMISE

He which testifieth these things saith, Surely I come quickly. Amen. Even so, come, Lord Jesus.   (Revelation 22:20)

Before His death, resurrection, and ascension, our Lord promised to return for His true church. The Bible is loaded with promises, but this is the most blessed promise of all.

6. THE LAST HEARTFELT PRAYER

Prayer permeates Scripture. John echoes the desire of the saints all down through the ages in his brief but heartfelt supplication, *"Even so, come, Lord Jesus."*

7. THE LAST SAINTLY BENEDICTION

The grace of our Lord Jesus Christ be with you all. Amen.
(Revelation 22:21)

The last book of the Bible, so heavy with wrath and judgments, ends with *grace* and not *curse*. *"Amen."* "So be it." The absolute certainty of truth is confirmed, and all the glories of eternity are to be ours through grace alone. As Christina Rossetti writes, "All that lies between has not effected towards ourselves its purpose unless we conclude the whole matter in a culminating grace by fearing God and keeping His commandments."

The hour is late, and the sands of time are sinking. May we be found living as children of the dawn, with our faces toward the eternal sunrise! May the things of earth grow strangely dim in the light of such glory and grace! As we linger amid the shadows, may we be found singing,

> I have a heritage of joy
> That yet I must not see;
> But the hand that bled to make it mine
> Is keeping it for me.[17]

---

17. Anna L. Waring, "My Heart Is Resting, O My God," 1854.

PART THREE:

THE FURTHER FACTS OF REVELATION

18

THE NUMBERS IN REVELATION

Numerals are a most fascinating aspect of Bible study, yet one that many people seem to neglect. From earliest times, educated people have found great delight in the study of numbers, and the strange fancies and extravagant speculations in the use of certain numbers reveal the superstition and philosophy of the ancient heathen world. Many of their assertions as to the significance of some numbers were completely false. Yet, the study of numbers in Scripture provides a great aid in the discovery of moral, dispensational, and prophetic glories. Speculation has no place in the Holy Spirit's use of numbers.

> God hath spoken once; twice have I heard this; that power belongeth unto God. (Psalm 62:11)

Ellicott observes that this is the usual Hebrew mode of emphasizing a numerical statement, and one growing naturally out of the structure of the verse, which loves a climax. The union of power and love is proven to the poet by the fairness and justice mentioned in the last clause.

Solomon also uses the numerical climax when he enumerates *six* things that God hates, and the *seventh* which He abhors most of all. (See Proverbs 6:16–19.) Confining ourselves to Revelation, let us trace the literal and symbolic significance of the numbers employed by John to express many facets of truth.

ONE

There is universal agreement as to the significance of this number. In all languages, it is the symbol of *unity*, and in Scripture, it is the sign of divine unity and absolute supremacy. *"Thou shalt have no other gods before me"* (Exodus 20:3). Such a command asserts that there is, in God, a sufficiency that needs no other and an independence that admits no other. In Ephesians 4:3–6, the apostle Paul describes a complete circle consisting of seven distinct unities as...

- One body
- One Spirit
- One hope
- One Lord
- One faith
- One baptism
- One God and Father of all

Three is the sign of divine manifestation, and *seven* of spiritual completeness. The first three unities are the *inward* manifestations of God, as only believers are included. The second three unities are the *outward* manifestations of God, as profession is contemplated. The *unity* and *supremacy* of the whole is maintained by God "above," "through," and "in" all.

Bullinger, in his most erudite work *Numbers in Scripture*, said, "As a cardinal number, *one* denotes *unity*; as an ordinal it denotes primacy. Unity being indivisible, and not made up of other numbers, *one* is therefore independent of all others, and is the source of all others. *One* excludes all difference, for there is no second with which it can either harmonize or conflict....The *first* is the only one. There cannot be two *firsts*."

The unity of the governmental attributes of Jehovah can be seen in the golden cherubim, which were *one* measure and *one* size. (See 1 Kings 6:25.) Does not the professing church need to be recalled to the meaning of this divine number? Is she not gradually slipping away from the unity of Christ's *one* sacrifice of Himself and her unity of worship—one altar?

Among the references to *one* in Revelation, we have these four conspicuous phrases:

+ *"One like unto the Son of man"* (Revelation 1:13).

+ *"One hour with the beast"* (Revelation 17:12).

+ *"One mind...unto the beast"* (Revelation 17:13).

+ *"In one hour is thy judgment come"* (Revelation 18:10).

+ *"In one hour so great riches is come to nought"* (Revelation 18:17)

+ *"For in one hour is she made desolate"* (Revelation 18:19)

It would seem as if the *"one hour"* in the foregoing passages cannot be limited to an hour of exactly sixty minutes. Probably the repeated cry is the same period spoken of as *"a short space"* (Revelation 17:10) or *"in one day"* (Revelation 18:8). Such a brief period indicates the terror and suddenness of God's judgment.

"One mind" (Revelation 17:13) refers to the unity of the kings in subjection to the authority and will of the beast.

Each of the twelve gates was made up of *"one pearl"* (Revelation 21:21). Although each pearl was distinct and different, there was *unity* in variety—unity, but not uniformity.

TWO

While one affirms that there is no other, two declares that there *is* another. It is a number with a twofold coloring. One writer suggests that this number can mean responsibility, weakness, or grace, depending on the context. Two individuals may be one in testimony and in fellowship, though different in character. It is tempting to linger over the pairs we find in Scripture, such as the two tablets of testimony (see Deuteronomy 4:13), and to thereby suggest that, in the majority of references, the number two is an expression of ample and competent testimony.

Consider the ministry of the two prophets Elijah and Elisha, and of the two soldiers Joshua and Caleb, who were faithful witnesses to the truth of God's Word. In the coming days of the great tribulation, testimony is to be borne to Christ in His royal and priestly rights by a fearless pair, described as...

+ *"two witnesses"* (Revelation 11:3)

+ *"two olive trees"* (Revelation 11:4)

+ *"two candlesticks"* (Revelation 11:4)

+ *"two prophets"* (Revelation 11:10)

The two hearts of these courageous warriors beat as one in their full testimony and in their devotion to the cause of Christ. When two are united in holy marriage, we speak about them as being one. Married to Christ, the two martyred witnesses were one in testimony, ridicule, death, resurrection, and ascension.

THREE

This number has a sacred association because it represents the Trinity—Father, Son, and Holy Spirit. (See Matthew 28:19.) Paul used the phrase *"these three"* when he dealt with the Christian graces of faith, hope, and love. (See 1 Corinthians 13:13.) Occurring frequently in Scripture, three offers the expositor of the Word a wealth of material for pulpit or classroom treatment. Here, for example, are a few instances to whet the appetite...

+ *Three* men appeared to Abraham (Genesis 18:2)

+ *Three* cities of refuge (Deuteronomy 4:41)

+ *Three* times a year (Deuteronomy 16:16)

+ *Threefold* priestly blessings (Numbers 6:24–26)

+ *Threefold* cry of the seraphim (Isaiah 6:3)

+ *Three* calls to earth (Jeremiah 22:29)

+ *Three* times a day, Daniel prayed (Daniel 6:13)

+ *Three* times Peter denied Christ (Mark 14:72)

+ *Three* measures of meal (Matthew 13:33)

+ *Three* days and *three* nights (Matthew 12:40)

+ *Three* times Peter saw the vision (Acts 10:16)

+ *Three* times Paul besought the Lord about his thorn (2 Corinthians 12:8)

The *triad* is a most integral part of Scripture, and wherever it is found, it can usually be regarded as the sign number of what is divine—as in the case of Paul's frequent salutation of grace, mercy, and peace. Divine testimony and divine completeness are often emphasized by the number *three*. There are certain Scriptures, however, where *three* can be regarded as the sign of resurrection in things moral, physical, and spiritual, as with…

+ The *third* day in creation.

+ The *third* day in Christ's resurrection.

+ The *third* day in Christ's revival.

As *three* dimensions of length, breadth, and height are necessary to form a solid object, the number *three* can be treated as the symbol of the cube—representative of that which is solid, real, substantial, complete, and entire. Altogether there are four perfect numbers that suggest completeness in Scripture…

+ *Three*, representing *divine* perfection

+ *Seven*, representing *spiritual* perfection

+ *Ten*, representing *ordinal* perfection.

+ *Twelve*, representing *governmental* perfection

The introductory section of Revelation has the divine seal of *three* stamped on it. In Revelation 1:1, this Revelation is...

+ divinely *given*

+ divinely *sent*

+ divinely *signified*

In Revelation 1:2, John bears record of...

+ the divine *Word of God*

+ the divine *Witness* (the testimony of Jesus Christ)

+ the divine *vision* (all the things that he saw)

The divine blessing of Revelation 1:3 is on...

+ the *reader*

+ the *hearer*

+ the *keeper*

In Revelation 1, verses 4 and 8, the divine Being is described as the Lord...

+ who *was*

+ who *is*

+ who *is to come*

In Revelation 1:5, the coming Lord is presented as...

+ the divine *prophet* ("*the faithful witness*")

+ the divine *priest* ("*first begotten of the dead*")

+ the divine *king* ("*the prince of the kings*")

In Revelation 1:5–6, the people of God are divinely...

+ *loved*
+ *cleansed*
+ *crowned*

In Revelation 1:17–18, Christ is presented as...

+ divinely *eternal*
+ divinely *living*
+ divinely *powerful*

In Revelation 1:19, the divine revelation was threefold, including...

+ things which thou *hast seen*
+ things which *are*
+ things *hereafter*

FOUR

Because global events are prominent in Revelation, the number *four*, the sign of universality, is used some thirty times. When the world, or the whole scene of creation, is contemplated, and when largeness and breadth of scope are in view, *four* is the number that is used, since it is associated with the earth with its geographic directions and seasons. In Isaiah 60:17, the fullness of material blessing in the earth is described in this fourfold way...

+ *For brass I will bring gold;*
+ *and for iron I will bring silver;*
+ *and for wood brass;*
+ *and for stones iron.*

If *three* is the signature of God, *four* is the signature of the world, which is made up of the four divisions *"of all nations, and kindreds, and peoples, and tongues"* (Revelation 7:9). *Four*, then, is the signature of man and of the material creation. There is an old Jewish saying to the effect that there are four things that take first place in the world:

+ *Man* among the creatures
+ *Eagles* among the birds
+ *Oxen* among the cattle
+ *Lions* among the beasts

FIVE

Although used less frequently than other numbers, *five* has its own significance. Weakness, in contrast to might, is suggested by some references: David's use of *five* smooth stones to smite Goliath (see 1 Samuel 17), *five* chasing a hundred (see Leviticus 26:8), and *five* loaves to feed five thousand (see Matthew 14:13–21; Luke 9:10–17; John 6:5–14). Other verses, however, such as Numbers 5:7 and Matthew 25:2, imply the thought of human responsibility. *Five* and its multiples occupy a conspicuous place in the measurements and arrangements of those parts of the tabernacle and temple that express human responsibility and testimony towards man.

SIX

Because it is one less than seven, the number of perfection, *six* has to do with man and implies his imperfection. It is the number of man without God. It is no surprise, therefore, that three *sixes* are the mark of the Satan's beast. (See Revelation 13:18.)

Created on the *sixth* day of creation, man is sealed with the number *six*. *Six* days he had to labor, and *six* is the number stamped on everything connected with human activity. The recurring references to *six* days of labor show the incompleteness of man's work—a work that can never reach a full and final result. Solomon's throne had *six* steps (see 1 Kings 10:19), and, because of the imperfection of his rule, his kingdom was divided. His glory came short of perfection. There were *six* waterpots of stone containing the water that Jesus turned to wine. (See John 2:6–10.)

SEVEN

The constant use in Scripture of the number *seven* demands careful study by all lovers of the Word. The important role that this number plays in Revelation is proven by the fact that John uses it no fewer than fifty times in its twenty-two chapters. *Seven* must be regarded as having special significance, since it is more frequently employed in the Bible as a whole than any other symbolic number. *Seven* also occurs in several multiples, as in *"seventy times seven"* (Matthew 18:22). At creation, God rested from His work on the *seventh* day—a Sabbath of rest.

As previously indicated, *seven* comes from a Hebrew root word meaning "to be full, satisfied; to have enough of," and it conveys the idea of perfection or completion, either of good or evil. Paul enumerates *seven* gifts and *seven* unities associated with the true church. (See Romans 12:6–8; Ephesians 4:4–6.) There were *seven* feasts of Jehovah. (See Leviticus 23.) Although we have already noted many of the *sevens* in Revelation, we now provide a list of perfections in Revelation that are associated with the number *seven*:

+ The *seven* Spirits of God—perfections of the Godhead

+ The *seven* golden candlesticks—perfection of light and truth, and of professed testimony for Christ

+ The *seven* stars—perfection in rule and oversight
+ The *seven* lamps—perfection in illumination of the Spirit
+ The *seven* seals—perfection of security and authority
+ The *seven* horns—perfection of divine power
+ The *seven* eyes—perfection of discernment
+ The *seven* trumpets—perfection of jurisdiction
+ The *seven* thunders—perfection of judgment
+ The *seven* plagues—perfection of divine wrath
+ The *seven* vials—perfection of destruction
+ The *seven* mountains—perfection of earthly power
+ The *seven* kings—perfection of earthly royalty

EIGHT

The derivation of this number suggests the idea of superabundance. It comes from a Hebrew root meaning "to make fat," "to superabound." As a participle, it implies "superabundant fertility" or "satiating." Because Christ rose on the *first* day of the week, which is also the *eighth* day, the number has come to represent resurrection. *Eight* is also the sign of eternity and of a new epoch. (See Genesis 21:4; Leviticus 14:23; 1 Peter 3:20; 2 Peter 2:5.)

TEN

Five indicates our responsibility toward men, and *twice five* measures our responsibility toward God, as its use in many parts of the tabernacle proves. The same idea is resident in the *Ten* Commandments. Israel's failure in the wilderness is described as consisting of *ten* times that they tempted God. (See

Numbers 14:22–23.) Pharaoh hardened his heart *ten* times and experienced the judgment of *ten* plagues.

As one of the perfect numbers of Scripture, *ten* signifies the perfection of divine order: nothing is lacking; the whole cycle is complete. Thus, in the *Ten* Commandments, we have the complete revelation of the requirements of God. In the physical realm, how perfectly suited we are with *ten* fingers and *ten* toes!

In John's vision of heaven, he numbered the angels around God's throne as *"ten thousand times ten thousand, and thousands of thousands"* (Revelation 5:11). In the same way, however, Satan's beast had *ten* horns, representing *ten* earthly kings. (See Revelation 17:12.)

In our treatment of the seven churches, we expressed the suggestion of the *"ten days"* (Revelation 2:10) of extreme tribulation as having a reference to the ten persecutions endured under successive emperors. The immediate meaning of the phrase, however, is the precious thought that the Lord knew how much His saints could bear and so limited the period of trial accordingly. *"He stayeth his rough wind in the day of the east wind"* (Isaiah 27:8).

TWELVE

This number, with its cognates, occurs over four hundred times in the Bible and is an exceptionally important figure. God has chosen it to signify the perfect administration of divine government in the world, Israel, and the church. (See Matthew 19:28; Revelation 21:12–21.) It was at the age of *twelve* that Jesus publicly announced His heavenly relationship and His task in a world of need. (See Luke 2:42.) *Twelve* legions of angels mark the perfection of angelic powers. (See Matthew 26:53.) In the Old Testament, the reader will find much to meditate upon in the frequent use of *twelve*...

+ The *twelve* cakes of showbread (Leviticus 24:5)

+ The *twelve* wells of water (Exodus 15:27)

+ The *twelve* precious stones in the breastplate (Exodus 28:21)

+ The *twelve* patriarchs (Acts 7:8)

+ The *twelve* stones (Joshua 4:8–9)

+ The *twelve* oxen (1 Kings 7:25)

+ The *twelve* gates (Ezekiel 48:31–34)

Occurring some twenty times in Revelation, the number *twelve* pervades patriarchal, apostolic, and national government. Thus, we have...

+ The *twelve* stars (Revelation 12:1)

+ The *twelve* angels, representing heaven's hierarchy (Revelation 21:12)

+ The *twelve* tribes, representing Israel as a nation (Revelation 21:12)

+ The *twelve* foundations, representing the faith (Revelation 21:14)

+ The *twelve* apostles, representing the church of Christ (Revelation 21:14)

+ The *twelve* fruits, representing bountiful provision in heaven (Revelation 22:2)

+ The *twelve* gates, representing freedom of entrance (Revelation 21:12, 21)

+ The *twelve* pearls, representing the glory of the city. (Revelation 21:21)

And among the multiples of *twelve*, we have...

+ *Twelve* thousand furlongs, the dimensions of the new city (Revelation 21:16)

+ *Twelve* thousand sealed—*twelve* thousand of each of the *twelve* tribes—144,000 in all (Revelation 7:5–8)

TWENTY-FOUR

Twenty-four is twice twelve and means the fullness of authority and representation.

+ The *twenty-four* elders (see Revelation 4:4) picture the representatives of law and grace.

+ The *twenty-four* seats (see Revelation 4:4; 11:16) represent the place of power and judgment.

FORTY-TWO

Six times seven is a number of prophetic significance, conveying the idea of limitation.

+ Tread underfoot *forty-two* months (Revelation 11:2)

+ Continue *forty-two* months (Revelation 13:5)

This period—representing 1,260 days, or three-and-a-half years, or "*a time* [one year], *and times* [two years], *and half a time* [six months]" (Revelation 12:14)—is associated with the antichrist and the time of Jacob's trouble. Bullinger remarks, "Being a multiple of seven, *forty-two* might be supposed to have some connection with spiritual perfection. But it is the product of *six* times *seven.* Six, therefore, being the number of man's opposition to God, *forty-two* becomes significant of the working out of man's opposition to God."

19

THE SYMBOLS IN REVELATION

In our study of Revelation, we attempted to explain many of the symbols used. In this section, we want to indicate the fact of symbolism and some principles governing the interpretation of symbols, as well as provide a classification of the many symbols John used.

Among the volumes guiding the preacher and student in this fascinating field of Bible exposition, special mention should be made of two works. First, there is the monumental work of E. W. Bullinger, *Figures of Speech Used in the Bible Explained and Illustrated*. This remarkable handbook, originally published in 1985, is a must for all ministers of the Word. Then, we have *Preaching from the Types and Metaphors of the Bible* by Benjamin Keach. Written around 1680, and now very hard to obtain, this is a treasure worth securing, despite the tendency Keach had of overloading his subjects with points and subpoints.

We must never forget that the Bible was written in the East, where language is more colorful and picturesque than in the West. This is one reason for its frequent use of symbols, types, and metaphors. Because the Bible is divinely inspired, and because its writers were borne along by the Spirit of truth, guidance was granted the writers in the choice of the symbolism they employed.

Because of His infinity, God had to resort to language that our finite minds could easily understand. Hence, the widespread use of illustrations taken from the world around us to illuminate and enforce divine truths. For example, God, who is *"immortal, invisible, the only wise God"* (1 Timothy 1:17), seems beyond the grasp of our comprehension. Our puny minds cannot penetrate such sublimity. But when He uses symbols to declare all that He is in Himself, then our minds are enlightened and our hearts are blessed.

How near to us God seems when He tells us that He is *"a sun and shield"* (Psalm 84:11)! We could not live without the light, heat, and power of the sun. Earth is so dependent upon this heavenly source of energy. Likewise, it is in God that we live and move and have our being. Even as we cannot do without the benefits of the sun, so, without God, we can do nothing and are nothing.

To the psalmist, the *shield* meant one thing: defense or protection in warfare. Being between its owner and the enemy, the shield warded off the thrust of a sword or the pointed arrow. God is indeed the *Shield* of His own people, standing between them and the enemy of their souls. Constantly, He is presented in Scriptures as the defense of those who trust in Him. Israel was assured that God was round about them as the mountains are round about Jerusalem.

Symbols, then, are windows to let the light in; these emblems suggest truths and thoughts by reason of their relationship or association. Webster describes the meaning of the word *symbol* as coming from two words: *syn*, meaning "with," and *ballein*, implying "to throw," and, in combination, suggesting "to throw together."

Often, a symbol is a visible sign of an invisible quality or idea. For example, a lion is the symbol of courage; a dove, of peace; a lamb, of meekness. Symbols, then, stand for, or represent, persons, things, or attributes, with the resemblance traceable between the symbol and the object symbolized.

It is not always easy to determine the difference between the literal and figurative. The Holy Spirit, however, makes possible that necessary spiritual insight that enables us to rightly interpret the beautiful and expressive symbolic language of the Bible. A safe principle to observe is that of taking everything literally, except where it is distinctly stated otherwise in the text. The locusts had on their heads *"as it were crowns like gold"* (Revelation 9:7). They were not actual crowns but had the *appearance* of crowns.

Another feature to bear in mind in the interpretation of a symbol is to trace its usage throughout the Bible, and then, by comparing Scripture with Scripture, to discover its full significance. If we take a frequently employed figure, that of *fire*, we will find that it describes God, Christ, the Spirit, the Word, prophetic authority, judgment, and so forth. As we group together the symbols of Revelation, remembering that there are almost three hundred quotations in it from the Old Testament, we realize how the roots of this final book of the Bible are embedded in the past, and how the past can interpret the present and the future.

SYMBOLS FROM THE ANIMAL KINGDOM

+ Bear—a hairy, shaggy, creature. (See Revelation 13:2.) A powerful and destructive enemy; the Persian Empire. (See Daniel 7:5.)

+ Beast—Greek *zoon*, "a living creature." Occurs eighteen times. (See, for example, Revelation 4:6–9.) Angelic beings of high order. Greek *therion*, "a wild beast." Occurs thirty-five times. Imperial power acting without reference to God. (See Daniel 4:16.)

+ Birds—speedy agents for good or evil. (See Revelation 18:2.) Sometimes represent spiritual wickedness. (See Isaiah 31:5.)

+ Calf—a symbol of youth, vigor, activity. (See Psalm 29:6; Hosea 14:2.) A type of Jesus, who served both God and man. (See Revelation 4:7.)

+ Dog—an expression of utter contempt. (See Matthew 15:27; Philippians 3:2.) Represents the lost, those without conscience or feelings. (See Psalm 22:16; Revelation 22:15.)

+ Dragon—cruel Egyptian power. (See Ezekiel 29:3.) Typical of cruel satanic power. (See Revelation 12:7; 13:2–4; 20:2.)

+ Eagle—swift invasions by kings. (See Ezekiel 17:2–7.) Type of Christ. (See Revelation 4:7.) Safety, tenderness, and care of Israel. (See Revelation 12:14.)

+ Frog—Egyptians were plagued by frogs because they believed that the reptiles were divinely inspired. (See Exodus 8:2.) Typical of unclean spirits. (See Revelation 16:13.)

+ Horse—connected with war and conquest. (See Revelation 6:1–8; 19:19.) Typical of power and strength. (See Psalm 66:12; Hosea 1:7.)

+ Lamb—gentle, meek, tender, unresisting animal. (See Isaiah 11:6; Luke 10:3.) Mentioned twenty-five times, mainly in relation to Christ. (See, for example, Revelation 5:6.)

+ Leopard—symbol of ferocity, swiftness, tenacity, and vengeance. (See Jeremiah 5:6; Daniel 7:6.) Represents earth's last cruel tyrant. (See Revelation 13:2.)

+ Lion—symbolic of righteous or evil rulers. (See 1 Peter 5:8; Revelation 5:5; 13:2.) Depicts the imperial greatness of Babylon. (See Daniel 7:4.)

+ Locusts—typical of destructive enemies permitted by God. (See Isaiah 33:4.) Agents of the torment of the godless. (See Revelation 9:3, 7.)

+ Serpent—in Hebrew, "hiss, whisper." In Greek, "sly, cunning." Satanic subtlety and mere worldly wisdom. (See Revelation 12:9; 20:2–3.)

+ Sheep—type of God's people. Used of Christ in Psalm 79:13 and Isaiah 53:6–7. Among the coveted but destroyed merchandise of Babylon. (See Revelation 18:13.)

SYMBOLS FROM COLORS

+ Black—used in personal and national mourning. (See Jeremiah 4:28). Symbol of famine and sorrow under the Man of Sin. (See Revelation 6:5, 12.)

+ Pale (green)—in Hebrew, "blanch." (See Isaiah 29:22; Jeremiah 30:6.) Symbol of death and future woe. (See Revelation 6:8.)

+ Purple—the color of royalty and wealth. (See Exodus 25:4; Luke 16:19; John 19:2). As worn by the great whore, it represents apostate Christendom. (See Revelation 17:4.)

+ Red—color of blood, but also of Communism and of Satan. (See Revelation 17:4; 12:3.)

+ White—occurs seventeen times in Revelation. Used of Christ and saints. Symbol of righteousness and victory. (See Revelation 19:14.)

SYMBOLS FROM THE MINERAL KINGDOM

+ Brass (copper)—withstands the test of fire, symbolizing endurance and strength. (See Deuteronomy 33:25.) Represents judgment upon sin. (See Numbers 21:4–9; Revelation 1:15.)

+ Gold—the most precious of metals. Especially related to deity. Symbol of wealth and kingship. (See Revelation 4:4; 9:7; 18:9–12.)

+ Iron—represents strength and irresistible power. (See Psalm 2:9; Daniel 7:7.) Symbol of a hardened conscience and the power to break. (See Revelation 2:27; 9:9; 12:5.)

+ Pearls (and jewels out of the earth)—precious stones and pearls adorn the eternal city. (See Revelation 21:11, 19–21.) Usually symbolic of God's people, His peculiar treasure. (See Malachi 3:17; Revelation 17:4; 18:12.)

+ Silver—used as currency. (See Exodus 30:12–16; Leviticus 5:15). It was among the corruptible and idolatrous things that Babylon lost by judgment. (See Revelation 9:20; 18:12.)

SYMBOLS FROM LUMINARIES

+ Candle (lamp)—symbolic of the Bible, knowledge, and salvation. (See Psalm 119:105; Isaiah 62:1). Represents testimony and message proclaimed. (See Revelation 1:12–20; 2:1, 5; 11:4.)

+ Lightning—obedience connected with the judicial power of God. (See Ezekiel 1:13–14; Nahum 2:4). Symbol of God's majesty (see Daniel 10:6) and of avenging and righteous wrath. (See Revelation 4:5; 8:5; 11:19; 16:18.)

+ Moon—reflects derived light of the sun. (See Psalm 81:3; Ezekiel 46:1.) A symbol of the witness of God's people. (See Song of Solomon 6:10; Revelation 6:12; 8:12; 12:1; 21:23.)

+ Stars—lesser luminaries suggesting subordinate rulers. (See Daniel 8:10–12.) Typical of heavenly and human beings, good or bad. (See Revelation 1:16–20; 3:1; 22:16.)

+ Sun—supreme in the heavens. In Hebrew, "brilliant." (See Malachi 4:2; Acts 26:13; 1 Corinthians 15:41.)

SYMBOLS FROM THE HUMAN BODY

+ Breast—in Hebrew, "firm part." Represents physical health, vigor, and power. (See Job 21:24). Typical of affections of Christ and our love for Him. (See Revelation 1:13; 15:6.)

+ Eyes—the windows to the soul. They stand for knowledge and insight. (See Numbers 10:31; Psalm 123:2.) Symbols of divine guidance, perception, and intelligence. (See Revelation 1:14; 4:6, 8; 21:4.)

+ Face—an indicator of character or expression. (See Genesis 3:19; Proverbs 21:29.) A symbol of reflected glory, intelligence, and omniscience (See Revelation 1:16; 4:7; 21:4.)

+ Feet—enable us to stand, walk, and run. "Under the feet" means subjection. (See Ephesians 1:22.) Symbol of Christlike walk and ways, character and conduct. (See John 13:1–10; Ephesians 6:15; Revelation 1:15, 17; 3:9; 11:11; 12:1; 13:2.)

+ Hair—Nazarites had long hair. (See Judges 16:17.) Short hair stood for masculine energy and dignity. (See Numbers 6:18–19; 1 Corinthians 11:14.) A symbol of Christ's glorified humanity and agelessness. (See Revelation 1:14.)

+ Hand—the right hand implies position and prestige. Hands represent labor. A symbol of possession, strength, action, and service. (See Revelation 1:16; 9:20; 10:5; 14:9, 14.)

+ Heart—the seat of emotion, affections, and purity. (See Psalm 40:8–12; 1 Timothy 1:5.) God is able to search motives, desires, and feelings. (See Revelation 2:23; 17:17; 18:7.)

+ Mind—the perceptive and thinking part of consciousness. (See Ezekiel 11:5.) A symbol of unity of decision (see Revelation 17:13) and of heavenly wisdom (see verse 9.)

+ Mouth—organ related to breathing, speaking, and eating. (See Job 33:2; Exodus 4:11.) Used of Christ, saints, antichrist, and Satan. (See Revelation 1:16; 3:16; 9:17; 12:15; 14:5.)

+ Voice—used forty-six times in Revelation. Great marvel of the body. Represents, for the most part, divine warnings to men. (See, for example, Revelation 4:5; 8:13.)

SYMBOLS FROM NATURE

+ Barley—as fashioned into bread. (See Judges 7:13; Numbers 5:15; Ezekiel 13:19.) A symbol of poverty, lowliness, and low estate. (See Revelation 6:6.)

+ Fig tree—a symbol of Israel's national and political life. (See Matthew 21:19–21; 24:32–33.) A symbol of security, prosperity, and peace. (See Zechariah 3:10; Revelation 6:13.)

+ Flour—in Hebrew, "to grind." Flour was crushed (see Numbers 28:20) and typified Christ in suffering. (See Numbers 28:28.) Was among the merchandise Babylon lost in judgment. (See Revelation 18:13.)

+ Fruits—symbolic of wealth, increase, and heavenly blessing. (See Psalm 21:10.) Also, the material things the soul lusts after. (See Revelation 18:14.)

+ Grapes—symbolizing blood or the fruit of the vine (see Genesis 49:11); Israel (see Jeremiah 2:21). Symbol of judgment of apostates. (See Revelation 14:18.)

+ Grass—in Hebrew, "green hay." Used for the frailty of flesh. (See Psalm 90:5; Isaiah 40:6–8.) Symbol of judgment as a necessity of life. (See Revelation 8:7; 9:4.)

+ Odors—fragrance of worship offered to God. (See Leviticus 26:31; Philippians 4:18.) Symbolic, as perfume, of prayers ascending to God. (See Revelation 5:8; 18:13.)

+ Olive trees—type of Israel. (See Judges 9:8–9; Psalm 52:8; Jeremiah 11:16; Romans 11.) Describes fruitfulness and testimony of witnesses. (See Revelation 11:4.)

+ Palms—in Hebrew, "erect." Sign of the flourishing state of the righteous. (See Psalm 92:12; Song of Solomon 7:7–8.)

+ Trees—applications of trees are as numerous as their uses. Symbol of judgment or of eternal sustenance. (See Revelation 2:7; 7:1, 3; 8:7; 22:2, 14.)

+ Wheat—figure used of Christ, God's Word, and the profession of saints. (See Jeremiah 23:28; Matthew 13:24–30.) This necessity of life was associated with judgment. (See Revelation 6:6; 18:13.)

+ Wine—in Hebrew, "pressed out." *Gethsemane* means "press of crushed olives." Used as a symbol of divine judgment. (See Revelation 14:8, 10; 16:19; 19:15.)

+ Wood—bountiful provision of nature. Look around you for uses of wood. Symbol of idolatry and judgment. (See Revelation 9:20; 18:12.)

+ Wormwood—a plant representing bitterness and depression. (See Jeremiah 9:15; Lamentations 3:15; Amos 5:7.) Symbol of divine curse resulting in bitterness of enemies. (See Revelation 8:11.)

SYMBOLS FROM THE FORCES OF NATURE

+ Clouds—because of their transitory nature, clouds represent divine movements. (See Psalm 18:11; 104:3.) Symbolic of divine presence, majesty, and glory veiled. (See Revelation 1:7; 10:1; 11:12; 14:14–16.)

+ Earthquake—in Hebrew, "vibration." Represents sudden calamity and tragedy. (See 1 Kings 19:11.) Prophetic of convulsion of earth's settled order. (See Revelation 6:12; 11:13; 16:18.)

+ Flood—in Hebrew, "deluge." Associated with God's judgment, as in Noah's day. (See Genesis 6:17.) Symbolic of Satan's hatred of Israel. (See Revelation 12:15–16.)

+ Hail—a scourge used to describe divine power in judicial acts. (See Isaiah 30:30.) Symbolic of the destruction of the works of evil men. (See Revelation 8:7, 11:19; 16:21.)

+ Heavens—occurs fifty-seven times in Revelation. Has threefold meaning: atmospheric, astral, and spiritual. Symbolic of source of authority and light. (See, for example, Revelation 6:13; 8:10.)

+ Lake—the phrase *"lake of fire"* occurs five times in Revelation. (See also Numbers 16:32–34; Isaiah 5:14.) Symbolic of immersion into never-ending agony. (See Revelation 19:20; 20:10, 15.)

+ Mountain—represents political and moral stability and greatness. (See Daniel 2:35; Psalm 125:1–2.) Symbolic of overthrow of national prominence. (See Revelation 6:14, 16; 8:8; 14:1; 17:9; 21:10.)

+ Pit—in Hebrew, "prison." Used of Sheol, or the place of departed spirits. (See Isaiah 14:15; 24:22.) Symbolic of abode of evil spirits and of Satan's captivity for a thousand years. (See Revelation 9:1–2; 20:1.)

+ Rainbow—in Hebrew, "bow in the cloud." (See Genesis 9:13.) Exists between heaven and earth. Symbolic of grace and mercy, and of our covenant-keeping God. (See Revelation 4:3; 10:1.)

+ River—usually represents spiritual gifts and blessings. (See Psalm 36:8; John 7:38–39.) Symbolic of eternal refreshment for saints. (See Revelation 8:10; 9:14; 16:4; 22:1.)

+ Sea—referred to twenty-five times in Revelation, both literally and symbolically. Symbol of heavenly transparency, as well as of peoples in a state of confusion. (See Revelation 4:6; 5:13; 8:8; 21:1.)

+ Thunder—in Hebrew, "to crash." Evidence of divine power. (See 1 Samuel 2:10.) Symbolic of God's voice in judgment. Occurs ten times in Revelation. (See, for example, Revelation 4:5; 6:1; 14:2.)

+ Waters—used of both good and evil influences. (See Psalm 1:3.) Symbolic of blessing, but also of nations satanically agitated. used eighteen times in Revelation. (See, for example, Revelation 8:11; 16:4–5; 17:15; 21:6; 22:1.)

+ Wind—used for the invisible, mighty power of God. (See Isaiah 11:15; John 3:8; Acts 2:2.) Symbolic of unseen yet powerful divine operations. (See Revelation 6:13; 7:1.)

SYMBOLS FROM PERSONALITIES

+ Elder—term applied to Jewish and Christian overseers. Symbolic of age, experience, wisdom (see 1 Peter 5:1–3), and heavenly saints in the character of royal priesthood. Used twelve times in Revelation. (See, for example, Revelation 4:4.)

+ Harlot—in Greek, *porne*, from which we have *pornography*. Symbolic of religious corruption and spiritual adultery. (See Revelation 17:1–16; 19:2; 21:8.)

+ Judge—administrator of justice and verdicts. (See 1 Kings 3:9.) Represents righteous judgment for saints and sinners. (See Revelation 6:10; 18:8; 19:2, 11; 20:13.)

- King—in Hebrew, "ruler." Used twenty-one times in Revelation—and six times as "kingdom." Possessor of supreme power and authority. (See 1 Timothy 1:17.) Symbolic of royal dignity of Christ and the saints. (See Revelation 1:5–6; 17:14; 19:16.)

- Man child—phrase indicating gender of a child. (See Leviticus 12:2; Job 3:3; Isaiah 66:7.) Represents Christ as the Son born to Mary. (See Revelation 12:5, 13.)

- Priest—a type of Christ. (See Hebrews 3:1.) All who are redeemed, both men and women, are included in the royal priesthood of believers. (See 1 Peter 2:9; Revelation 1:6; 5:10; 20:6.)

- Prophet—Old Testament prophets forthtold and foretold divine messages. Term is used twelve times in Revelation, of both true and false prophets. (See Revelation 2:20; 10:7; 16:13; 20:10.)

SYMBOLS FROM INANIMATE OBJECTS

- Books—represent a written or printed narrative or record. Used twenty-eight times in Revelation. Covers records of deeds, decisions, and rewards. (See Revelation 1:11; 10:2; 17:8; 20:12; 22:18.)

- Breastplate—used for the purpose of defense. (See Exodus 25:7; Isaiah 59:17; Ephesians 6:14.) Symbolic of a safeguard for the heart and conscience. (See 1 Thessalonians 5:8; Revelation 9:9, 17.)

- Gates—in Hebrew, "opening." An open gate denotes security and access. (See Isaiah 60:11.) Symbolic not only of government (see Genesis 19:1) but also of free entrance into a city. (See Revelation 21:12–14.)

+ Horns—used to represent kingly power and glory. (See Psalm 75:10; 132:17; 1 Samuel 2:1.) Symbolic of power and the authority of the Man of Sin. (See Revelation 5:6; 13:1; 17:12, 16.)

+ Key—suggests the right to exercise authority and symbolizes possession of knowledge. (See Isaiah 22:22; Matthew 16:19; 18:18.) Symbolic of divine knowledge, authority, and government. (See Revelation 1:18; 3:7; 9:1; 20:1.)

+ Linen—in Hebrew, "carded, bleached, twisted." (See Genesis 41:42.) Symbolic of Christ's righteousness and our purity. (See Revelation 19:8, 14.)

+ Seal—in Hebrew, "to close." Usually implies a finished transaction. (See Esther 8:8; Ephesians 1:13.) Symbolic of security, preservation, and judgment. (See Revelation 5:1–10; 6:1–17; 7:2; 9:4.)

+ Sword—represents magisterial authority and power. (See Romans 13:4). Symbolic of Christ, the Word, war, and judgment. (See Revelation 1:16; 2:12, 16; 6:8; 19:15, 21.)

+ Tabernacle—a temporary structure (see 2 Corinthians 5:1, 4; 2 Peter 1:14) and dwelling (see John 1:14). Represents the place where God localized His presence. (See Revelation 13:6; 15:5; 21:3.)

+ Temple—the permanent abode set apart for worship. (See 1 Kings 6:1–14; Psalm 68:29.) Occurs sixteen times in Revelation. Symbolic of God's eternal habitation among His people. (See Revelation 3:12; 7:15; 11:19; 21:22.)

+ Trumpet—used for various reasons of public summons and gatherings. (See Isaiah 27:13; Zechariah 9:14.) Symbolic of rapture and judgment. (See 1 Thessalonians 4:16; Revelation 1:10; 8:2; 9:14.)

20

SERMON OUTLINES
OF REVELATION

Here are a few bones for you to clothe with flesh. As a whole, the book of Revelation is loaded with homiletical material, as shown in our previous treatment of the sevens.

AMAZING WONDERS

In *Heroes and Hero-Worship,* Thomas Carlyle uses the striking phrase "Worship is transcendent wonder." There is not much worship, however, associated with the objects of wonder in the apocalypse. In the first three references, the word *"wonder"* implies a "sign" and is in keeping with the term *"signified"* in Revelation 1:1:

+ The wonder of Israel's existence and preservation (Revelation 12:1)

+ The wonder of the devil's person and power (Revelation 12:3)

+ The wonder of the false prophet's miraculous acts (Revelation 13:13)

In the following references, a different Greek word is used for *"wonder"* or *"wondered."* It is a word expressing amazement or astonishment.

+ The wonder of the beast's resuscitation (Revelation 13:3)

+ The wonder of the murderous harlot church (Revelation 17:6)

♦ The wonder of the fatal end of Gentile world power (Revelation 17:8)

TRIALS AND TRIBULATIONS

Care must be taken to distinguish between *tribulation* and *the great tribulation*. Jesus said that all His saints must expect tribulation as they linger in a troubled world. (See John 16:33.) Paul, who suffered much tribulation, gloried in it (see Romans 5:3) and experienced divine comfort in it (see 2 Corinthians 1:4). He could also rejoice in it. (See 2 Corinthians 7:4.) But while tribulation has always been the lot of the righteous, "the great tribulation" covers a specific prophetic period (see Matthew 24:15, 21, 29), the terrible course that runs for three-and-a-half years (see Daniel 7:25; 9:25–27), embracing Jews and Gentiles alike. Here are a few examples:

♦ The tribulation of John and fellow saints under Nero (Revelation 1:9)

♦ The tribulation of the Smyrna church under pagan Rome (Revelation 2:9–10)

♦ The tribulation of an extreme order, which the apostates of Thyatira experienced. (Revelation 2:22)

♦ The tribulation, the period of hitherto-unknown trouble predicted by the prophets and our Lord, which is described as *"the time of Jacob's trouble"* (Jeremiah 30:7) (Revelation 7:14; 11:2–3)

A COLLECTION OF EVERLASTINGS

The finite mind of man cannot fully comprehend all that is associated with eternity. Being mortal, he judges everything by time. Yet, because he will exist beyond the grave, he should be found living under the impact of eternal realities. *"For ever and ever"* (1 Chronicles 16:36) means to the ages of ages and is from a Hebrew term implying "from eternity to eternity." Here are examples from Revelation:

+ The eternal glory and dominion of God (Revelation 1:6; 7:12)

+ The eternal existence of God (Revelation 4:9–10; 10:6; 15:7)

+ The eternal adoration of the Lamb (Revelation 5:13–14)

+ The eternal reign of God (Revelation 11:15)

+ The eternal gospel (Revelation 14:6)

+ The eternal torment of the lost (Jude 6, 13; Revelation 14:11; 19:3; 20:14)

+ The eternal doom of the unholy trinity (Revelation 20:10)

+ The eternal service of the redeemed (Revelation 22:5)

SEALS—BROKEN AND UNBROKEN

In *Antony and Cleopatra*, Shakespeare spoke of "this kingly seal" and has the phrase "Seal, then, and all is done." Here, we have the ideas of security, finality, and attestation, which a seal suggests. (See 2 Timothy 2:19; 1 Corinthians 9:2; Ephesians 4:30.)

+ The seven-sealed book (Revelation 5:1–7; 6:1–17; 8:1)

+ The saints sealed by God (Revelation 7:2, 4–8)

+ All divinely sealed ones are appropriated as preserved for God.

+ The woe of the unsealed (Revelation 9:4)

    As the sealed are marked for blessing and preservation, so the unsealed are singled out for just punishment.

+ The sealed thunders (Revelation 10:4)

+ The sealed pit (Revelation 20:3)

As the tomb was sealed, seeming to indicate that Jesus could not rise again (see Matthew 27:66), so Satan is sealed and cannot come forth from the abyss for a thousand years. (See Revelation 20:1–3.)

+ The unsealed prophecies of the apocalypse (Revelation 22:10)

A GALAXY OF STARS

Luminaries, both actual and symbolic, have a prominent place in this final book of the Bible.

+ The seven stars (Revelation 1:16–20; 2:1; 3:1)
+ The morning star (Revelation 2:28; 22:16)
+ The heavenly stars (Revelation 6:13)
+ The great star (Revelation 8:10–11; 9:1)
+ The third part of stars (Revelation 8:12; 12:4)
+ The twelve stars (Revelation 12:1)

THE DOXOLOGIES

Although the bulk of Revelation is taken up with judgment, it has surprisingly much to say about praise, singing, and rejoicing. Amid its cries of anguish, there are hallelujahs! A profitable meditation could be developed along the line of apocalyptic anthems.

1. Doxology exalting the power and possessions of the Lamb (Revelation 5:11–14)
2. Doxology of the host of heaven for God's salvation (Revelation 7:10–12)

3. Doxology for the universal dominion of God and Christ (Revelation 11:15–18)

4. Doxology for victory over Satan (Revelation 12:7–12)

5. Doxology from heaven and earth for the new song (Revelation 14:2–5)

6. Doxology of the saints for Him who is the King of saints (Revelation 15:3–4)

7. Doxology from the small and great for divine omnipotence (Revelation 19:1–6)

A BOOK OF THRONES

The words *seat, seats, throne,* and *thrones* are synonymous terms. In the majority of cases, a throne is associated with heaven and implies divine authority, power, and judgment.

+ The throne of Satan (Revelation 2:13)

+ The throne of the Father (Revelation 3:21)

+ The throne set in heaven (Revelation 4:1–11)

+ The throne to be feared (Revelation 6:16)

+ The throne of the beast (Revelation 13:2; 16:10)

+ The thrones of the redeemed (Revelation 20:4)

+ The great white throne (Revelation 20:11–15)

+ The eternal throne (Revelation 22:1)

THE LAKE OF FIRE

While *Hades* is the present abode of all lost souls, the *lake of fire* is to be the final depository of all that is alien to God's mind and will. The occupants of this dread place are specifically mentioned as...

+ The beast (Revelation 19:20; 20:10)
+ The false prophet (Revelation 19:20; 20:10)
+ The devil (Revelation 20:10)
+ The last enemy, death (Revelation 20:14)
+ Hades (Revelation 20:14)
+ All unbelievers (Revelation 20:15; 21:8)
+ The goat nations (Matthew 25:31–46)
+ The devil's angels (Matthew 25:41)

A LIBRARY OF BOOKS

Within the book of Revelation, we have mention of several books and records:

+ The book John wrote (Revelation 1:11, 19)
+ The book of overcomers (Revelation 3:5)
+ The book sealed with seven seals (Revelation 5:1–7)
+ The little book (Revelation 10:2, 8–11)
+ The book of life (Revelation 20:12–15)
+ The book of the redeemed (Revelation 21:27)

THE BEATITUDES OF THE BELOVED

We are all familiar with the renowned beatitudes of Christ's Sermon on the Mount (see Matthew 5:1–12), but not as many of us give thought to the beatitudes of Revelation. Scattered throughout Revelation are beatitudes and benedictions that we can fitly add to those that the Master enunciated to His hearers gathered around the mountain.

+ The beatitude of reading and of obedience (Revelation 1:3)
+ The beatitude of the righteous dead (Revelation 14:13)
+ The beatitude of the holy watcher (Revelation 16:15)
+ The beatitude of the bride (Revelation 19:9)
+ The beatitude of the resurrected (Revelation 20:6)
+ The beatitude of prophecy lovers (Revelation 22:7)
+ The beatitude of eternal reward (Revelation 22:14)

THE THINGS ABSENT FROM HEAVEN

John found that human language was most inadequate to describe all that he saw in heaven. The best of words fell short when it came to unveiling the glory of the unseen. He felt it more comforting to tell us what would *not* be in heaven than to tell us what we could expect there.

+ No more hunger or thirst (Revelation 7:16)
+ No more sun or heat (Revelation 7:16; 21:23; 22:5)
+ No more tears or crying (Revelation 7:17; 21:4)
+ No more sea (Revelation 21:1)
+ No more death (Revelation 21:4)
+ No more sorrow (Revelation 21:4)
+ No more pain (Revelation 21:4)
+ No more temples (Revelation 21:22)
+ No more moon (Revelation 21:23)
+ No more night (Revelation 21:25; 22:5)
+ No more sin (Revelation 21:27; 22:15)
+ No more curse (Revelation 22:3)
+ No more lamps (Revelation 22:5)

A BATCH OF BEHOLDS

The frequent Bible exclamation *"behold,"* meaning "to gaze intently and consider," appears over four hundred times in the Bible and is used in its past, present, and prospective tenses. *Behold* also occurs as a herald of hope or of horror. This word occurs twenty-five times in Revelation.

1. Behold the coming majesty (Revelation 1:7)

2. Behold immortality (Revelation 1:18)

3. Behold satanic antagonism (Revelation 2:10)

4. Behold the great tribulation (Revelation 2:22)

5. Behold opportunity (Revelation 3:8)

6. Behold false worship (Revelation 3:9)

7. Behold advent readiness (Revelation 3:11)

8. Behold gracious entreaty (Revelation 3:20)

9. Behold heavenly access (Revelation 4:1)

10. Behold sovereignty (Revelation 4:2)

11. Behold triumph (Revelation 5:5)

12. Behold sacrificial royalty (Revelation 5:6)

13. Behold universal adoration (Revelation 5:11)

14. Behold mock peace (Revelation 6:2)

15. Behold desolation (Revelation 6:5)

16. Behold death (Revelation 6:8)

17. Behold divine wrath (Revelation 6:12–17)

18. Behold salvation (Revelation 7:9)

19. Behold woes (Revelation 8:13; 9:12; 11:14)

20. Behold satanic hatred (Revelation 12:3)

21. Behold the beasts (Revelation 13:1, 11)

22. Behold Armageddon (Revelation 14:14)

23. Behold preparation (Revelation 16:15)

24. Behold the glorious (Revelation 19:11–16)

25. Behold the new creation (Revelation 21:5)

THE MYSTERIES UNFOLDED

Young's Analytical Concordance of the Bible, by Robert Young, interprets the word *mystery* as meaning "what is known only to the initiated." All who are spiritually initiated can understand many of the mysteries of Scripture. (See 1 Corinthians 13:9–12.) The word is used exclusively in the New Testament (twenty-seven times), and John employs it four times:

1. The mystery of the seven stars (Revelation 1:20)

2. The mystery of God (Revelation 10:7)

3. The mystery of Babylon the Great (Revelation 17:5)

4. The mystery of the woman (Revelation 17:7)

The student of Revelation finds himself embarrassed with riches when it comes to expositional material. The theological content of the book is almost inexhaustible. Yet what a sadly neglected book of the Bible it is! Many preachers are afraid to expound this book of Revelation. But the experience of this writer of well over fifty years of preaching experience is that audiences respond most eagerly when the book is sanely expounded. Advertise a series of sermons on the book of Revelation, and Bible-lovers gather like bees around a honey pot.

BIBLIOGRAPHY

Brooke, Hubert. *The Vision of the Candlestick*. London: Marshall, Morgan & Scott, 1880.

Darms, Anton. *Tomorrow: Studies in the Revelation*. Chicago: Moody Press, 1943.

DeHaan, M. R. *Revelation*. Grand Rapids: Zondervan, 1967.

Dice, A. *The Revelation: A Book for Today*. London: Elliot Stock, 1894.

Hislop, Alexander. *The Two Babylons*. New York: Loizeaux Brothers, 1943.

Kuyper, Abraham. *The Revelation of St. John*. Grand Rapids: Eerdmans, 1935.

Larkin, Clarence. *The Book of Revelation*. Published by the author, 1920.

Mitchell, Fred. *The Lamb upon His Throne*. London: Marshall, Morgan & Scott, 1951.

Newell, William R. *The Book of the Revelation*. Chicago: Moody Press, 1939.

Pentecost, J. Dwight. *Things to Come*. Grand Rapids: Zondervan, 1958.

Ramsay, W. M. *The Letters to the Seven Churches*. New York: A. C. Armstrong & Son, 1909.

Rossetti, Christina G. *The Face of the Deep: A Devotional Commentary on the Apocalypse.* London: Society for Promoting Christian Knowledge, 1902.

Scott, Walter. *Exposition of the Revelation of Jesus Christ.* London: Pickering & Inglis, 1930.

Seiss, J. A. *The Apocalypse* (3 vols.) New York: Charles C. Cook, 1900. (Also available in reprint edition by Zondervan.)

Stanton, Gerald B. *Kept from the Hour: Biblical Evidence for the Pretribulational Return of Christ.* Grand Rapids: Zondervan, 1956.

Stier, Rudolf. *The Words of the Angels.* London: Swan, Lowrey Co., 1886.

Tatford, F. A. *God's Programme of the Ages.* Grand Rapids: Kregel, 1967.

——*Prophecy's Last Word.* London: Pickering & Inglis, 1947.

Walvoord, John F. *Israel in Prophecy.* Grand Rapids: Zondervan, 1978.

——*The Millennial Kingdom.* Grand Rapids, Zondervan, 1959.

——*The Rapture Question.* Grand Rapids: Zondervan, 1970.

——*The Return of the Lord.* Grand Rapids: Zondervan, 1983.

——*The Revelation of Jesus Christ.* Chicago: Moody Press, 1966.

ABOUT THE AUTHOR

When Dr. Herbert Lockyer (1886–1984) was first deciding on a career, he considered becoming an actor. Tall and well-spoken, he seemed a natural for the theater. But the Lord had something better in mind. Instead of to the stage, God called Herbert to the pulpit, where, as a pastor, Bible teacher, and author of more than fifty books, he touched the hearts and lives of millions of people.

Dr. Lockyer held pastorates in Scotland and England for twenty-five years. As pastor of Leeds Road Baptist Church in Bradford, England, he became a leader in the Keswick Higher Life Movement, which emphasized the significance of living in the fullness of the Holy Spirit. This led to an invitation to speak at the Moody Bible Institute's fiftieth anniversary in 1936. His warm reception at that event led to his ministry in the United States. He received honorary degrees from both the Northwestern Evangelical Seminary and the International Academy in London.

In 1955, he returned to England, where he lived for many years. He then returned to the United States, where he spent the final years of his life in Colorado Springs, Colorado, with his son, the Rev. Herbert Lockyer Jr., a Presbyterian minister who became his editor.